AF555949

Teaching Thinking Skills

Teaching Thinking Skills

Gurpreet Kaur

RANDOM PUBLICATIONS
NEW DELHI (INDIA)

Teaching Thinking Skills

ISBN 978-93-5111-474-1

Published in 2015 in India by

RANDOM PUBLICATIONS

4376-A/4B, Gali Murari Lal, Ansari Road
New Delhi-110 002
Phone : +9111-43580356, 011-23289044, 011-43142548
e-mail: sales@randompublications.com,
info@randompublications.com, randomexports@gmail.com

Reprinted 2026

Type Setting by : Friends Media, Delhi-110089

Preface

Throughout history, philosophers, politicians, educators and many others have been concerned with the art and science of astute thinking. Some identify the spirit of inquiry and dialogue that characterized the golden age of ancient Greece as the beginning of this interest. Others point to the Age of Enlightenment, with its emphasis on rationality and progress. In the twentieth century, the ability to engage in careful, reflective thought has been viewed in various ways: as a fundamental characteristic of an educated person, as a requirement for responsible citizenship in a democratic society, and, more recently, as an employability skill for an increasingly wide range of jobs.

Teaching children to become effective thinkers is increasingly recognized as an immediate goal of education. If students are to function successfully in a highly technical society, then they must be equipped with lifelong learning and thinking skills necessary to acquire and process information in an ever-changing world. Thinking skills are necessary tools in a society characterized by rapid change, many alternatives of actions, and numerous individual and collective choices and decisions. The societal factors that create a need for well developed thinking skills are only part of the story, however.

This book presents practical and universal strategies for the teaching of thinking skills and problem-solving, using examples of topics from the curriculum, classroom techniques, and tried-and-tested activities which systematically develop pupils' thinking and problem-solving skills. While accommodating the need of all learners to develop effective thinking skills, the book also caters to the need to differentiate learning activities to extend the more able learners. This accessible, jargon-free book will be welcomed by teachers, students and researchers alike.

Author

Contents

1

Thinking Skills Programmes

There are many strands in what has become known as the 'thinking skills' tradition. An important one in the present context is the 'critical thinking' tradition, which is commonly traced back to John Dewey, the American psychologist, philosopher and educator. On a related but different tack, the (mathematical) 'problem solving' tradition has rather obscure beginnings but the Hungarian mathematician Georg Polya is widely credited with originating it as a teachable skill; unusually for a book on mathematics, his classic *How to Solve It* has sold over a million copies.

A quite different strand, which has been very influential in schools, derives from the work of the Israeli psychologist, Rueben Feuerstein on 'Instrumental Enrichment'. The work of Edward De Bono, especially on divergent thinking, otherwise often known as 'lateral thinking', is different again and has been widely implemented. There is also Matthew Lipman's Philosophy for Children programme, which is similar to the critical thinking tradition in some respects. Again in the United States, the work on 'multiple intelligences' developed by Howard Gardner at Harvard, has been enormously influential and aims to develop different intelligences by teaching thinking skills.

In Britain, one of the most significant developments has been the CASE programme (Cognitive Acceleration Through Science Education) developed by Adey and Shayer, and based on the work of Piaget. There is also the Somerset Thinking Skills programme, derived from Feuerstein, the work on critical thinking, embodied in the AS level examination in Critical Thinking and the work emanating from the Newcastle School of Education.

These are only some of the strands in the thinking skills tradition. Some originate from work in psychology (e.g., instrumental enrichment and CASE) whilst others derive from philosophy (e.g., critical thinking and Philosophy for Children). In some programmes, thinking skills are taught in 'standalone' courses, separate from ordinary school subjects (e.g., instrumental enrichment, Philosophy for Children) whilst others are 'infused' into the teaching of ordinary school subjects (e.g., CASE, Thinking Through Geography). In all cases the teaching aims to teach thinking skills *explicitly* and *directly*, rather than assuming that they get developed *indirectly* and *implicitly* in the course of studying the normal school curriculum.

Whether thinking skills are taught through standalone courses or through being 'infused' into redesigned subject lessons, a key concern of all such work is to ensure that students 'transfer' the skills learned in one context to other contexts. This will involve 'bridging' work, in other words explicitly 'teaching for transfer'. Despite their differences, the key to nearly all 'thinking skills' programmes is 'metacognition' -thinking about one's thinking. They all require the participant to self-consciously adopt 'good' ways of thinking when faced with problems of whatever kind. For example, in the critical thinking tradition, if you face a decision, you need to ask yourself questions about objectives, alternatives, consequences, risks etc. In the same way, Polya gives students key questions to ask themselves when faced with any mathematical problem.

There are many variations on the themes mentioned above and some of these will be discussed below. There is also growing evidence of the effectiveness of many of these programmes in delivering improved student performance and this is also given below.

Motivation of Thinking Skills Programmes

The basic motivation for all developments in the 'thinking skills' tradition has always been much the same, whatever the details of the resulting programme. Here are four, rather different, examples.

1. Matthew Lipman, was a distinguished Professor of Philosophy in Columbia University in New York in the 60/70s. He became increasingly frustrated because he found that his university students lacked a number of basic thinking skills, like the ability to construct

an argument, to clarify ideas, to see things from others' points of view and the like. He was also convinced that it was too late to change their thinking habits at the university level so he designed the Philosophy for Children Programme which aims to teach these and other thinking skills to schoolchildren aged 5 - 15 This is a stand-alone programme - in which thinking skills are taught separately from normal school subjects.

2. The impetus for the CASE (Cognitive Acceleration through Science Education programme) came from a survey of 14,000 pupils in 45 schools in England and Wales, which showed that only 16% of 16 year olds were showing evidence of even early 'formal operational thinking' (a fundamental idea of Piaget's). Since this kind of thinking is required to understand how to test hypotheses effectively, to judge critically between the merits of two arguments or to cope with proportionality, the implication was clear - that the vast majority of pupils cannot think at the level required for the science curriculum (or indeed many other areas). CASE is a programme where the teaching of thinking skills is embedded in the teaching of subject matter, namely the science curriculum for 12-13 year olds

3. Rueben Feuerstein created his Instrumental Enrichment (IE) programme, which was initially developed nearly 50 years ago, explicitly to help overcome the thinking deficiencies in culturally disadvantaged, low-performing Israeli adolescents, many of who had been traumatised by their early experiences during and after the Second World War. Despite its distinctive origins, Instrumental Enrichment, which is a standalone programme, or programmes derived from it, are now widely used with a much wider range of abilities and ages, often with successful results.

4. Georg Polya, himself a brilliant mathematician and teacher, noticed that his students (even at Stanford University) didn't know how to solve unfamiliar problems. He became convinced that, although they knew a lot of mathematics, they didn't know how to direct their own thought processes in ways that could be fruitful. They didn't realise that there are strategies for solving mathematical problems. That lead him to write *How to Solve It* (and some other books) which explain what he calls *heuristic strategies* for solving problems. Though teaching Polya-type problem solving heuristics is not greatly in fashion at the moment, many university teachers refer their students to *How to Solve It* at some stage.

Similar stories lie behind the work of nearly all those who have contributed to the development of the thinking skills tradition. They notice some deficiency in the thinking of their students and devise some teaching interventions which aim at directly addressing those thinking deficiencies - ie at teaching thinking explicitly and directly. Of course, different original concerns can lead to quite different educational proposals - often for students at different stages of intellectual development and in very different contexts.

However the resulting programmes have similar objectives (to teach thinking skills directly) and usually have other similarities too, for example, as we said above, the key to nearly all of them is 'meta-cognition' - thinking about one's thinking and explicitly trying to direct one's thinking to follow some good model. (To explain with an analogy; just as you can try to improve your golf swing (a motor skill) by self consciously trying to swing like Tiger Woods, so you can improve your skill in decision making by self consciously trying to follow a good decision making model -and similarly with other thinking skills). Another common element is practice; just like any other skills, the way to develop thinking skills is to start with easy tasks and to practice the skill in more and more complex situations.

The thinking skills tradition argues that thinking skills *can* be taught and *should* be taught. Furthermore, it is claimed, these skills are *transferable,* i.e., if students learn general thinking skills in one context, they will be able to (and actually will) apply them to many other contexts, provided the teaching specifically aims at such transfer. Critics of the thinking skills tradition most commonly challenge this transferability claim. The most famous advocate of this opposition is John McPeck in his *Critical Thinking and Education.* Rather than responding to his arguments directly we shall review the evidence for believing that 'teaching thinking' can deliver what it promises.

Evidence on Teaching Thinking

There is extensive evidence (both in the UK and elsewhere) that thinking skills can be developed through direct and explicit teaching, that they contribute to improved performance in a wide range of subject areas and that transfer does occur under the right circumstances.

Some of the most striking evidence comes from the work of Philip Adey and Michael Shayer on their CASE (Cognitive Acceleration Through Science Education) project. In this project, which builds on Piaget's work, thinking skills are taught to 12-13 year old pupils over a period of two years in carefully redesigned National Curriculum science lessons. The results are fully documented in Adey and Shayer. In short they show remarkable evidence that students who received this teaching did far better in their subsequent GCSE examinations than control groups of students who did not (on average, they obtained a whole grade higher). Furthermore, not only did they do better in their science examinations, but they also did significantly better in their other GCSE exam subjects, so transfer had occurred across a wide range of subjects.

Interestingly, when students who had received CASE teaching were tested immediately after the CASE programme, they showed relatively little improvement over the control groups, but the GCSE results suggest that the thinking skills interventions take time to have their effect.

The most recent UK evidence on the effectiveness of teaching thinking skills comes from researchers in the Centre for Learning and Teaching, Newcastle University. They conducted a 'meta-study', looking at hundreds of published papers reporting 'thinking skills' interventions with school pupils aged 5-16. The study investigated the 'quantitative impact of thinking skills interventions on

(i) pupils' cognitive achievement,

(ii) pupils' curriculum attainment, and

(iii) pupil's affective states' (eg., motivation and engagement).

The authors expected that 'intervention effects would be positive, since the vast majority of educational innovations have a positive effect' but they were particularly interested in whether the effect sizes 'would exceed the 0.4 level cited by Hattie as the average intervention size effect from his meta-analysis of 200,000 effect sizes'. Given that his study included interventions with effect sizes ranging from 0.6 to over 1 Hattie considers that 0.5 is a minimum for an intervention to be considered 'educationally significant'.

Though the Newcastle researchers reviewed hundreds of published papers, they restricted their meta-study to ones in which control groups had been used and effect sizes were (or could be) quantified. There were 30 of these and the results are summarised as follows:

> 'Analysis of these studies indicate that thinking skills approaches are effective in improving pupils' learning. A meta-analysis of this impact found an overall effect size of 0.71 on cognitive measures (such as tests of

> reasoning or non-verbal measures such as Ravens Progressive matrices) and an effect size of 0.66 for curriculum outcomes (such as mathematics or science tests). These effect sizes indicate that an 'average' class of pupils who received such interventions would move from 50th place in a rank of 100 similar classes to about 26th on curriculum tests and to about 24th place on cognitive measures.'
>
> 'The identification of 'thinking skills' has identified a collection of research studies which have an above average impact on learning outcomes. This suggests that teachers' interest and enthusiasm for such approaches is well-founded … as such approaches tend to have a positive effect, over and above what you would usually expect from an educational intervention.'

There is also extensive evidence from the United States, involving a similar meta-study methodology. This evidence shows that adopting approaches which make thinking explicit, or which focus on particular kinds of thinking, are successful at raising attainment, particularly those based on metacognitive approaches or cognitively demanding interventions such as problem solving and hypothesis testing.

The evidence cited here shows that significant educational gains are *possible* from teaching thinking skills. Of course, these positive results show what *can* be done - but it is equally obvious that 'teaching thinking' can be done poorly and ineffectively. Carol McGuinness, in her DfES Research Report spells some of the conditions for success in this kind of teaching as follows,

> '..the general framework [of ideas for developing thinking skills] now includes: the need to make thinking skills explicit in the curriculum; teaching through a form of coaching; taking a metacognitive perspective; collaborative learning (including computer-mediated learning); creating dispositions and habits of good thinking; [and] generalising the framework to thinking curricula, thinking classrooms and thinking schools.'

Furthermore, whatever approach is adopted, [it] must maximise transfer, that is, adopt strategies (eg bridging, deliberate teaching for transfer) which ensure that learning transfers beyond the context in which it is learned.

Of course, even positive results like those cited above need to be interpreted with caution. This is partly because of the differences in the thinking skills programmes included in the studies and partly because a meta-study is only as good as its contributing studies. However, the important point is that there are many studies now giving incontrovertible evidence that 'thinking skills' interventions *can* be very effective in raising standards.

Assessing Thinking Skills for University Admission

No doubt the evidence just outlined will be welcome in universities for its own sake, but there is another reason why work on thinking skills is interesting to them.

Universities want to admit those students who will be most successful on their courses. In order to do this, they need information which helps them judge/predict how well applicants are likely to do once they are admitted - how well they are equipped to cope with the special demands of university work and of particular courses.

The UCAS form gives university admission officers quite a lot of information about students' ability to work hard and learn material in given subject areas from their A level results (either predicted or known). Indeed, A level results have been the main determinant of university admission ever since they were first introduced in 1951. Admissions officers also have information from head-teachers reports (on the UCAS form) and perhaps from interviews (which are notoriously unreliable, though few universities research the reliability of their interviews). Sometimes they set their own tests, though these are usually subject matter tests (like STEP papers taken for admission to mathematics in Cambridge and some other universities).

Given these sources of information, many university admissions are decided reasonably straightforwardly. However, in recent years there has been a tremendous increase in the number of university applicants who have very good A-level results. As a result, increasing numbers of universities and courses have been faced with the problem of choosing between 'too many' good applicants and their methods have generated considerable controversy. So, how might this be done both skilfully and fairly? If one talks to admissions officers who are faced with choosing between 'very able' applicants, they commonly say something like the following,

> 'Of course our candidates are very good at learning what their teachers tell them (they have or are predicted to get very good A-level results), but they fall into two groups when you ask them questions outside what they have 'done for A-level', questions which require them to show how they think in such situations. Some candidates simply flounder - they haven't 'done it' so they have little to say about it. Others welcome such questions; they are ready to think about possible solutions, will talk around the problem, try different approaches - and so on. They show a readiness to think on their own account and they know how to do that. These are the ones we want to admit.'

To put the point differently, when students move from school to a university, many will find that they have to think a great deal for themselves. University teachers will assume a whole range of thinking skills - an ability to argue a case, to solve problems, to judge credibility, and much more. Other things being equal, students will perform better at university if they have been taught these skills explicitly and know how to deploy them in novel situations.

There is no doubt that these 'thinking skills' are teachable (though not commonly taught), helpful (especially in the modern world where knowledge becomes obsolete so quickly and what is needed is people who are good at thinking things through for themselves), examinable (OCR/ CIE are already doing this quite extensively) and the kinds of things university admissions officers are looking for but receive little information about from the UCAS form.

Thus, an assessment of suitable 'thinking skills' could be just what university admissions officers are looking for if they are faced with the problem of too many able applicants. At present, universities have no direct information about how good applicants are at *thinking things through on their own account* - at tackling novel situations of just the kind they will often encounter in university and subsequently. This ability is just what the new Thinking Skills Assessment aims to measure.

Working back from what students have to do in university, it seems reasonable to assume that a reliable measure of this ability could be very helpful in the admissions process and evidence is beginning to emerge to support this view.

Measuring Intelligence versus Assessing 'Thinking Skills'

Intelligence and the Scholastic Aptitude Test (SAT)

Work on *measuring* 'intelligence' is usually traced back to the pioneering work of the French psychologist, Alfred Binet. This work was taken up and developed in the US in the 20s and 30s by Stanford Professor Lewis Terman and Harvard professor Robert Yerkes. In this tradition, 'intelligence' is usually taken to be a fairly fixed endowment and intelligence tests are taken to assess something fixed. Of course, intelligence develops over time - as one grows older - but an individual's position in any overall ranking is likely to remain much the same at different ages. As a corollary, on this conception it is not thought possible to significantly 'improve' one's level of intelligence through teaching.

By contrast, the thinking skills tradition believes that many of the skills commonly identified with intelligence can be taught and developed by direct teaching of the right kind.

Thus, there are quite different views about cognitive development underlying the two traditions and there is mounting evidence that the 'thinking skills' tradition is on the right track - that performance of school pupils can be considerably improved by teaching thinking skills - that it is possible to 'really raise standards' in this way.

Following in the tradition of Binet's work, an instrument, called the Scholastic Aptitude test (SAT), was developed in the United States, to help with the process of university admissions. Its development began in 1926 but it became widely used after the second World War, when admissions to higher education in the US were greatly expanded. It is now called the Scholastic Assessment Test and has been well-established for over 60 years.

The problem faced by colleges in the United States was that there has never been anything like the UK National Curriculum or national examinations like the UK A-levels, so how should they compare applicants from different States, with different curricula, different examinations and different standards? The SAT was designed as an 'objective' measure of 'intelligence' (seen as a fairly fixed endowment), which would be a good indicator of academic aptitude and which could greatly assist admissions officers in North American universities.

It has long been designed to measured two abilities, 'verbal reasoning' and 'mathematical reasoning', which are seen as

(i) developed abilities which grow slowly over the years,

(ii) relatively independent of what the student is currently learning in the classroom and

(iii) general academic skills necessary for successful college work.

The SAT is widely used in the United States and elsewhere (eg Canada, Sweden and Israel) to provide *supplementary* predictive information in the college admission process. It is combined with the Grade Point Average to predict performance and its predictive validity is usually measured in terms of performance one year after admission. (And there are now several similar instruments used for similar purposes, including the Graduate Record Examination (GRE), the Law Schools Admission Test (LSAT) and others.)

Thinking Skills and the Thinking Skills Assessment (TSA)

Arising out of the thinking skills tradition, instruments called the Biomedical Admissions Test (BMAT), a medical and veterinary schools entrance test, and the more general Thinking Skills Assessment (TSA) have been developed by UCLES, also to help with the process of university admissions. These tests have been developed on the basis of the work done by UCLES on assessing thinking skills over the past 25 years.

The problem faced by some universities in the UK and for which these instruments were designed is quite different from the problem for which the SAT was designed in the US. In short, the problem in the UK is to differentiate between very large numbers of candidates with similar and excellent A level results. The TSA and the BMAT are designed to assist admissions officers in British universities faced by 'over-subscription' in discriminating skilfully and fairly between such candidates.

The Thinking Skills Assessment is currently designed to measure two skills, 'critical thinking' and 'problem solving', which are seen as

(i) skills/abilities which are *teachable* - (with significant pay-off for A levels and university work)
(ii) skills which can be developed through special approaches to subject matter teaching or through stand-alone courses
(iii) general/transferable academic skills which are vital to successful university work

The TSA is currently being piloted by 22 colleges in 5 disciplines in the University of Cambridge. It provides *supplementary* predictive information in the college admission process. Scores are combined with A-level scores to predict performance and the predictive validity of both tests is being measured in terms of performance one year after admission. The BMAT also has a thinking skills component and it is currently being used by faculties in five leading universites.

Scholastic Assessment Test

Some extra information about students' thinking skills could be of great assistance in the admission process in British universities. Some people have suggested that the North American Scholastic Assessment Test (SAT) could be used to provide that extra information. But this would be a mistake, for several reasons:

(i) The British and North American educational systems are very different. In particular, there is nothing akin to the National Curriculum in the US and each of the 50 States has its own curricula and State examinations. As a result, there are no national examinations like our A-levels.

(ii) Furthermore, admission to university in North America is normally to the first year of a four year course, where the first year teaching is broader and more general in nature than the first year of most British university courses, which are more specialised. In that context, far more students will change direction or leave university during and at the end of the first year in North America than happens here.

(iii) Because there are no national examinations like A levels in North America, the problem faced by admissions officers in the institutions of higher education in the US is how to compare the qualifications of applicants from a huge variety of backgrounds. The SAT is designed to deal with this problem. Thus, it aims to provide an 'objective' standard with which to weigh different standards which might be applied in different schools, in different States across a large and very diverse country.

(iv) In Britain, the problem for institutions of higher education is quite different. A levels have existed since 1951; they are national examinations which are very well established - and are based on national curricula. Admission to British universities has been decided mainly on the basis of performance in these examinations ever since they were first introduced. Most university admissions are decided quite straightforwardly on the basis of predicted A-level grades and the Head-teacher's report provided on the UCAS form. However, increasing numbers of universities and courses need to discriminate between 'too many' able applicants. Thus, in the UK, the problem is to find a method of differentiating skilfully and fairly between candidates with very high A-level scores.

(v) The SAT is designed for the North American educational context. Educational Testing Service, who produces it, works very closely with educational institutions to ensure that it meets their needs. It is unlikely to provide an 'off the peg' instrument to help selection in the very different UK context, where the problem to be addressed is different.

(vi) One of the most important differences between the SAT and the TSA is that the skills assessed in the TSA are teachable skills which are valuable in higher education. The SAT on the other hand has long claimed to measure 'innate' or 'native' ability. Of course, it is well known that candidates can be 'coached' to do better on the SAT than they would without such practice. Clearly, candidates taking any test will benefit from doing similar tests (usually past test papers), which show the structure of the test and the kind of questions it contains. However, most of the strategies for getting higher marks on the SAT do not involve gaining more knowledge or skills that will benefit students in the HE courses to which they aspire. They simply involve learning what to look for in the test and how to use its structure to the candidate's advantage. By contrast, learning thinking skills leads to the enhancement of students' performance in all parts of the curriculum as well as preparing them to get the best from Higher Education. Furthermore, such study will pay dividends in bringing candidates' thinking skills up to a suitable level for the purposes of BMAT or TSA.

(vii) The SAT is commonly criticised for the effect it has on the attitudes of students to education - that it devalues real education, etc. This is not true of teaching and assessing thinking skills.

(viii) Thinking Skills assessments are also useful in being able to screen out those that have been 'crammed' for a knowledge-based test but do have the required level of thinking skill and are thus not likely to succeed at a selective faculty. They might also supply useful information about those without 'standard' 'A' Levels.

To summarise: the SAT is very well suited to the North American context and the problems it faces. The British context and problems are quite different.

What is Critical Thinking?

The thinking skills assessed in the BMAT and TSA instruments introduced above are 'critical thinking' and 'problem solving'. It is time to explain how these are conceived. A key reason for doing this is that these assessments of thinking skills are intended to have a 'face validity' for university academics (especially those involved in the admissions process). That is to say the questions are intended to look like the kinds of questions students need to address in university work and perhaps similar to the sorts of questions admissions officers would like to put to candidates in interview precisely to see how well they think in unfamiliar situations, when facing novel problems.

The thinking skills which are taught in the critical thinking tradition include arguing a case, decision-making, problem solving, explaining causes, evaluating, comparing and contrasting, judging credibility, clarifying and interpreting ideas and many other 'higher order' thinking skills (cf Bloom (ed) for an account of 'higher order' thinking).

In the UK, the Qualifications and Curriculum Authority has established 'subject criteria' for critical thinking teaching and examinations and these say that AS level specifications should require students to:

1. understand the language of reasoning
2. clarify expressions and ideas
3. identify reasons and conclusions
4. recognise and evaluate different kinds of claims
5. judge the credibility of sources
6. understand and use different patterns of reasoning as well as different standards for evaluating arguments
7. recognise and evaluate special kinds of reasoning: causal explanations, justifying decisions, reasoning from different points of view, basic ethical reasoning
8. recognise assumptions
9. present relevant arguments
10. understand basic forms of statistical reasoning appropriate to informed citizens.

In addition, A level students should be able to:

1. evaluate rhetorical and persuasive language, including some classic fallacies
2. understand forms of statistical reasoning appropriate to informed citizens

3. understand and use features of hypothetical reasoning such as for example what if, suppositional reasoning, testing hypotheses
4. identify and evaluate ethical arguments, making reference to principles
5. recognise and apply some basic logical ideas, such as for example excluded middle, converse, contradiction, consistent, circularity, counter example, necessary and sufficient conditions, imply/entail, generalisation
6. use images, symbols and other non-verbal stimuli in reasoning such as for example those in news reporting, advertising, political and similar cartoons.

It is not difficult to see from such a list that these are skills which are fundamental to many intellectual activities and are also skills which are taken for granted in many university courses. Thus, on the face of it, if one could get reliable information about applicants' critical thinking skills, this information could be very relevant in the university admission process.

The critical thinking tradition is now very well established. John Dewey is usually regarded as the founder of this tradition, but many other scholars have made important contributions. Edward Glaser conducted the first scientific experiment to see if critical thinking skills could be taught and was responsible for the *Watson Glaser Critical Thinking Appraisal*, still the most widely used test of critical thinking in the world. Robert Ennis (and) has made many important contributions, as have Scriven, Swartz, Costa and many others in the last 30 years. In the United States, student reaction to the Vietnam War is widely credited with giving impetus to the teaching of critical thinking in universities and elsewhere. Students demanded instruction in how to combat bad reasoning and how to construct good arguments - hence the development of many courses claiming to teach 'critical thinking'.

Despite all this good work, it is important to note however that when something like critical thinking becomes 'fashionable', as it has in the United States in the past two decades, poor quality teaching and testing becomes a serious problem and risk discrediting the good work, so measures of the effects of teaching critical thinking (like other thinking skills) need to take this into account..

Among UK organisations, UCLES has given a significant lead in developing assessments of critical thinking and of problem solving skills. The history of their involvement goes back to the 1980s when they devised a British version of the North American Law Schools Admission Test to assist in selecting students to read Law at Cambridge University. In 1997 they asked Dr Alec Fisher to design a new AS level examination in critical thinking. This was first piloted in 1999 and has been taught and examined successfully ever since. The number of students who took the examination in 2004 was 14,315. UCLES has also had an Advanced Extension Award since 2002 and the AS is currently being extended to an A-level to be first taught from September 2005 and first examined in June 2006.

What is Problem Solving?

The basic idea behind this tradition is that reasoning and thinking about numbers, shapes, and other 'mathematical' objects and structures is quite different from verbal reasoning (in the 'intelligence' tradition) or critical thinking (in the 'thinking skills' tradition) and needs to be differently taught and assessed. In the tradition which owes so much to Polya, the kind of problem solving with which are concerned here includes the ability,

- to read and understand material with mathematical/quantitative/ graphical content
- to clarify and interpret such information when it is unclear or ambiguous,
- to evaluate reasoning about such information,
- to identify assumptions,
- to identify counter-examples and other flaws in reasoning,
- to understand different logical relationships (negation, implication, quantifiers, etc)
- to construct solutions to (unfamiliar) problems which use such information,
- to identify *relevant* or *necessary* information for solving a problem,
- to differentiate between possible, necessary and other logical relationships,
- to compute, visualise and estimate,
- to find procedures for solving an unfamiliar problem,
- to formulate hypotheses and conjectures (e.g., suggesting patterns from examples),
- draw conclusions from given data,

- to write and express themselves using mathematical/quantitative/ graphical ideas.

Again, it is not difficult to see that such skills are fundamental to work in many sciences, social sciences, engineering and other intellectual activities. They are also skills which are taken for granted in many university courses. Thus, on the face of it, if one could get reliable information about applicants' problem solving skills, this information could be very relevant in the university admission process.

Some people would trace the 'problem solving' tradition back to Binet's work on measuring intelligence. But, insofar as we are speaking of a teachable skill, most people who have worked in this field would identify Georg Polya and his book *How to Solve It* as the origin of this tradition. Polya's work has since been taken up by various mathematics educators and much work has been done in this tradition, notably by the American mathematics educator, Alan Schoenfeld. A good example of British work in this field is *Problem Solving: The School Mathematics Project 16-19,* published by Cambridge University Press in 1989 which remains a source of excellent ideas and material.

The critical thinking tradition includes the skill of 'problem solving' but this is normally a non-mathematical kind of problem solving, (like deciding which universities to apply to). So this should not be confused with the 'quantitative' problem solving with which we are dealing here.

The UCLES Thinking Skills Assessment (TSA) sees the problem solving skills it assesses as being 'parallel' to critical thinking skills - but about numerical, quantitative and spatial data or subject matter. Comparison of the two lists of skills above shows many similarities, though critical thinking uses only ordinary language whilst problem solving uses 'quantitative' language and different reasoning techniques. For example, a distinctive feature of the problem solving domain is that the reasoning skills involved are nearly all *deductive* reasoning skills, whereas in the case of critical thinking deductive reasoning is rare.

The 'problems' in the TSA currently fall into three groups, called Finding Procedures, Relevant Selection and Identifying Similarity (Willmott Appendices, B and C) but the fundamental point about them is that they are 'novel' problems, of a kind students will not have encountered at school and for which there is no ready 'off the peg' solution. To tackle these problems, students will have to have problem solving strategies available to them - of the kind Polya gives.

Of course, many university courses have among their admission requirements a pass in GCSE or A level mathematics (perhaps at particular grades), because they require the *content and problem solving skills* of GCSE or A level mathematics. But, again, it seems reasonable to assume that specific information about problem solving skills could be of help to admission officers in many university fields, and evidence to that effect is beginning to emerge.

Parallel to the case of testing critical thinking, testing problem solving skills could help admission officers distinguish between applicants who have been well-drilled to pass mathematics examinations and those who can solve quantitative problems of a novel, unfamiliar kind who have a skill which is needed in many university courses. Its problems would require that the candidate could use problem solving strategies and *understood* how to solve new kinds of problems (at a given level)

What is needed now is consultation with those for whom the TSA is intended, especially teachers in higher education, about the mathematical/ quantitative/logical/ problem solving skills which are needed in various areas of academic work with reference to questions of the types discussed above. As I said earlier, it is important that questions have 'face validity' for university teachers.

Clearly, some university subject areas require almost no problem solving skills of the kind outlined above (e.g., English Literature); others require a relatively low level and others quite a high level (e.g., Physics, Computing).

There is a view among many involved in education that students' thinking skills simply develop slowly and fairly independently of what is being studied in their normal school subjects - history, physics etc. The 'thinking skills' tradition argues that these skills are better taught *explicitly* and that doing so can really *raise educational standards*.

There are many strands in what has become known as the 'thinking skills' tradition, including the *critical thinking* and *problem solving* traditions. Thinking skills programmes are nearly always prompted by the realisation that students lack some thinking ability and are designed to remedy that deficiency by teaching the skills in question *explicitly* and *directly*.

The essential ideas behind nearly all of these programmes is '*metacognition*' - self consciously directing ones own thinking to be more skilful - and practice (just as one can improve a motor skill, like a playing golf).

There is increasing *evidence* that thinking skills can be developed through direct teaching and that they can significantly improve performance in ordinary school subjects. And this evidence is outlined above, citing some important sources.

These results are welcome to universities for their own sake, but are also of interest to them for another, more specific, reason. In recent years there has been a tremendous increase in the number of university applicants with very good A-level results. Thus, increasing numbers of universities and courses have been faced with the problem of choosing from among 'too many' able candidates and their methods have generated considerable controversy. Some are now experimenting with tests of 'thinking skills' to provide them with the extra information they need to make these choices *wisely* and *fairly*.

At present, candidates' UCAS forms give admissions officers a great deal of information, but provide no direct information about how good applicants are at *thinking things through on their own account* - at tackling novel situations of just the kind they will often encounter in university work. Thus, working backwards from what students will have to do in university, it seems entirely reasonable to assume that a reliable measure of this ability could be very helpful in the admissions process and evidence is beginning to emerge to support this view.

There is a question about what should be assessed by such tests. Should they assess *'intelligence'*, thought of as being something *fairly fixed*, like the North American Scholastic Assessment Test (SAT)? Or should they assess 'thinking ability' seen as being both *teachable* and *fundamental to success in university work*?

The SAT works very well in the North American context but is not the instrument for the different problems faced in the UK. What is required here is a test of thinking skills; these are vital for success in university, teaching them would raise standards and assessing them gives information not otherwise available to admissions officers. Working back from the 'thinking skills' required by university, what is needed is a test of 'critical thinking' and 'problem solving' (and perhaps others).

These constructs are explained sufficiently fully for university teachers to see that they are fundamental to success in many university courses.

As we have argued, these skills can be taught and should be taught explicitly. They can improve performance in school subjects and are vital at the university level. The UCLES Thinking Skills Assessment, which is built on 25 years work in this field, is designed to assess just these thinking skills and could therefore provide valuable information to help in the admission process of many universities. Evidence on this instrument is published in Willmott.

Thinking skills assessments of the right kind could be valuable to British universities in making admission decisions wisely and fairly. The BMAT and the TSA are already well-developed and evidence about their utility is emerging. UCLES also envisages producing *similar thinking skills assessments* (besides the TSA and BMAT) for other subjects, in consultation with interested academics. There is much work to be done but this is an interesting development which deserves to be taken seriously and followed up.

References

Adey, P.S., Shayer, M (1994) *Really Raising Standards: Cognitive intervention and academic achievement.* London: Routledge.

Binet, A., and Simon, T. (1916) *The development of intelligence in children.* Baltimore: Williams and Wilkins.

De Bono, E (1976) *Teaching Thinking*. London: Maurice Temple Smith.

Ennis, R. H. (1996) *Critical Thinking* New Jersey; Prentice Hall.

Fisher, A (2001) *Critical Thinking: An Introduction* Cambridge: Cambridge University Press.

2

Higher Order Thinking Skills

Higher order thinking skills include critical, logical, reflective, metacognitive, and creative thinking. They are activated when individuals encounter unfamiliar problems, uncertainties, questions, or dilemmas. Successful applications of the skills result in explanations, decisions, performances, and products that are valid within the context of available knowledge and experience and that promote continued growth in these and other intellectual skills. Higher order thinking skills are grounded in lower order skills such as discriminations, simple application and analysis, and cognitive strategies and are linked to prior knowledge of subject matter content. Appropriate teaching strategies and learning environments facilitate their growth as do student persistence, self-monitoring, and open-minded, flexible attitudes.

This definition is consistent with current theories related to how higher order thinking skills are learned and developed. Although different theoreticians and researchers use different frameworks to describe higher order skills and how they are acquired, all frameworks are in general agreement concerning the conditions under which they prosper.

Useful learning strategies include rehearsal, elaboration, organization, and metacognition. Lessons should be specifically designed to teach specific learning strategies. Direct instruction (teacher-centered presentations of information) should be used sparingly. Presentations should be short (up to five minutes) and coupled with guided practice to teach subskills and knowledge.

Teacher- and/or student-generated questions about dilemmas, novel problems, and novel approaches should elicit answers that have not been learned already.

Sincere feedback providing immediate, specific, and corrective information should inform learners of their progress.

Small group activities such as student discussions, peer tutoring, and cooperative learning can be effective in the development of thinking skills. Activities should involve challenging tasks, teacher encouragement to stay on task, and ongoing feedback about group progress.

Computer-mediated communication and instruction can provide access to remote data sources and allow collaboration with students in other locations. It can be effective in skill building in areas such as verbal analogies, logical thinking, and inductive/deductive reasoning.

Valid assessment of higher order thinking skills requires that students be unfamiliar with the questions or tasks they are asked to answer or perform and that they have sufficient prior knowledge to enable them to use their higher order thinking skills in answering questions or performing tasks. Psychological research suggests that skills taught in one domain can generalize to others. Over long periods of time, individuals develop higher order skills (intellectual abilities) that apply to the solutions of a broad spectrum of complex problems.

Three item/task formats are useful in measuring higher order skills: (a) selection, which includes multiple-choice, matching, and rank-order items; (b) generation, which includes short-answer, essay, and performance items or tasks; and (c) explanation, which involves giving reasons for the selection or generation responses.

Classroom teachers recognize the importance of having students develop higher order skills yet often do not assess their students' progress. Several performance-based models are available to assist them in teaching and assessing these skills. Comprehensive statewide assessment of higher order skills is feasible but would be expensive. Florida and a number of other states now incorporate the measurement of higher order skills in their statewide assessments.

Defining Thinking Skills

The challenge of defining "thinking skills, reasoning, critical thought, and problem solving" has been referred to as a conceptual swamp in a study by Cuban, and as a "century old problem" for which "there is no well-established taxonomy or typology". In addition, explanations of how learning occurs have been viewed as inadequate, with no single theory adequately explaining "how *all* learning takes place".

Several factors may account for these views about thinking and learning. First, different types of learning require different teaching strategiesCno single method works for all learning, although specific strategies work for specific types. Second, intelligence is no longer seen as an unchanging general ability but rather a kaleidoscope of abilities that can be affected by a variety of factors, including teaching strategies. Third, the understanding of the thinking process has shifted to a multidimensional view—much more like a complex network of interactive capabilities rather than a linear, hierarchical, or spiral process. Fourth, the research over the last two decades has focused on more specialized topics such as insight, wait time for problem solving, visual imagery and metaphors, and schemata.

Despite the challenges related to defining higher order thinking, educators, administrators, and evaluators in Florida and across the nation have expressed agreement about the value of teaching it. There is a renewed awareness that, although information and memory provide "a refrigerator in which to store a stock of meanings for future use," it is judgment that "selects and adopts the one to be used in an emergency..." Complex real-life problems often demand complex solutions, which are obtained through higher level thinking processes. Teaching higher order thinking, then, provides students with relevant life skills and offers them an added benefit of helping them improve their content knowledge, lower order thinking, and self-esteem.

The need to set standards for higher order thinking skills has been documented throughout the 1980s and 1990s. In the 1980s, documentation came from the National Assessment for Educational Progress (NAEP); the National Commission on Excellence in Education in *A Nation at Risk;* Goodlad's *A Place Called School*, which focused on social studies and science; the 1985 Commission on Reading report called *Becoming a Nation of Readers*; and the 1986 Carnegie Forum on Education and the Economy's Task Force on Teaching.

Reports written in the 1990s have documented similar results. According to Kent Ashworth, the director of dissemination for the NAEP, little has changed in the last 20 years. Linn reported that the state-by-state NAEP results in mathematics signaled another "wake-up America call, along with stumbling verbal SAT scores in the fall of 1991". Such deficits stem from too much focus on lower-level objectives and not enough on meaningful learning and higher order thinking.

Nationwide responses to these grim reports included creation of the National Council on Education Standards and Testing (NCEST), the Bush Administration's America 2000 proposals (U.S. Department of Education), and the Department of Labor's Secretary's Commission on

Achieving Necessary Skills (SCANS) report. In Florida, standards for learning outcomes and the Florida Comprehensive Assessment Test (FCAT) series were established to shift attention to the development of higher order thinking skills. Florida expresses the goal of enabling students "to make well-reasoned, thoughtful, and healthy lifelong decisions". This goal aligns with the foundation skills and workplace competencies from SCANS, in which education will be considered successful when each student "thinks creatively, makes decisions, solves problems, visualizes, knows how to learn, and reasons". Examples of the Florida Sunshine State Standards related to higher order thinking are listed below.

- *Reading*: "analyzes the validity and reliability of primary source information and uses the information appropriately"
- *Math:* "uses and justifies different estimation strategies in a real-world problem situation and determines the reasonableness of results of calculations in a given problem situation"
- *Language Arts:* "selects and uses strategies to understand words and text, and to make and confirm inferences from what is read, including interpreting diagrams, graphs, and statistical illustrations"
- *Science:* "understands the interconnectedness of the systems on Earth and the quality of life"
- *Social Studies:* "uses maps, globes, charts, graphs, and other geographic tools, including map keys and symbols to gather and interpret data and to draw conclusions about physical patterns"

In the FCAT, the focus on higher order thinking skills has been particularly noticeable in mathematics, where word problems are more complex and address real-life situations more than previous tests.

Several recent initiatives by the DOE have also sharpened the focus on higher order thinking skills. In November 1997, the DOE completed an assessment feasibility study on listening and verbal communication skills, information literacy skills, and problem-solving skills. This current study extends the previous and ongoing initiatives by the DOE by reporting on the analysis of research and discourse on thinking processes. The study has identified the major theorists and provided an overview of their concepts and theories. To assist classroom teachers, the study provides definitions, teaching strategies, assessment strategies for both statewide and classroom assessment, sample teaching assignments, test questions, and an extensive resource list.

Several major concepts relevant to the higher order thinking processes are to follow, based on three assumptions about thinking and learning. First, the levels of thinking cannot be unmeshed from the levels of learning; they involve interdependent, multiple components and levels. Second, whether or not thinking can be learned without subject matter content is only a theoretical point. In real life, students will learn content in both community and school experiences, no matter what theorists conclude, and the concepts and vocabulary they learn in the prior year will help them learn both higher order thinking skills and new content in the coming year. Third, higher order thinking involves a variety of thinking processes applied to complex situations and having multiple variables.

Context

The level of thinking depends upon the context, with a real-world situation offering multiple variables to challenge thinking processes. Going through a cafeteria line and making decisions about types and amounts of food one should eat requires a much more sophisticated thinking process than counting carbohydrates and fats in a classroom. Successful higher order thinking depends upon an individual's ability to apply, reorganize, and embellish knowledge in the context of the thinking situation.

Metacognition

The self-correcting nature of thinking is called "metacognition." Metacognition includes awareness of one's thinking processes, self-monitoring, and application of known heuristics and steps for thinking. One's success with metacognition depends, in part, on a belief in one's ability to get smarter as well as the beliefs of others, such as teachers, in one's ability.

Procedural Knowledge

Procedural knowledge sometimes is misunderstood as a higher order thinking skill. While it may be a prerequisite for higher order thinking, it actually is a type of knowledge—specifically, knowledge of rules and their application. The ability to recite a rule or set of procedures is "information learning"; the ability to apply a rule or procedure to a routine single-variable situation is "application." Neither of these capabilities involves higher order thinking. Instead, applications of procedural knowledge that also involve analysis and synthesis of two or more concepts would be considered higher order thinking. Examples include

> "constructing map projections and grids, writing clear and concise case reports, calculating the fixed overhead costs for a project, designing spreadsheets, drawing conclusions about the impact of social reform on the universality of social programs, and establishing meaningful relationships with coworkers".

Comprehension

Comprehension, a part of lower order thinking skills, is integral to higher order thinking skills development. In fact, some research and teaching strategies focus on comprehension as if it were within the higher order domain. While it is an important prerequisite, it is not a higher order thinking skill. Comprehension remains the process by which individuals construct meaning from information and form new "schemata" through specific activities, including, but not limited to,

- generating and answering questions that demand higher order thinking about old and new ideas;
- confronting conflicting ideas and information, problems, or dilemmas;
- exploring and making discoveries;
- conducting systematic inquiries;
- summarizing, reciting, and discussing new ideas and their relationships;
- relating new understandings to other concepts;
- applying new ideas and information in basic problem-solving activities; or
- reflecting and verbalizing about cognitive processes involved in comprehension.

CREATIVITY

Although some references do not explicitly include creativity as higher order thinking, it cannot be unmeshed from the process. The very act of generating solutions to problems requires the creative process of going beyond previously learned concepts and rules. Creativity involves divergent and convergent thinking to produce new ideas. Its place in the network of higher order thinking skills was well articulated in Pasteur's observation that "chance favors only the prepared mind" because "only a trained mind can make connections between unrelated events, recognize meaning in a serendipitous event," and produce a solution that is both novel and suitable.

Major features of creativity are listed below.

- Creativity involves the consistent use of basic principles or rules in new situations, such as Benjamin Franklin's application of conservation and equilibrium; Picasso's creation of "Guernica," resulting from sketches and modifications of previous work; Watson and Crick's discovery of the DNA double helix structure; and Edison's invention of an electric lighting system.
- Creativity involves discovering and solving problems. Innovative approaches are used to accurately evaluate shortcomings, and actions are taken to remedy those weaknesses.
- Creativity involves selecting the relevant aspects of a problem and putting pieces together into a coherent system that integrates the new information with what a person already knows. In a basic sense, it involves a series of decision-making choices between "two or more competing alternatives of action," each having "several pros and cons associated with it".
- Creativity overlaps with other characteristics, such as "intelligence, academic ability, dependability, adaptiveness, and independence" and can "evolve within each of the seven intelligences".
- Creativity requires many of the same conditions for learning as other higher order thinking skills. The learning processes are enhanced by supportive environments and deteriorate with fears, insecurities, and low self-esteem. Creativity deteriorates with extrinsic motivation, restraint on choice, and the pressure of outside evaluation.

Insight

Insight is the sudden unexpected solution to a problem. Complexity seems to be the spark for solving problems through insight. Noninsight solutions require using rules, while insight solutions require problem-solving and cognitive strategies as defined by Gagné, Briggs, and Wager. From another perspective, noninsight solutions require comprehension and application, while insight solutions require analysis, synthesis, and evaluation as defined by Bloom. Other research on higher order thinking also applies directly to the concept of insight as follows:

- Insight involves many of the same features as creativity, including examining all factors that could be causing a problem, searching for a new way to state the problem, finding alternative approaches, persevering, taking risks, applying broad knowledge, and recognizing analogies.
- Playfulness, creativity, and an ability to unify separate elements are major parts of insight. Causes of impasses include failure to recognize relevant cues or patterns, overemphasis on irrelevant cues, underemphasis of relevant cues, and searches in the wrong spaces.
- Dimensions of learning support insight in (1) both pattern recognition and reasoning, (2) the second dimension of acquiring and integrating diverse knowledge, (3) the third dimension of extending and refining knowledge through purposefully widened observation and reasoning, (4) the fourth dimension of making choices among alternatives, an especially (5) the fifth dimension of developing productive habits of mind with systematic control of reasoning and scientific methods.

A study by Beyth-Maron found that critical thinking underscores the ability to make good choices.

- As with creativity, the "emotional tone of the person solving problems" affects insight (Sternberg & Davidson, 1995, p. xi). Metacognition and cognitive strategies, such as persevering, address the attitudes and habits of mind involved in insight. Motivation and fear of failure influence risk taking and persevering.

Intelligence

In the past decade, intelligence has been defined more broadly. Intelligence is

- no longer limited to the idea of a single ability or global capacity to learn, adapt, and think rationally;
- inclusive in its general and specific abilities to embrace general knowledge, comprehension, thinking, and problem solving;
- multidimensional in mental processes involving convergent and divergent thinking; and
- multilevel, including linguistic-verbal, logical-mathematical, spatial, musical, bodily-kinesthetic, interpersonal, and intrapersonal abilities that influence one's approaches to problem solving and thinking.

Problem Solving

A problem is "a situation in which the individual wants to do something but does not know the course of action needed to get what he or she wants". The process of problem solving requires "a series of successive decisions, each of which depends on the outcomes of those that precede it". In a review of research and reports, King, Rohani, and Goodson have identified 31 problem-solving tasks, from problem finding through evaluation.

Critical Thinking

Some researchers and scholars use the terms "critical thinking" and "higher order thinking" interchangeably, while others define "critical thinking" as a form of higher order thinking. Some use the terms "critical thinking" and "problem solving" interchangeably; yet for others, critical thinking is a form of problem solving. Still others define "critical thinking" as a part of the process of evaluating the evidence collected in problem solving or the results produced by thinking creatively. Critical thinking is a particular domain that has been defined in detail through Gubbins' *Matrix of Critical Thinking,* Facione, P. (n.d.), and the McREL Institute. Critical thinking also has been described in the following ways:

- goal-directed, reflective, and reasonable thinking, as in evaluating the evidence for an argument for which all the relevant information may not be available
- an essential component in metacognitive processes
- analysis, inference, interpretation, explanation, and self-regulation; requires inquisitive, systematic, analytical, judicious, truth-seeking, open-minded, and confident dispositions toward critical-thinking processes

- the disposition to provide evidence or reasoning in support of conclusions, request evidence or reasoning from others, and perceive the total situation and change one's views based on the evidence

Theories of Learning and Higher Order Thinking Skills

No one has yet explained the process of thinking much better than Dewey, who described it as a sequenced chaining of events. According to Dewey, this productive process moves from reflection to inquiry, then to critical thought processes that, in turn, lead to a "conclusion that can be substantiated" by more than personal beliefs and images. Thought can straighten out entanglements, clear obscurities, resolve confusion, unify disparities, answer questions, define problems, solve problems, reach goals, guide inferences, shape predictions, form judgments, support decisions, and end controversies.

According to Dewey, thinking does not occur spontaneously but must be "evoked" by "problems and questions" or by "some perplexity, confusion or doubt." The observations or "data at hand cannot supply the solution; they can only suggest it". Furthermore, it is this "demand for the solution" that steadies and guides the entire process of reflective thinking; the "nature of the problem fixes the end of thought, and the end controls the process of thinking". Dewey's conceptualization parallels current discussion and research about problem solving and metacognitive strategies and the importance of teaching students to think about their own thinking processes. As students become aware of their thinking processes, they realize how their own personal makeup can play a role in how they make their choices and interpret situations. Factors such as culture, experience, preferences, desires, interests, and passions can radically alter the decision-making process. Nevertheless, with time and more experience in systematic thinking, individuals and groups can develop the principles to guide decision making so that "a certain manner of interpretation gets weight, authority" as long as "the interpretation settled upon is not controverted by subsequent events".

The following section provides explanations of the work of key learning theorists, practitioners, and researchers in the field of thinking and learning. Researchers and teachers choose from a variety of frameworks for learning, with each framework approaching learning from simpler to more complex stages. However, the frameworks are artificial—they are only meant to be a means of defining the thinking/learning process; they can in no way capture the intricacies of the thinking process. "The boundaries separating the forms of complex thinking are sometimes blurred and somewhat artificial, often reflecting the particular interest of individual investigators".

Piaget

According to Piaget, the developmental stages are the key to cognitive development. School-age and adolescent children develop operational thinking and the logical and systematic manipulation of symbols. As adolescents move into adulthood, they develop skills such as logical use of symbols related to abstract concepts, scientific reasoning, and hypothesis testing. These skills are the foundation for problem solving, self-reflection, and critical reasoning. Recent research shows that children perform certain tasks earlier than Piaget claimed, vary in how rapidly they develop cognitively, and seem to be in transition longer than in the cognitive development stages. However, research also shows that biological development, together with instructional techniques, affects the rate of movement from one stage of learning to the next.

Bruner

According to Bruner, learning processes involve active inquiry and discovery, inductive reasoning, and intrinsic motivation. Stages of cognitive development are not linear; they may occur simultaneously. Bruner introduced the "spiral curriculum" in which learners return to previously covered topics within the context of new information learned. Both Piaget and Bruner focus on active learning, active inquiry and discovery, inductive reasoning, intrinsic motivation, and linkage of previously learned concepts and information to new learning. Stages include enactive (hands-on participation), iconic (visual representations), and symbolic (symbols, including math and science symbols).

Bloom

In each of Bloom's three taxonomies (cognitive, affective, and psychomotor), lower levels provide a base for higher levels of learning. Comprehension and application form linkages to higher order skills; here, the learner uses meaningful information such as abstractions, formulas, equations, or algorithms in new applications in new situations. Higher order skills include analysis, synthesis, and evaluation and require mastery of previous levels, such as applying routine rules to familiar or novel problems. Higher order thinking involves breaking down complex material into parts, detecting relationships, combining new and familiar information creatively within limits set by the context, and combining and using all previous levels in evaluating or making judgments. There also appears to be some interaction across taxonomies. For example, the highest level of the psychomotor taxonomy involves the use of our body's psychomotor, affective, and cognitive skills to express feelings or ideas as in the planning and execution of a dance performance or song designed to convey a particular message.

Gagné

According to Gagné, intellectual skills begin with establishing a hierarchy according to skill complexity. Within this structure, discriminations are prerequisites for concrete and defined concepts, simple rules, complex higher order rules, and then problem solving. Cognitive strategies may be simple or complex. Attitudes and motor skills, related varieties of learning, may involve lower as well as higher order thinking—spanning from a simple application of a tool to a complex systems analysis and evaluation. Bloom and Gagné and Briggs allow for greater possibilities of teaching complex skills to younger learners and the possibility that learners can be "young" at any age, starting at lower levels and connecting to higher levels of thinking. This variation for learning capabilities does not fit as well in Piaget's and Bruner's frameworks.

Marzano

To Marzano, the dimensions of thinking feed into dimensions of learning, both of which build upon contributions from other scholars and researchers. For example, Gagné refers to the generalizations that describe relationships between or among concepts as "rules", while Marzano calls them "principles". The book *Dimensions of Thinking* has been designed as a practical handbook with definitions, examples, and classroom applications.

Dimensions of learning evolved from constructs expressed by scholars and researchers in a 1988 framework on dimensions of thinking and the follow-up experiences of educators in classroom situations. These dimensions parallel early concepts expressed by Dewey.

Rather than differentiate levels of thinking skills, the dimensions of learning establish a learner-centered framework with

> ... a set of practical, research-based instructional strategies that infuse critical thinking and self-directed learning into curriculum and instruction; a flexible planning approach that allows teachers to focus on (1) knowledge to be learned, (2) broad issues and their applications to contemporary life, and (3) the meaningful use of knowledge....

Educators have used the dimensions of learning as a resource for instructional strategies, managing school improvement, planning instruction and assessment, making systematic reforms, and defining what students must be able to do in order to solve problems and make decisions in many situations. In studies conducted by Huot, Marzano et al., and McREL, the dimensions of learning are identified as follows.

- *Dimension 1:* fostering positive attitudes and perceptions about learning in a supportive and safe learning environment (Dewey emphasized open-mindedness, wholeheartedness, and responsibility for thinking in environments of freedom, curiosity, variety, spontaneity, and novelty, and with joyful, structured, and integrated learning about thinking in all subjects.)
- *Dimension 2:* acquiring and integrating knowledge, with emphasis on procedural knowledge (Dewey xplained that thinking must include access to "past experience and a fund of relevant knowledge" to unravel confusion or generate a solution; it requires integration of character and mind through infusion of intellectual subjects with "so-called 'informational' subjects"; students use what they already know to attend to new knowledge)
- *Dimension 3:* extending and refining knowledge through thinking (Dewey emphasized that changes in knowledge and belief rest upon careful and extensive study, purposeful widening of the area of observation, reasoning out the conclusions of alternative conceptions and "personal examination, scrutiny, and inquiry")
- *Dimension 4:* using knowledge in meaningful tasks, including systems analysis (ecosystems, systems of government, number systems, etc.) and authentic tasks over a period of time (Dewey observed that students use the power of thought to enrich meaning and cannot learn to think via drill and practice on isolated tasks that have nothing in common with or too much familiarity with their earlier life experiences; students learn best "when something beyond their ken is introduced" to which they can apply "the old, the near, the accustomed".

- *Dimension 5:* developing habits of mind that help one organize new information, think, and learn, such as seeking accuracy, avoiding impulsiveness, and persisting when answers are not apparent (Dewey proposed that "correct habits of reflection" are a central factor in thinking, involving systematic movement from one thought to another, instead of an "irresponsible stream of fancies"; noting or observing facts instead of just "something... brought to mind"; using quality proof and logic as the "basis of belief," and carefully looking into things, instead of reckless or impatient glances "over the surface"; following up ideas and outcomes of discovery instead of "haphazard, grasshopper-like" guessing; and "suspending judgments till inferences have been tested by the examination of evidence" instead of "whim, emotion, or accidental circumstances".)

The McREL Institute makes the dimensions framework a practical tool by offering a teacher's manual, a newsletter, and other resources to teachers that link their teaching strategies in the dimensions to standards and benchmarks. These resources show teachers how to apply the dimensions in real classroom situations and how to integrate the dimensions in curriculum frameworks across a variety of subject areas. Tips on how to apply the dimensions are specific and evolve from a dialogue with teachers entrenched in the process of learning. Marzano's 1994 book, *Assessing Student Outcomes: Performance Assessment Using the Dimensions of Learning*, includes a detailed list of questions corresponding to each reasoning process.

Glaser

Much of the structure and information in "dimensions of thinking" and "dimensions of learning" relates not just to the work of Dewey but also to Glaser. Glaser drew upon concepts articulated by Dewey and reported research from the 1930s and 1940s. Their work, together with contemporary research, shows the stability of several major concepts for higher order thinking. Glaser reported that the type of thinking required for problem solving originates in a perceived difficulty, state of doubt, or perplexity. It begins with "making acquaintance with the particular facts that create a need for definition and generalization," in order to see "the correct difficulty to be overcome", not with "definitions, rules, general principles, classifications, and the like". Furthermore, the way a problem is "apprehended or defined limits the kind of answers that will occur to the thinker. To get out of the rut requires a reformulation of the issue". This perspective suggests that higher order thinking involves more than a simple hierarchy or continuum. The importance of dispositions like attitudes and habits of mind also come into play in steering the thinking process in the right direction or taking it off course through aberrations of analysis, selection, association, inference, generalization, and language comprehension, such as

- ambiguity or misunderstanding of directions, word elements or language, or simple lack of information, material, or statements beyond the educational level of the individual;
- habits of thinking, false analogies, and logical errors; previously conceived orientations, rigid mind sets, and the tendency to block the correct response; perhaps egocentric perceptions of relationships, particularly by young children; or to read one's own beliefs or prejudices into interpretations; and
- failing to see what has to be solved; to isolate and define values of a problem; to consider all data, fallacies of inspection, observation, generalization, and confusion; and the influence of feelings and temporary physiological conditions.

Vygotsky

Vygotsky seems to have consolidated major concepts of cognitive development.

- Cognitive development progresses as children learn; biological maturity accounts for "elementary processes" such as reflexive responses.
- When learning a specific skill, students also perceive the underlying principles.
- Social interaction and social culture play major roles in learning and cognitive development; children internalize knowledge most efficiently when others, such as teachers, parents, or peers, guide and assist them; significant people in an individual's life contribute to the development of "higher mental functions"; people's cognitive processes function differently when working on their own versus working in groups.
- Everyone has a "zone of proximal development," and asking certain questions or giving suggestions will move the individual toward potentially higher levels; such support helps students in solving

problems until they can solve them independently and may include hints, questions, behavior modeling, rewards, feedback, information giving, self-talk, or peer tutoring.

Haladyna

Haladyna expressed the complexity of thinking and learning dimensions by classifying four levels of mental processes (understanding, problem solving, critical thinking, and creativity) that can be applied to four types of content (facts, concepts, principles, and procedures). Applying a set of skills across dimensions of content fits well with the actual complex, recursive, and systemic processes of higher order thinking. Although his terminology often varies from other theorists', the territory is similar:

Haladyna's terms	*Gagné's terms*	*Bloom's terms*
facts	information	knowledge
concepts	concepts	comprehension
principles, procedures	rules	application
critical thinking	problem solving	synthesis and evaluation
creativity	no direct match	no direct match

Gardner

According to Gardner, multiple intelligences form a major part of an individual's dispositions and abilities. These intelligences are independent of each other and account for the spectrum of abilities used in different fields of work, such as teaching, surgery, athletics, dancing, art, or psychotherapy.

Gardner's theory, which regards intelligence as having seven dimensions (Table 1), has been receiving recent attention related to teaching. Schools are shifting curricula and teaching methods to accommodate the diverse abilities and talents of students. Teachers may have a greater impact by creating lessons that "use the various types of intelligence in classroom activities". Although Gardner is commonly credited with theories related to multiple intelligences, others also have developed models of thinking that reflect the multifaceted nature of intelligence.

Certain components of models or theories of intelligence are similar to factors identified in models and theories of learning. For example, Guilford's products resemble the learning outcomes described by Gagné, Briggs, and Wager. "Units" are like the lower levels of discriminations and verbal information, "classes" are like the classification of concepts, "relations" are like the rules formed by relating one concept to another, and "systems" are like the systems of rules integrated into problem-solving strategies.

Table 1: Activities and Abilities Related to Intelligences

Types of Intelligence	*Forms and Textures*
linguistic-verbal	language, rhythms, inflections, meaning, and order of words (stories, books, humor, rhymes, songs)
logical-mathematical	reasoning with strings and patterns of symbols (pattern blocks, activities to form numbers and letters, building, measuring, cooking, gardening, other math-logic applications)
musical	pitch, melody, tone, and sound movements in time (rhythm sticks, varieties of music, interaction with musicians, dance exercises)
spatial	visual perception, transformation, modification, and creations (colors, shapes, spaces, games with movement and coordination)
bodily-kinesthetic	body motion and manipulation of objects (games with movement and manipulation, hands-on projects, dance exercises, sports, tactile activities)
interpersonal	relationships with others (cooperative games or exercises, peer or paired activities, public performances, conversation, exercises to focus on sensitivity to diverse needs)
intrapersonal	knowledge of self (exercises to express and acknowledge feelings, possibly journals or speeches or drawings; resources and exercises to identify and analyze one's own thinking processes, skills, interests, and feelings)

Similarly, Guilford's "content areas" are ways of receiving and perceiving information and instruction, and Guilford's "operations" parallel the mental processes that teaching strategies attempt to influence. There also are parallels with the notion of learning capabilities, in that Gagné and Briggs refer to stating, classifying, demonstrating, generating, and originating as the functions associated with different learning outcomes (i.e., stating verbal information, classifying concepts, demonstrating rules, generating problem solving, and originating cognitive strategies). These functional terms guide instructional designers in their specification of learning strategies and test items and have meanings that are similar to Guilford's terms of cognition, memory retention, memory recording, and divergent and convergent production.

It is often difficult to distinguish intelligence from the higher order thinking processes. McPeck, in examining the dimensions of critical thinking as defined by Watson and Glaser, found the characteristics identified "to be very similar to what we normally mean by general scholastic ability, or intelligence". This observation illustrates the type of interdisciplinary extensions that have been occurring through dialogue and research about how to describe "the intimate connection between the kinds of knowledge and their corresponding kinds of skills". McPeck concludes that it is just as important to teach the structure of a discipline as to teach thinking skills, and that "most problems are in fact 'multicategorical' and not domain-specific".

The concept of multiple dimensions of thinking has long-standing stability in teaching and learning when viewed in a larger context. For example, Symonds, in his 1936 book *Education and the Psychology of Thinking*, stated that "Thinking is not the application of independent units, one at a time, but rather a skillfully conducted interplay of habits and skills". This skillful interplay of habits and skills matches the concepts of Dewey as well as the more contemporary "dimensions of learning" of McREL. Another dimension, "content and context," provides the individual with something to think about, but serves primarily as "the vehicle that carries" the thinking skills.

References

Blagg, N., Ballinger, M. and Gardner, R. (1988) *Somerset Thinking Skills Course Handbook* Oxford: Basil Blackwell

Bloom, B. S. (Ed.) (1956) *Taxonomy of Educational Objectives, the classification of educational goals - Handbook I: Cognitive Domain.* New York: McKay

Costa, A (2001) *Developing Minds: A Resource Book for Teaching Thinking* (3rd edition) Alexandria, VA. Association for Supervision and Curriculum Development

De Bono, E (1987) *CoRT thinking programme: workcards and teachers' notes* Chicago: Science Research Associates

Dewey, J. (1909) *How We Think* Boston, MA: D.C. Heath and Co.

Ennis, R. H. (1958) 'A Concept of Critical Thinking' *Harvard Educational Review* Vol. 32, No.1, pp.81-111.

3

Teaching Strategies

Some fundamental principles of learning should guide all teaching strategies, whether focused on higher order or lower order thinking. The American Psychological Association (APA) summarized recent changes in perspectives on learning in a report entitled *Learner-Centered Psychological Principles: Guidelines for School Redesign and Reform*.

Table 1. Basic Principles of Learning

Nature of Learning	Learners freely and actively pursue personally meaningful goals and construct meaning through internal mediation, discovery, perceptions, thoughts, and beliefs.
Goals of Learning	Learners seek meaningful, coherent representations of knowledge.
Construction of Knowledge	Learners link new information and its meaning with past and future-oriented knowledge.
Higher Order Thinking	Metacognition facilitates creative thinking, critical thinking, and development of expertise.
Motivational Influences	Motivation for learning results from individual beliefs about personal control, competence, and expectations for success or failure; ability; clarity and saliency of values, interests, and goals; and general feelings and mental states.
Intrinsic Motivation	Learners have natural enthusiasm, curiosity, and joy for learning that can be undermined by fear of failure, insecurity, self-consciousness, fear of punishment, or ridicule.

Motivational Learning Tasks	Relevant and authentic learning tasks of optimal difficulty and novelty for the individual student will stimulate curiosity, creativity, and higher order thinking.
Constraints and Opportunities	Genetic and environmental factors affect physical, intellectual, emotional, and social development.
Social Acceptance and Self-Esteem	Respectful, caring relationships that express belief in individual potential, appreciation of individual talents, and acceptance of individuality will lead to greater learning and self-esteem.
Individual Differences	Learners have different capabilities and ways of learning due to environment and heredity; basic principles of learning, motivation, and effective instruction apply to all learners.
Cognitive Filters	Learners construct reality and interpret life experiences filtered through their personal beliefs, thoughts, and understandings.

These principles suggest that learning is a very individual activity—goals and learning tasks that are meaningful for one teacher or learner may not be meaningful for another. In the learning process, individuals seek coherent representations of knowledge that both fit into what they already know and also have future usefulness. How well they progress depends in great part upon the teacher; the climate the teacher establishes and the instructional strategies the teacher uses can motivate students to learn and think on higher levels.

A major factor in the growth of higher order thinking capability is a student-centered classroom. It supports the open expression of ideas, provides active modeling of thinking processes, develops thinking skills, and motivates students to learn. Without it, students will not persist in higher level thinking processes. In this open environment, a teacher's awareness of student motivation can dramatically affect a student's progress. A teacher who incorrectly assumes that a student lacks motivation to think at a higher level may miss the real reason for nonperformance—a lack of prerequisite knowledge and skills or lack of interest in the content or activities; or the teacher may not understand that a learner's motivation is sometimes influenced by cultural differences of values placed on learning (however, motivational differences are not due to race, ethnicity, or economic status).

In the student-centered environment, great expectations lead to greater achievement. Teachers who expect more of their students express more positive interactions; smile more frequently; use more eye contact; have closer proximity to students; provide clearer and more thorough explanations; give more enthusiastic instruction and follow-up questions; require more complete and accurate answers; provide more prompting and encouragement; allow more time to answer questions; and give more praise, less criticism, more complete feedback, and more conceptual evaluations.

The teacher avoids comparing students with each other. Constructive critical responses to student work are meant to provide strategies to overcome a student's learning difficulty— "procedures such as displaying students' grades, exhibiting student assignments, or sharing in other ways the accomplishments of successful students decrease rather than increase the motivation level of low-achieving students". The successful teacher conveys the message that "making mistakes is okay; in fact, it is an important part of learning".

In lesson planning, the teacher sets appropriate short- and long-term instructional goals because unrealistic expectations can increase anxiety. Students will persist in achieving goals that are "challenging, specific, and attainable in the near future" through reasonable effort and persistence. There is no busywork in this student-centered, thinking classroom, and student progress is monitored using several methods—not just tests.

Specific Methods to Enhance Thinking Skills

Once the teacher establishes the student-centered classroom and creates a framework for incorporating thinking skills into lessons, he or she can then consider strategies and methods that can enhance students' thinking ability.

Instructional Communications

To reduce the risks of ambiguity and confusion and improve student attitudes about thinking tasks, the teacher should provide students clear instructions for assignments as suggested in the studies by Hines, Cruickshank, and Kennedy; and Snyder et al.. For this reason, careful lesson planning is essential. Factors to consider in lesson planning include organization of activities, clarity of explanations, modeling of thinking skills in action, examples of applied thinking, feedback on student thinking processes, instructional alignment of objectives and activities, and adaptations for diverse student needs.

Kauchak and Eggen found that the following strategies contribute to the particular kinds of instructional communications necessary for developing higher order thinking skills.

1. Align learning goals, objectives, content ideas and skills, learning tasks, assessment activities, and materials and aids.
2. Establish organized activities and routines.
    a. Prepare a task analysis of the thinking skill to be learned: identify the particular thinking skill to be learned, the prerequisite knowledge and skills, the sequence of related subskills, and the readiness of students to learn (diagnosis of prerequisite knowledge and skills).
    b. Prepare sample problems, examples, and explanations.
    c. Prepare questions that go beyond simple recall of factual information to focus on advanced levels of comprehension, such as How? Why? and How well?
    d. Plan strategies for diagnosis, guidance, practice, and remediation.
    e. Explain and follow established routines, such as starting on time and following the planned sequence of activities.
    f. Convey enthusiasm, genuine interest in a topic, warmth, and a businesslike approach with thorough preparation and organization, minimal transition time between activities, clear expectations, and a comfortable, nonthreatening atmosphere.
3. Explain the task clearly.
    a. Set goals at the beginning of an assignment.
    b. Provide examples of finished products.
    c. Avoid vague, ambiguous terminology such as "might," "a little more," "some," "usually," and "probably." These terms suggest disorganization, lack of preparation, and nervousness.
    d. Introduce tasks with a clear and simple organizing framework such as a diagram, chart, preview, or one paragraph overview.
    e. Introduce key concepts and terms before further explanation and study.
    f. Use questions that focus attention on important information.

g. Give emphasis with verbal statements, nonverbal behaviors, repetition, and written signals.

h. Make ideas vivid with pictures, diagrams, examples, demonstrations, models, and other devices.

4. Give transition signals to communicate that one idea is ending and another is beginning.

5. Provide feedback at frequent intervals with a corrective feedback to clarify incorrect or partially incorrect responses.

Scaffolding

Scaffolding involves giving students support at the beginning of a lesson and then gradually turning over responsibility to the students to operate on their own. This limited temporary support helps students develop higher order thinking skills. It functions in much the same way that scaffolding does when providing safety and access for a window washer or painter. However, scaffolding must be limited to "only enough support so that learners make progress on their own" (Kauchak & Eggen, 1998,). Too much or too little support can interfere in the development of higher order thinking skills. For example, when teachers give students help even though the students do not ask for it, as reported in a study by Graham, students get the message that they cannot do the task on their own.

Students differ in the ways that they organize knowledge and events in their memories (also known as their "schemata" or "script knowledge"). These differences influence how they understand current information and events and are "partially explained by cultural background", but are not fixed. Scaffolding can change the schemata and scripts by which students learn new information and skills. The following strategies provide the type of structural support needed for developing thinking skills.

1. Use scaffolding at the following times :

    a. During initial learning, use scaffolding along with a variety of examples to describe the thinking processes involved.

    b. Use scaffolding only when needed, by first checking for understanding and, if necessary, providing additional examples and explanations.

    c. Use scaffolding to build on student strengths and accommodate weaknesses.

2. Provide structured representations and discussions of thinking tasks.
   a. Visually represent and organize problems in concrete examples such as drawings, graphs, tables, hierarchies, or tables.
   b. Demonstrate how to break up a thought problem into convenient steps, using a number of examples and encouraging students to suggest additional examples.
   c. Discuss examples of problems and solutions, explaining the nature of problems in detail and relating the worked-out solutions to the problems. This practice reduces the student's need for additional teacher assistance.
3. Provide opportunities for practice in solving problems.
   a. Provide teacher-directed practice before independent practice, spot-checking progress on practice and providing short responses of less than 30 seconds to any single request for assistance.
   b. Assign frequent, short homework assignments that are logical extensions of classroom work (not more than 20 minutes for elementary students; 10 problems a night works better than 50 a week).
   c. Link practice in the content area to complex, real-life situations.

Learning and Thinking Strategies

Learning strategies, sometimes referred to as cognitive strategies, include rehearsal, elaboration, organization, and metacognition to assess and regulate one's own thinking. They may involve skills such as highlighting, diagramming, visualizing, or using mnemonics. Some learning strategies are more complex, such as "multipass," a strategy used to improve reading comprehension. Multipass also would apply to the initial learning of new concepts, rules, and principles by means of written information. In the first "pass," students survey material for a general idea of what the information covers and how it fits together. In the second "pass," students size up the important points, looking for "contextual cues to important information." In the third "pass," students attempt to answer questions about a passage.

The following strategies have been known to help develop individual learning and thinking capabilities.

1. Deliberately design lessons or programs for the express purpose of teaching specific learning and thinking strategies.

2. Teach self-reflection and self-evaluation about thinking processes. The following effective approaches were reported in several studies by Crowl et al.,
   a. Challenge preexisting ideas (beliefs, concepts, and misconceptions) by presenting situations that students are unable to explain—paradoxes, dilemmas, and perplexities.
   b. Guide students in how to do systematic inquiry, allowing them to think independently, but preventing them from pursuing dead ends and simplistic answers.
   c. Encourage students to reflect upon and make sense of new information by making judgments in writing or discussions about its relevance, telling in their own words how to integrate their findings with their previously existing ideas, opinions, or approaches.
   d. Encourage and guide students to formulate hypotheses, speculate on consequences, guess, brainstorm, and discuss how their thinking processes have worked to change their ideas.
   e. Monitor and correct inefficient strategies.
   f. Encourage continuous reflection of beliefs about thinking, thinking processes, and evaluation of effectiveness.
3. In approaching different learning and thinking tasks, use cognitive maps and advance organizers to show the major steps or parts.
4. Teach the initial and rehearsal strategies for complex tasks.
   a. Teach how to preview, question, read, reflect, recite, and review (PQ4R) when learning from written materials.
   b. Provide instruction in "abstracting, analyzing, outlining, summarizing, and generalizing"; this improves "both reasoning and reading ability"
   c. Emphasize broad problem-solving strategies, algorithms (specified set of steps for solving problems), or heuristics (widely applicable problem-solving strategies such as using means–end analysis for ill-defined problems, working backward when parameters are known, and drawing analogies for unfamiliar problems).
   d. Provide practice for routines of different strategies, algorithms, and heuristics until they are overlearned, so that their use becomes fast, effortless, and consistent.

e. Teach specific learning strategies by talking about the strategy, modeling it while thinking out loud, and providing opportunities for practice. Show persistence in thinking things through and confidence in the thinking process; students who hear teachers express self-confidence in reasoning actually develop greater confidence in themselves. The following strategies were reported in a study by McTighe.

- Provide names and definitions for each thinking skill.
- Ask students for synonyms and examples.
- Model steps for using each skill.
- Explain appropriate and inappropriate contexts for using each skill.
- Arrange practice of skills in cooperative learning groups.

5. Strengthen comprehension and skills in applying related concepts, rules (principles and procedures), decision-making processes, and problem-solving strategies.

a. Diagnose students' existing schemata (conceptions and misconceptions) by asking probing questions.

b. Provide hands-on situations for students to "mess around" with interpreting raw data or generating new explanations.

c. Provide examples of questions or stems of questions that require higher order thinking and encourage students to answer them independently, in pairs, or in groups.

d. Redirect, probe, and reinforce the development of critical and creative thinking skills.

e. Provide practice, without the expectation of extrinsic rewards, grades, or tests, in making choices, brainstorming, finding problems, experimenting with chosen themes and approaches, and developing tentative solutions to a variety of problems involved in areas such as painting, music, storywriting, and other art challenges, as well as scientific and mathematical undertakings.

f. Provide practice on how and when to apply procedural knowledge, including rules and facts.

- Provide opportunities for discovery of procedural knowledge.
- Explain the goals of the procedure.

- Define problems/situations for which the procedure is appropriate.
- Explain why particular strategies are appropriate for the problems/situations.
- Demonstrate the step-by-step application of a procedure.
- Provide students with practice in choosing appropriate procedures and carrying out the steps of procedures.
- Provide feedback on student performance of procedure.s.g.Include individualized options in lesson plans designed to teach higher order thinking.
- Provide choices among assignments, such as having 70% required and 30% optional.
- Create multidimensional classrooms with learning tasks that encourage intellectual diversity, using modalities for several kinds of intelligences, such as linguistic, logical-mathematical, musical, or spatial.
- Vary sequence of instruction and application. Students with low induction aptitude benefit from receiving training before performing an application task, while those with high induction aptitude benefit from performing the application task first
- Use cultural/community resources and information to express the acceptance and valuing of different perspectives that are necessary for successful learning by all students.
- Use participation tasks that are open-ended, involving several ways to solve problems, such as tasks that include opportunities for students to make different kinds of contributions, call on a variety of knowledge and skills (including reading, writing, constructing, and designing), and incorporate multiple media
- Use multiability tasks with varied activities to accommodate differences in language proficiency, abstract thinking, and influence of emotion.
- Help students see themselves as effective learners so they can develop a greater internal locus of control

- Provide alternate learning materials with additional support and guidance for those who need it and additional enrichment activities for the others.
- Use mastery skills test management: Students who pass the quizzes are allowed to continue; those who do not pass are moved into additional activities.
- Use peer tutoring to allow more able students to work with other students on specific skills.
- Use cooperative learning such that each member investigates independently and later explains a different concept, process, or skill to the others.
- Use collaborative problem solving for problem analysis, not for problem solution.
- Use team-assisted individualization that combines cooperative and mastery learning. Students in mixed-ability learning teams receive direct teacher instruction on how to proceed, work on individual assignments with assistance and support from other members, and receive rewards for team performance.
- Use computer programs that target specific concepts and skills

Direct Instruction

Direct instruction, involving teacher-centered presentations of information, generally does not work well for developing higher level thinking skills. Nevertheless, the following strategies can make direct instruction more effective.

1. Limit direct teaching methods to the introduction of strategies and skills.
2. Combine direct instruction with guided practice to teach students well-structured subskills and knowledge, such as teaching the learning strategies of rehearsal, elaboration, organization, monitoring, or metacognition.
3. Avoid long lectures and use minilectures instead. Keep lectures very short (up to five minutes). The amount learned from a lecture decreases as the length of the lecture increases. Minilectures should be even

shorter for younger, slower, or poorly motivated students or for complex or abstract content. A study by Kauchak & Eggen offered the following suggestions:

- Introduce new content with a familiar frame of reference. Analogies work well for this purpose. "The closer the fit of the analogy, the more learning is facilitated.... Red blood cells are our bodies' oxygen railroad"
- Express briefly what will be learned, why it is important, when it will be useful, and how it should be applied.
- Break up segments with questions, discussions, and other devices because attention increases when a question is asked.
- Keep student responses to questions short because attention decreases when a student is called on.
- Use visual displays to organize information—networks, hierarchies, schematic diagrams, and matrices show relationships among ideas or concepts.
- Include demonstrations, debates, and student-initiated questions. These improve student attention and involvement.
- Develop and link content to the overall section or purpose of learning.
- Include transition signals between topics.
- Provide review and closure through summaries, both verbal and visual.

Questioning Strategies

To generate higher order thinking processes, questions must elicit answers that have not already been presented. Planning the questions in advance of actual learning time helps assure questions go beyond simple recall of information. Recalling the steps in a major procedure or skill may be useful, but memorization of steps does not help the learner understand why or how the steps should be used, nor does it help the learner apply the steps in a problem situation.

The following strategies for asking questions have been shown to improve the development of thinking skills.

- Ask questions of all students equally, calling on nonvolunteers as well as volunteers.
- To stimulate curiosity or demand problem solving, ask questions about paradoxes, dilemmas, and novel problems and approaches.
- Have students generate their own questions about topics.
- Start with lower-order questions, remediating as needed, and lead up to higher-order questions.
- Provide wait time after a question because students differ in the rate at which they respond.

FEEDBACK

Feedback informs learners of their progress. Thc following strategies for providing feedback are effective.

- Use informal checks such as thumbs up or thumbs down to show who got a problem right.
- Provide immediate, specific, and corrective information, using a positive emotional tone.
- Avoid expressions of low expectations such as "That was a good first effort".
- Avoid insincere feedback or excessive praise because they do not work except for very young children. Praise is effective only when students believe they have earned it. Use praise to help students "develop their own standards for success".
- Adjust feedback to response. For correct quick, firm answers, use short, general praise (e.g., "good answer"). For correct but hesitant answers, respond with encouraging feedback and explanation (e.g., "Yes, the apostrophe in this case indicates a contraction, not a possessive. We see there is no possession suggested in the sentence"). For incorrect answers due to carelessness, simply correct the error. For incorrect answers due to misunderstanding, provide more explanation and questioning, but do not overexplain. Take this approach with every student. For a number of incorrect errors by several students, reteach the material. When a student is unable to respond, prompt the student until an acceptable answer is given—do not redirect the question to another student. Reinforce desired behaviors, and at the same time, use appropriate behavioral strategies to eliminate undesirable behaviors.

Team Activities

Group size must be limited to six or fewer for group work to remain manageable and focused. Before they can work well in teams or groups, students must learn skills such as listening carefully, maintaining focus, and providing support and encouragement. Students must also receive challenging tasks, encouragement to stay on task when grappling with open-ended questions, and ongoing feedback about their progress.

Team or group work facilitates knowledge construction through social interaction. Team and group work profit from careful strategic planning, including development of tasks, group procedures, materials, and assessment methods. Student performance improves with monitoring of student activities and minimized transitional periods from one activity to another.

The forms of group work found to be effective for the development of thinking skills include student discussions, peer tutoring, and cooperative learning. In any of these situations, using introductory activities to develop rapport or "warm up" for the team or group can facilitate group interaction. At the start of a group, use some team-building activities such as name-learning games with follow-up quizzes on naming partners. Use additional time for students to do getting-to-know-you interviews (interests or hobbies) or "something that no one else knows about me" activities for group members. Use this information to introduce group members to the rest of the class.

Student Discussions

Student discussions "stimulate thinking, challenge attitudes and beliefs, and develop interpersonal skills". When organized and managed well, discussions allow students "to develop critical thinking abilities and investigate questions that don't have simple answers". For best results, assure the presence of student background knowledge before using discussions. Begin with moral dilemmas to develop understanding and clarification of values or use other types of dilemmas to develop other critical thinking and problem-solving skills. Arrange groups for face-to-face discussion, such as in semicircles or circles, so that the teacher is included as part of the semicircle or circle.

Peer Tutoring

Peer tutoring pairs up students of different abilities to increase understanding and skill learning. Make sure tutors are trained; untrained tutors sometimes imitate the worst from their teachers, such as punitiveness or a lack of helpful feedback. Students should learn how to explain objectives, stay on task, encourage their peers to talk about the lesson, and provide supportive comments, praise, and positive feedback. Place cross-age or same-age students in one-to-one pairs and supply them with structured learning materials for practice and feedback. Provide clear structure through student worksheets, including a focused agenda for tutor and tutee. Provide teacher monitoring, feedback, and guidance during peer tutoring to check progress and correct mistakes or misunderstandings. Restructure whenever a peer tutoring pair is not working.

Cooperative Learning

Cooperative learning is effective for developing cognitive, affective, and interpersonal skills through individual accountability. It involves more students and teamwork than peer tutoring and capitalizes on student diversity by placing students on learning teams and rewarding the group's planning and inquiry performance. Cooperative learning increases motivation, time on task, and student involvement and improves student self-esteem. Learning tasks should require cooperation and communication. Provide useful resources for study such as the Internet, textbooks, and reference books. Use student-generated charts or worksheets to support the organization of inquiry results and rotate student roles. Cooperative learning includes group investigation, student teams-achievement divisions (STADs), and Jigsaw II.

Group investigation involves placing students in study groups to investigate a common topic. Group investigation gives students "the chance to wrestle with ill-structured tasks, which are the kinds of problems we face in real life" and to "clarify and then structure the problem" To help students engage and stay involved, introduce the topic and ask students to identify subtopics that each group will investigate; divide students into groups according to student interest and balance of achievement, gender, and cultural background; arrange for group presentations to share the information gained; and provide feedback to groups and individuals on results and presentations.

STADs group students into teams and subteams as study groups. STADs study groups use four- or five-member teams, subdivided into pairs or trios, to study and master basic skills topics. These are more structured than group investigation teams. Using STADs can support the learning of concepts and rules in areas such as language arts, math, science, social studies, and health. Plan activities by identifying content and skills to be mastered, presentation and practice activities, assignments to groups, improvement points, and group rewards. Prepare worksheets (and answers) that require direct application of the concepts, principles, or rules taught. Create quizzes for each student to parallel the worksheet information but with changes to prevent students from merely memorizing and providing rote responses. Before organizing into groups, teach students "quiet talk" and explain how to use it during discussions. The following are strategies for STADs:

- Organize teams in work spaces and divide each team into two pairs or a trio and a pair.
- Provide one worksheet to each pair or trio and focus attention on the use of the worksheets for studying, so that everyone on the team can explain each item on the worksheet.
- Focus on improvement points from quiz scores so that groups compete against themselves rather than each other and explain the purpose of this process to the students.
- Instruct students to work individually and discuss their problem-solving strategies within each pair and trio.
- During teamwork time, focus on promoting cooperation and providing encouragement and praise.
- Calculate team improvement points from individual scores and give team rewards; improvement can be reflected in individual team grades.

Jigsaw II is more structured and involves group goals, individual accountability, and equal opportunity for success. In Jigsaw II, assignments require individual members to investigate specific areas of expertise and then to return to the group to share results. Jigsaw II strategies are as follows:

- Divide content into roughly equal subtopics and organize them into worksheets or charts. Assign topics in which individuals are expected to obtain expertise and reflect assignments on worksheets.
- Locate and organize resources.
- Divide students into groups for balance of achievement, gender, and cultural background.
- Explain procedures.

- Monitor study activities and make appropriate rescues available.
- Convene groups to discuss and compare information.
- Administer and score quizzes using improvement points.
- Provide feedback on group performance.

Computer Mediation

Computer-mediated communication provides opportunities for access to remote data sources, collaboration on group projects with students in other locations, and sharing of work for evaluation or response by other students.

Computer-assisted instruction (CAI) and computer-based instruction (CBI), when combined with regular instruction, "improves students' attitudes, motivation, and academic achievement". The following applications of such computer-mediated communication have been shown to be effective in improving learning of prerequisite and higher order thinking skills:

- practicing inferencing skills and problem-solving strategies;

  skill building in areas such as verbal analogies, logical reasoning, and inductive/deductive thinking; and
- drilling and practicing, which incorporate probes or tests.

Lessons involving higher order thinking skills require particular clarity of communication to reduce ambiguity and confusion and improve student attitudes about thinking tasks. Lesson plans should include modeling of thinking skills, examples of applied thinking, and adaptations for diverse student needs. Scaffolding (giving students support at the beginning of a lesson and gradually requiring students to operate independently) helps students develop higher order learning skills. However, too much or too little support can hinder development.

Useful learning strategies include rehearsal, elaboration, organization, and metacognition. Lessons should be specifically designed to teach specific learning strategies. Direct instruction (teacher-centered presentations of information) should be used sparingly. Presentations should be short (up to five minutes) and coupled with guided practice to teach subskills and knowledge.Teacher- and/or student-generated questions about dilemmas, novel problems, and novel approaches should elicit answers that have not been learned already.Sincere feedback providing immediate, specific, and corrective information should inform learners of their progress.

References

Dawes, R. M. (1988).*Rational Choice in an Uncertain World.* Orlando, Fla.: Harcourt Brace.

Glaser, R. (1984)."Education and Thinking: The Role of Knowledge." *American Psychologist.*

Halpern, D. F. (1996).*Thought and Knowledge: An Introduction to Critical Thinking.* (3rd ed.) Mahwah, N.J.: Erlbaum.

Halpern, D. F. (1998)."Teaching Critical Thinking for Transfer Across Domains: Disposition, Skills, Structure Training, and Metacognitive Monitoring." *American Psychologist.*

Lochhead, J., and Whimby, A. (1987). "Teaching Analytic Reasoning Through Think-Aloud Pair Problem Solving." In J. E. Stice (ed.), *Developing Critical Thinking and Problem-Solving Abilities.* New Directions for Teaching and Learning, no. 30. San Francisco: Jossey-Bass.

Mayer, R. E. (1992).*Thinking, Problem Solving, Cognition.* New York: Freeman.

4

Assessment of Thinking Skills

Higher order thinking skills include critical thinking, problem solving, decision making, and creative thinking. They encompass the skills defined in Bloom's Taxonomy of Educational Objectives; the hierarchy of learning capabilities propounded by Briggs and Wager, Gagné, and Gagné, Briggs, and Wager; and a number of other less well-known conceptualizations. An example is Gubbins' *Matrix of Critical Thinking Skills,* which includes

(1) problem solving,

(2) decision making,

(3) inferences–inductive and deductive reasoning,

(4) divergent thinking,

(5) evaluative thinking, and

(6) philosophy and reasoning.

Assessment methods for measuring higher order thinking include multiple-choice items, multiple-choice items with written justification, constructed response items, performance tests, and portfolios. These methods can be used in both classroom and statewide assessments, but for convenience, consider the two kinds of assessments separately.

Validity of Thinking Skills and Dispositions

Assessing the validity of measures of higher order thinking skills is more difficult than assessing those of lower order thinking skills. It is necessary to verify that higher order processes were used in arriving at correct answers.

For example, some items (especially multiple-choice) must be answered through the use of higher order thinking by students who have not previously encountered the problems presented. Other students can arrive at correct answers to the same items by calling on prior knowledge. In addition to those related to the influence of prior knowledge, questions concerning the generalizability of higher order skills remain to be answered.

A comprehensive definition of validity was formulated by Messick. Validity is an overall evaluative judgment of the degree to which empirical evidence and theoretical rationales support the *adequacy* and *appropriateness of interpretations* and *actions* based on test scores or other modes of assessment. Validity is not a property of the test or assessment as such, but rather of the meaning of the test scores.

The scores are a function not only of the items or stimulus conditions, but also of the *persons* responding as well as the *context* of the *assessment*. In particular, what needs to be valid is the meaning or interpretation of the scores as well as any implications for action that this meaning entails. The extent to which score meaning and action implications hold across persons or population groups and across settings or contexts is a persistent and perennial empirical question. This is the main reason that validity is an evolving property and validation a continuing process.

Norris considered two questions of importance in determining the validity of tests of critical thinking: "(a) Is critical thinking generalizable? and (b) What is a critical thinking disposition?". He also raised the question of whether critical thinking dispositions are generalizable. Students may have the skills to think critically but may not employ them in testing situations because of other factors such as lack of subject-specific knowledge or their religious or political beliefs.

Generalizability of critical thinking skills has two aspects—epistemological and psychological. Epistemological generalizability holds that there are skills such as inductive reasoning that apply to all subject matter contents. Critics of this point of view argue that each subject matter area has a unique epistemology and that each area has its own set of critical thinking skills. Psychological generalizability presumes that epistemological generalizability exists and that skills acquired in one subject matter can be applied in others.

An important goal of education should be the production of critical thinking dispositions in students.

> Critical thinkers are disposed to seek reasons, try to be well informed, use credible sources and mention them, look for alternatives, consider seriously points of view other than their own, withhold judgment when the evidence and reasons are insufficient, seek as much precision as the subject permits, among other activities.

Much of the evidence for generalizability of higher order thinking skills comes from psychological studies of transfer. Perkins and Salomon summarized a considerable amount of research conducted during the last 30 years that indicated that cognitive (higher order) skills are context bound. However, they pointed out that

> ... recent research shows that, when general principles of reasoning are taught together with self-monitoring practices and potential applications in varied contexts, transfer often *is* obtained.

In summary, recent research and theorizing concerning transfer put the negative findings cited earlier in a different light. These findings do not imply either that people have little ability to accomplish transfer or that skill is almost entirely context bound.

Rather, the negative results reflect the fact that transfer occurs only under specific conditions, which often are not met in everyday life or laboratory experiments. When the conditions are met, useful transfer occurs.

The work of Perkins and Salomon suggests that instruments can be constructed that are both valid for the measurement of higher order skills and sensitive to instruction.

Lohmann argued that while intelligence test scores have most often been used as predictors of educational attainment, their most important use may be as measures of educational outcomes. Many studies have shown that intelligence and educational attainment are positively correlated and it is reasonable to conclude that increases in education cause increases in intelligence. "Intelligence tests (particularly the so-called performance variety) often measure something Cattell and others call fluid ability (Gf). General academic achievement tests, on the other hand, usually measure something Cattell calls crystallized abilities (Gc)". Lohmann pointed out that transfer of old learning to new situations is greater for fluid than for crystallized intelligence. Thus, both kinds of abilities are the products of education, but fluid abilities are more closely akin to higher order thinking skills than crystallized abilities. He cited the results of the Follow-Through

Study in which highly structured projects were more successful in producing crystallized abilities than more unstructured ones, while the reverse was true for fluid abilities. Similar results were cited for other investigations.

Haladyna and Sternberg adopted much the same view as Lohmann. Haladyna characterized abilities (Gf) as being developed over long periods of time compared to achievement (Gc), which can be developed in a shorter time frame. He defined abilities as "complex combinations of what we have called knowledge and skills, but they also include affective components like motivation and attitude". Examples of abilities are critical thinking, problem solving, and creativity.

Sternberg conceptualized abilities as being forms of developing expertise. He pointed out that ability tests measure achievement of content that students encountered in previous grades. He viewed abilities as educational outcomes and not as the causes of such outcomes.

> Individual differences in developing expertise result in much the same way they result in most kinds of learning—from (a) rate of learning (which can be caused by amount of direct instruction received, amount of problem solving done, amount of time and effort spent in thinking about problems, and so on) and from (b) asymptote of learning.

Peterson employed a real-life problem in each of 3 academic content domains (social sciences and humanities, social sciences and natural sciences, and social sciences and psychology) crossed with 6 generic problem-solving skills (decision making, communication, analysis, synthesis, valuing, and execution) to conduct a multitrait-multimethod study of the structure of these 18 skill/task observations. Subjects were university students: lower level, 20; upper level, 26; and graduate level, 16. Confirmatory factor analysis was used to evaluate a model that contained a general second-order factor, 6 skill factors, and 3 subject content factors. This model provided a moderately good fit to the data, but most of the common variance was accounted for by the general factor. A model containing only skill and subject matter factors did not provide a good fit. Peterson concluded that a general reasoning test, a vocabulary test, or a general knowledge test would provide as much information as a test of generic problem-solving skills. However, he pointed out that because all variables were measured by written responses, a general writing ability could have inflated the influence of the general problem-solving factor.

Whimbey reported correlations of three reasoning tests (the *Cornell Critical Thinking Test*, the *Whimbey Analytical Skills Inventory,* and the *New Jersey Test of Reasoning*), with achievement scores from the New Jersey College Basic Skills Placement Test (NJCBSPT).

Correlations of achievement with the Cornell test were lower than with the other two tests, perhaps because it measures some special ability or possibly because of its low reliability (reported to be below.70). Whimbey concluded that special tests of higher order abilities are unnecessary because they have so much overlap with achievement tests. "There are numerous time-proven, standardized academic aptitude and achievement tests, such as the Degrees of Reading Power, California Achievement Tests, Differential Aptitude Tests, and the Scholastic Aptitude Test, which are practical indicators of students' analytical skills".

Kosonen and Winne studied the effects of teaching statistical laws of reasoning in two experiments with college undergraduates and one with 7th- and 10th-grade students. Students were taught abstract rules of probability and asked to apply them to everyday problems. Statistical results in all three experiments indicated that the posttest means of instructed student were significantly higher than those of the control students. Standardized treatment effect sizes were all above.5 and most were above 1.0 (one standard deviation larger). With respect to the question of whether formal statistical rules are domain-specific, the authors state

> A larger claim that statistical reasoning transfers or generalizes across domains is more difficult to support because the definition of domain is unclear. Students in our studies addressed problems that ranged over various everyday activities including hiring people with particular qualifications, conducting a survey of attitudes, playing a recreational board game, choosing restaurants with good food, judging people's nature on the basis of brief social interactions, generating a marketing strategy on the basis of business competitors' profits, monitoring equipment in a fast-food restaurant, predicting a child's aptitude for sports, and so forth. We believe that these topics represent a broad spectrum of domains and, on this interpretation, we conclude that our and other studies demonstrate that students who receive effective instruction in abstract, formal rules of reasoning can transfer those rules across domains.

The psychometric generalizability of performance tasks was studied by Shavelson, Baxter, and Gao. They used one data set in elementary science and two in math to study the effects of different tasks, methods of measurement, and raters on the assessment scores of elementary students obtained from the same subject matter domain. They found that the greatest inconsistency in student scores was due to task variability. Depending on the data set, they estimated that in order to reach acceptable levels of generalizability, between 8 and 23 tasks would be required. They also found that student performance was dependent, in part, on different methods (expert observation, student notebooks, computer simulation, and short answer questions) of measuring student performance in the same subject matter content.

Linn also studied the psychometric generalizability of performance tasks in math at grades 4 and 8. Twelve tasks were used at the 4th-grade level and 16 at the 8th-grade level. Tasks were administered to students in "bundles" of 2 to 4 tasks. Administration times for bundles ranged from 4 to 6 hours. Linn's results were in agreement with those of Shavelson et al.. Approximately 15 tasks or more, depending on the grade level and data set, would be required to achieve an acceptable level of generalizability.

Published Measures of Thinking Skills

Ennis listed 7 possible purposes for which published tests of critical thinking may be used. These purposes are listed as follows:

1. Diagnosing the levels of students' critical thinking.
2. Giving students feedback about their critical thinking prowess.
3. Motivating students to be better at critical thinking.
4. Informing teachers about the success of their efforts to teach students to think critically.
5. Doing research about critical thinking instructional questions and issues.
6. Providing help in deciding whether a student should enter an educational program.
7. Providing information for holding schools accountable for the critical thinking prowess of their students.

Ennis suggested that published tests could be used for the first 5 purposes but not the last 2 because they are not comprehensive in their coverage of critical thinking skills and they are not secure. He listed 10 published tests that measure a variety of skills and 4 that measure only one aspect of critical thinking.

The *California Critical Thinking Skills Test* (CCTST) is based on a definition of critical thinking skills identified as a result of a two-year Delphi study conducted by the American Philosophical Association. It consists of two forms, each containing multiple-choice questions that measure five subskills (analysis, evaluation, inference, deductive reasoning, and inductive reasoning) and an overall critical thinking score. Internal consistency reliabilities for the total scores of Forms A and B were reported to be.70 and.71 respectively. Jacobs's study yielded total score alpha reliabilities of.56 and.59 for Forms A and B, respectively. Subscore reliabilities ranged from.04 to.53. Facione and Facione reported results of a quasi-experimental validation study of college students who were enrolled in a critical thinking course and control students who had not fulfilled that requirement. Significant pre- and postcourse gains were reported for the experimental students but not for controls. Significant pretest correlations were found between the CCTST and SAT Verbal (.550), SAT Math (.439), Nelson-Denny Reading (.491), and college grade point average (.200). These results were also reported by Facione.

The *California Critical Thinking Disposition Inventory* (CCTDI) is a 75-Likert item measure derived from the American Philosophical

Association study. It produces several scale scores and a total score. The scales are "discipline neutral" (i.e., they can be used in liberal arts, sciences, and professional disciplines). Descriptions of scales follow.

- The *Inquisitiveness* scale on the CCTDI *measures one's intellectual curiosity, and one's desire for learning even when the application of the knowledge is not readily apparent.*
- The *Open-mindedness scale addresses being tolerant of divergent views and sensitive to the possibility of one's own bias.*
- The *Systematicity* scale measures *being organized, orderly, focused, and diligent in inquiry.*
- The *Analyticity* scale targets *prizing the application of reasoning and the use of evidence to resolve problems, anticipating potential conceptual or practical difficulties, and consistently being alert to the need to intervene.*
- The *Truth-seeking* scale targets the disposition of *being eager to seek the best knowledge in a given context, courageous about asking questions, and honest and objective about pursuing inquiry even if the*

findings do not support one's self- interests or one's preconceived opinions.

- The CT *Self-Confidence* scale measures the trust one places in one's own reasoning processes. CT *self-confidence allows one to trust the soundness of one's own reasoned judgments and to lead others in the rational resolution of problems.*
- The *Maturity* scale targets the disposition to be judicious in one's decision making. The CT-mature person can be characterized as one who *approaches problems, inquiry, and decision making with a sense that some problems are necessarily ill- structured, some situations admit of more than one plausible option, and many times judgments must be made based on standards, contexts, and evidence which preclude certainty.*

Internal consistency reliabilities for the seven scales were reported to be between.71 to.81. The reliability for the total score was.91. In separate studies, correlations between the CCTDI and the CCTST were.67 for 20 highly motivated college students,.21 for 106 nursing students,.38 for 238 high school students, and.14 for 191 native Spanish-speaking high school students.

The *Ennis-Weir Critical Thinking Essay Test* was used by Davidson and Dunham to assess the effectiveness of a yearlong instructional program in intensive English with Japanese students. Treatment students (n = 17) received training in critical thinking skills while control students (n = 19) received only intensive English instruction. Total scores on the test can range from -9 to +29. The mean of the treatment students was 6.6, which was significantly higher (p <.001) than the 0.06 mean of the control students.

Reed and Palumbo and Reed, Palumbo, and Stolar used sections of the *Ross Test of Higher Cognitive Processes* (*Analysis of Relevant and Irrelevant Information* and *Analysis of Attributes*) and sections of the *Watson-Glaser Critical Thinking Appraisal* (*Deduction* and *Interpretation*) as pre- and posttests to evaluate the effects of computer programming instruction on problem-solving ability. The first investigation involved 23 college students who were given 81 hours of instruction in BASIC over an 8-week period. Significant pre- and postdifferences (pretest mean = 44.00, SD = 8.22; posttest mean = 45.65, SD = 7.74) were found. A significant reduction in computer anxiety was also found. The second investigation involved 21 college students enrolled in a BASIC programming course and 8 students in a Logo class. Statistically significant gains were found for both the Logo and BASIC groups. For the Logo group, the pretest mean was 43.75, *SD* = 9.74; the posttest mean was 46.63, *SD* = 10.25. In the BASIC group, the pretest mean was 45.40, *SD* = 6.13; the posttest mean was 47.15, *SD* = 5.39. No differences were found between the 2 groups. Failure to include control groups in these studies makes it impossible to rule out effects due to testing. However, the authors of the first study interviewed randomly selected students to determine whether or not they could recall, at posttest time, the exact answers they had given on the pretest. In all cases, students indicated that they could not recall previous answers.

Gadzella et al. reported results of a 14-week study in which college students were pre-tested with Form A of the Watson-Glaser, received instruction in critical thinking skills and in analyzing critical thinking examples, and were posttested with Form B of the Watson-Glaser. Significant pre- and posttest differences were found for the total score and 2 of the subscores (Interpretations and Evaluation of Arguments) but not for the 3 other subscores (Inference, Recognition, and Deductions). Pre- and posttest means and standard deviations were 47.69, 10.03 and 51.00, 7.88, respectively.

Item/Test Formats

Higher order thinking skills can be measured by a variety of item and test formats. Sugrue integrated information from three research-based, domain-specific problem-solving models and identified three response formats for measuring higher order thinking skills:

(1) selection (multiple-choice, matching),

(2) generation (short answer, essay, performance), and

(3) explanation (giving reasons for selection or generation of a response).

Multiple-Choice Items

Prominent investigators of critical thinking have endorsed the use of the multiple-choice format in measuring at least some higher order skills. Paul and Nosich recommended the use of multiple-choice, multiple-rating, and short-essay items in constructing an instrument for the national assessment of higher order thinking. Multiple-choice items could be used for assessing "micro-dimensional critical thinking skills, like identifying the most plausible assumption, recognizing an author's purpose, selecting the most defensible inferences, and such like".

Facione, Norris, and Ennis all recognized that subjects can select keyed responses to multiple-choice items for the wrong reasons and distractors can be chosen for valid reasons. Facione and Norris recommended that a think-aloud procedure be employed to investigate the construct validity of multiple-choice items during test construction. Subjects are asked to tell what they are thinking as they select their answers. When correct responses were chosen through faulty thinking or incorrect responses through valid thinking, items could be modified or discarded. Norris and King used this methodology in constructing the *Test on Appraising Observations.*

Simpson and Cohen used a think-aloud procedure in connection with item analytic data to demonstrate the validity of multiple-choice items categorized as knowledge or thinking items based on Bloom's taxonomy. A medical pathology course was the context for their procedure.

Ennis suggested that answer justification be incorporated into the actual test. Subjects would be asked to select correct responses and then to provide written justifications for their choices. An advantage of this procedure is that subjects could be given credit for nonkeyed responses if they provided adequate justification. Answer justification for higher order thinking items was first recommended by Bloom, who cast both item and justification in multiple-choice format.

Hancock cited a number of empirical studies in which multiple-choice and constructed-response tests measured the same higher order skills. He constructed multiple-choice and constructed-response items to measure the knowledge, comprehension, application, and analysis skills of undergraduate and graduate students in introductory educational measurement and research statistics courses. His findings indicated that the two-item formats were generally comparable for all four skill levels.

Killoran illustrated a variety of ways that multiple-choice items can be used to assess both lower and higher order thinking skills in social studies. Standard multiple-choice items can be developed to measure

(1) recognition of important terms and persons,

(2) comparisons and contrasts,

(3) cause and effect,

(4) generalizations,

(5) chronology, and

(6) special item types, such as fact and opinion and use of sources.

Data-based questions, including maps, tables, outlines, cartoons, etc., can measure:

(1) comprehension,

(2) explanation,

(3) conclusion or generalization, and

(4) prediction.

Writing Test Items to Evaluate Higher Order Thinking Skills is an important resource for teachers who want to construct items for measuring higher order skills. The book gives instructions on how to write and score multiple-choice and constructed-response items, performance tasks, and portfolios in three domains—cognitive, affective, and psychomotor. Procedures for item review and statistical analysis of item responses are presented.

Performance Tests

Performance tests, including hands-on tasks (e.g., laboratory problems), essays, short-answer constructed-response measures, and portfolios, have been widely recommended for measuring higher order thinking skills. They have been proposed as replacements for multiple-choice tests, which have been criticized as placing "too much emphasis on factual knowledge and on the application of procedures to solve well-structured, decontextualized problems". With few exceptions (e.g., the *Ennis-Weir Critical Thinking Essay Test*), performance tests are domain-specific measures. They can be "authentic" in that they can be highly related to instruction and serve as good examples of teaching procedures. They can deal with complex, real-life problems that require students to employ several higher order skills in their solution. They can generate student interest and motivation.

Performance tests also have limitations. They can be costly and time consuming and they can lack generalizability. In addition, Facione noted that the application of many critical thinking subskills, particularly inference and evaluation, may not be apparent in the final version of an essay or report.

By its very nature the essay omits claims considered and judged irrelevant, arguments evaluated as not of sufficient significance to the issues at hand to warrant mention, evidence queried but not used in the final form of the essay, alternatives conjectured but ultimately abandoned, and conclusions drawn but ultimately reconsidered and disregarded.

Newmann constructed an essay test of higher order thinking skills in social studies that required students to write persuasively about constitutional issues. Its purpose was to assess students' interpretation, analysis, and use of knowledge in the social sciences rather than to measure "discrete thinking skills such as hypothesis testing or evaluating the reliability of sources". It was designed to permit "comparisons of students over time, and between teachers, schools, districts, and states". The task consisted of (1) a two-page narrative, which described a court case involving the search of a student's purse and locker by a high school principal who suspected her of smoking and selling marijuana, (2) background information on constitutional rights, and (3) instructions for responding. Each essay was assigned one of five scores: (1) unsatisfactory, (2) minimal, (3) adequate, (4) elaborated, or (5) exemplary. The test was used in fifty-one classrooms of thirty-eight teachers of the diverse social studies subjects in grades 9–12 in seven high schools. Although the classes covered U.S. history, world history, politics, sociology, economics, etc., we tested all students on the constitutional exercise. In spite of the fact that none of the classes focused teaching on this particular civic competence, we found that teachers' promotion of thinking in their daily lessons, regardless of the subject taught, had a strong positive relationship to students' persuasive writing on the constitutional issue, even after controlling for student writing ability and general social studies knowledge.

Newmann concluded that the exercise requires higher order thinking and understanding of relevant content. Success on the test is related to the extent to which higher order thinking is stressed in the classroom.

Enright and Beattie developed a five-step model called SOLVE for assessing critical thinking skills in mathematics. The five steps are Study the Problem (S), Organize the Data (O), Line Up a Plan (L), Verify the Plan (V), and Evaluate the Match (E).

Portfolios

Portfolios are collections of student assignments and projects (essays, performance tasks, etc.), which are gathered over an extended period of time, usually one academic year. Depending on its purpose, the portfolio may also contain teacher evaluations, standardized test scores, and student reflections on their accomplishments. Portfolios that are intended to demonstrate growth and proficiency are often limited to single subject matter areas. Lankes cited an example of one school at which students were required to complete 14 portfolios in various content areas. However, portfolios may also contain real-world assignments that cut across many subject areas and allow students the opportunity to employ higher order skills in completing them. Portfolio performances are different from the performance tasks cited above in that they may occur over long periods of time and may be revised by students as a result of teacher input or self-reflection. Disadvantages of portfolios for formal assessment include high costs of scoring and questions about the authorship of portfolio entries.

Haladyna provided a template to aid teachers in designing an evaluation portfolio. It should contain (1) a table of contents; (2) a provision for a reflective letter that allows the student to summarize his or her successes, frustrations, insights, feelings, etc.; (3) the specific tasks to be accomplished and evaluated; (4) the page limit; (5) the extent of collaboration allowed with other students; (6) a statement of the permissibility of editorial assistance; (7) an indication of whether or not an appendix containing preliminary drafts, etc., is required; and (8) grading criteria (the scoring rubric) that make the student aware of how points will be assigned to the various sections of the portfolio.

Classroom Assessment of Thinking Skills

Stiggins, Griswold, and Wikelund summarized a number of studies, which suggest that assessments based on teacher observation and judgment and teacher-made tests are not generally of high quality and that teacher assessment of higher order thinking skills is rare. Few items written by teachers measure skills above the three Bloom taxonomy levels of knowledge, comprehension, and application and a high percentage of them are recall (knowledge) items. Stiggins et al. studied the assessment practices (use of oral and test questions) of 36 teachers who taught mathematics, science, social studies, and language arts at grade levels 1 to 12. Excluding math items, over one-half of the test questions at all grade levels were recall measures (55%) followed by inference (19%), analysis (16%), comparison (5%), and evaluation (5%). In math, 72% of the questions measured inference, 19% measured recall, and 9% measured comparison. Oral questions followed the same pattern, with slightly less than half of them measuring recall. Teachers who had received training in teaching and/or testing higher order thinking skills tended to use fewer recall questions than teachers who had no training.

More recently, Bol and Strage studied the relationships between the instructional goals and the assessment practices of 10 high school biology teachers. Individual interviews with the teachers indicated that they wanted students to acquire an understanding and appreciation of biology and its real-world applications. They also stressed the importance of having students develop higher order thinking skills (distinguishing important from unimportant information, integration and interpretation of information, critical thinking and problem solving, and time and effort management). Examination of test items used by the teachers revealed that more than half required only factual information and almost none required application skills.

Assessment Models

Baker, Aschbacher, Niemi, and Sato

Baker, Aschbacher, Niemi, and Sato developed a performance-based model for assessment of student understanding of subject matter content. They suggested that it may assist others who need to develop similar measures. They illustrated the model through the development of instruments on the Civil War era of U.S. history and the analysis of an unknown substance in chemistry. A major purpose of the model is to generate tasks that are comparable by design rather than by statistical equating. The structure of the measures and the production of scoring rubrics are thought to reduce variability from topic to topic. The model consists of four assessment components:

- a prior knowledge measure, which assesses (and activates) students' general and topic-relevant knowledge;
- provision of primary source materials (text), that is, new information in written text for students to read;
- a writing task in which students integrate prior and new knowledge to explain subject matter issues in response to a contextualized prompt; and
- the scoring rubric for the writing task.

The prior knowledge measure consisted of 20 short-answer constructed-response items. They measured basic concepts, principles, and background knowledge related to the task. In the history example, items included "states rights" and the "Kansas-Nebraska Act."

Text materials are primary sources that students must use in responding to the prompt. In the example, the texts used were the speeches of Abraham Lincoln and Stephen Douglas. The writing task was an essay written in one class period by a student who had no help from peers, parents, or teachers. The task could be modified to extend over longer periods of time and include collaboration with others.

The essay scoring rubric consists of six dimensions, a General Impression of Content Quality scale that focuses on the overall quality of the content understanding, and five analytic scales, which are listed as follows. prior knowledge (facts, information, and events outside the provided texts used to elaborate positions)

- number of principles or concepts (number and depth of description of principles)
- argumentation (quality of the argument, its logic and integration of elements)
- text (use of information from the text for elaboration)
- misconceptions (number and scope of misunderstandings in interpretation of the text and historical period)

Students are allowed 15 minutes to respond to the prior knowledge items, 25 minutes to read primary sources, and 50 minutes to read the prompt and write the essay.

Baker et al. provided detailed specifications for developing assessments (prior knowledge test, essay task, and text materials) and for rater training, scoring, and reporting. They also provided samples of training materials and student responses at different performance levels.

Sugrue

Sugrue's problem-solving model contains three major interacting components: knowledge structures, cognitive functions, and beliefs about oneself. For good problem solvers, knowledge structures are well organized. Concepts and principles are integrated and linked to applications by conditions and procedures.

Concepts are categories of things, people, events, etc., that are similar with regard to some important attributes. They share the same name.

According to studies by de Kleer and Brown, Genter and Stevens, Glaser, and Merrill,

> A principal is defined as a rule, law, formula, or if-then statement that characterized the relationship (often causal) between two or more concepts. Principals can be used to interpret problems, to guide actions, to troubleshoot systems, to explain why something happened, or to predict the effects a change in some concept(s) will have on other concepts as reported in studies by de Kleer and Brown, Gentner and Stevens, Glaser, and Merrill.
>
> Procedures and conditions are links from concepts and principles to applications.
>
> A procedure is a set of steps that can be carried out to achieve some goal. Conditions are aspects of the environment that indicate the existence of an instance of a concept, or that indicate that a principle is operating or might be applied, or that a particular procedure is appropriate. Good problem solvers should be able to recognize situations where a principle is operating; they should also be able to recognize situations where procedures can be performed to identify or generate instances of a concept; and they should be able to carry out those procedures accurately. Good problem solvers should be able to assemble a procedure based on a principle to engineer a desired outcome in an unfamiliar situation.

The cognitive functions assessed by the model are planning and monitoring. Planning consists of laying out the steps to be followed in solving the problem. Monitoring refers to being aware of different parts of one's performance, including time spent and time available, progress toward the solution of the problem, and changes in tactics when necessary.

Three beliefs about oneself and the task are important in problem-solving assessment. Perceived self-efficacy (PSE) refers to the student's assessment of his or her ability to solve the problem. Perceived demands of the task (PDT) involves the student's belief about the difficulty of the task. Perceived attraction of the task (PAT) refers to the student's interest and motivation in completing the task. Assessment of these beliefs is necessary to complete a profile of problem-solving performance.

Sugrue recommended that multiple item formats for measuring multiple aspects of the content domain to which the task belongs be used to assess problem solving. Tasks presented to students should not be ones they have encountered previously. A student profile based on multiple formats and multiple aspects could help determine the extent to which the overall assessment is novel for individual students.

Content Analysis

A content analysis is a major requirement for developing an assessment. The Overview Content Analysis Form that follows was developed by Sugrue and completed for problem solving in solution chemistry.

Sugrue provided sample multiple-choice, open-ended, and hands-on items for solution chemistry.

The Mid-Continent Regional Educational Laboratory

The Mid-Continent Regional Educational Laboratory (McREL) authentic assessment model is organized around 14 complex reasoning processes within 6 general competencies. The competencies are listed below.

1. Knowledge of concepts, generalizations, processes, and strategies that are considered critical to specific content areas.
2. Ability to utilize complex reasoning processes.
3. Ability to gather and utilize information from a variety of sources in a variety of modes.
4. Ability to communicate effectively through a variety of products.
5. Ability to regulate one's own learning and development.
6. Ability to work in a cooperative/collaborative manner.

A number of subcompetencies are contained within each competency. The 14 complex reasoning processes and questions that students could ask in relation to them are as follows.

— *Comparing:* How are these alike? How are they different?

— *Classifying:* What groups can I put things into? What are the rules governing membership in these groups?

— *Structural Analysis:* What is the main idea or what is the most important information? What is the dominant pattern? What are the supporting patterns? What are the supporting pieces? How are the pieces related?

— *Supported Induction:* What conclusions/generalizations can you draw from this and what is the support for these conclusions? What is the probability for this and what is the support for that conclusion?

— *Supported Deduction:* What has to be true given the validity of this principle? What is the proof that this must be true?

— *Error Analysis:* What's wrong with this? What are specific errors that have been made? How can it be fixed?

— *Constructing Support:* What is the support for this argument? What are the limitations of this argument?

— *Extending:* What's the general pattern of information here? Where else does this apply? How can the information be represented in another way (graphically, symbolically)?

— *Decision Making:* What/whom would be the best or worst? Which one has the most or least?

— *Investigation:* What are the defining characteristics (definitive)? Why/how did this happen (historical)? What would/would have happen/ed if (projective)?

— *Systems Analysis:* How does this operate? What are the relationships among components? What effect does one part have on another?

— *Problem Solving:* How can I overcome this obstacle? Given these conditions, what can I expect the answer to be?

— *Experimental Inquiry:* What do I observe? How can I explain it? What can I predict from it?

— *Invention:* How can this be improved? What new thing is needed here?

Although the competencies and reasoning processes apply to all subject matters, Marzano et al. emphasize that they always apply to domain-specific content. It is important that students acquire sufficient declarative knowledge (e.g., concepts and facts) and procedural knowledge (e.g., strategies and algorithms) within a specific content domain before they can be expected to engage in the complex reasoning processes that may be required by performance measures. They provide details for (1) constructing authentic classroom tasks and examples of them, (2) securing tasks to maximize reliability for districtwide or state-level assessment, and (3) generalizing rubrics for rating declarative and procedural knowledge and complex reasoning skills.

Advanced International Certificate of Education

The Advanced International Certificate of Education (AICE) (University of Cambridge, Local Examinations Syndicate, 1997a) is an assessment model for college-bound students who are 18 years of age or older. Schools that fully participate in the program offer courses in 3 broad areas: mathematics and sciences (9 courses), languages (8 courses), and arts and humanities (9 courses). To receive an AICE certificate, students must take examinations in at least 5 courses (all courses include critical thinking and other higher order thinking skills). One course from each broad subject area must be included. Assessment requirements for each course typically include some combination of externally scored examinations and school-based assessments, which can include essays, performance tests, and portfolios. Successful students may receive college credit or be eligible for advanced courses at many colleges and universities.

As an example, the assessment objectives of the AICE course in economics (University of Cambridge, Local Examinations Syndicate, n.d.) cover all levels of Bloom's taxonomy. The curriculum on which the assessments are based include

- resources and the economic problem (factors of production and scarcity, choice and opportunity cost);
- allocative mechanisms (market system, command economy, mixed economy);
- the circular flow of national income (the circular flow model, consumption and saving, economic fluctuations);
- specialization, trade, and exchange (the open economy: trade and exchange);
- international trade (protection, commodity agreements, exchange rates, international monetary system, balance of payments, multinational companies);
- economic development (living standards, developing economies); and
- policy objectives and instruments (full employment, price stability, economic growth).

International Baccalaureate Diploma Program

The International Baccalaureate (IB) Diploma Program (International

Baccalaureate North America) is a curriculum and assessment model for high schools. Students will acquire knowledge in the areas of language, literature, mathematics, science, and social studies with particular recognition and emphasis on the interrelatedness of the various disciplines by

- developing a proficiency in the communication skills of reading, writing, and speaking and listening;
- developing a proficiency in the process of calculating, problem solving, observing, measuring, and estimating;
- developing a proficiency in the intellectual skills of analysis, synthesis, induction, deduction, and critical and aesthetic judgment; and
- developing the skills and attitudes that contribute to intelligent and productive participation in the economic system as well as developing an appreciation for both unique and common characteristics of other individuals and cultures.

The curriculum and examinations consist of six subject matter areas, a special course entitled Theory of Knowledge, the Creative Action and Service project, and an extended essay. The six subject matter areas are (1) Language A1, the student's native or strongest language; (2) Language A2, a second modern language; (3) Individuals and Societies, social studies, philosophy, business, etc.; (4) Experimental Sciences; (5) Mathematics; and (6) the Arts and Electives. The Theory of Knowledge course is taken by students in their senior year to help them integrate the knowledge, skills, and understandings attained from all their IB course work. The Creative Action and Service project can emphasize sports, theater, community service, or other extracurricular activities. The extended essay "offers the opportunity to investigate a topic of special interest and acquaints students with the kind of independent research and writing skills expected at a university".

Both internal and external assessments are made of a student's course work. Teacher assessments (internal) can make up to 20% of a student's grade. The IB program is offered by a number of Florida high schools. IB graduates are eligible for advanced placement or course credit at a large number of American universities.

Statewide Assessment Models

Sternberg and Baron indicated that the measurement of students' thinking abilities should be accompanied by a curriculum that included thinking skills instruction. He concluded that collaboration by state department personnel, cognitive psychologists, and testing organizations provided a good model for future efforts to develop statewide assessment of higher order thinking skills..

Paul and Nosich were commissioned by the U.S. Department of Education and the National Center of Educational Statistics to develop a model for the national assessment of higher order thinking. Their report (a) identified 21 criteria for higher order skills testing, (b) developed a concept of critical thinking that meets these criteria, (c) identified 4 domains of critical thinking, and (d) recommended ways to measure the 4 kinds of critical thinking skills.

The 21 criteria are given as answers to the following questions (italics theirs):

1. Can it be used for information processing skills?
2. Can it be used to test flexible skills and abilities that can be used in a wide variety of subjects, situations, contexts, and educational levels?
3. Can it account for important differences among the subject areas?
4. Can it be used to focus on fundamental abilities fitted to the accelerating pace of change and embedded in intellectual history?
5. Can it be used to improve instruction?
6. Can it make clear the interconnectedness of our knowledge and abilities, and why expertise in one area cannot be divorced either from findings in other area or from a sensitivity to the need for interdisciplinary integration?
7. Can it be used to assess those versatile and fundamental skills essential to being a responsible, decision-making member of the workplace?
8. Can it generate clear concepts and well thought-out, rationally articulated goals, criteria and standards?
9. Can it account for the integration of adult-level communication skills, problem-solving, and critical thinking, and legitimately assess all of them without compromising essential features of any of them?
10. Does it respect cultural diversity by focusing on the common-core skills, abilities and traits useful in all cultures?

Does it test for thinking that promotes "the active engagement of students in constructing their own knowledge and understanding?"

11. Does it concentrate on assessing the fundamental cognitive structures of communication?
12. Can it be used to assess the central features of making rational decisions as a citizen, a consumer, and a part of a world economy?
13. Can it avoid reducing a complex whole to oversimplified parts?
14. Can it articulate what is central to basic skills for the future?
15. Can it provide the kind of skills that are seen as valuable outside the school as well as inside it?

17 and 18. Can critical thinking be assessed in a way that requires evaluation of

authentic problems in realistic contexts where the abilities assessed include those of formulating the problem and initial screening of plausible solutions?

19. Can critical thinking be assessed nationally in a way that is financially affordable?

20 and 21. Can critical thinking be assessed so as to gauge the improvement of students over the course of their education and to measure the achievement of students against national standards?

Paul and Nosich proposed an assessment that could meet the criteria implied by the 21 questions. It would consist of multiple-choice, multiple-rating, and essay items. Multiple-choice items are limited to reasoning skills such as recognition of assumptions, inferences, and detection of faculty reasoning.

Paul and Nosich proposed that a higher order skills examination be composed of both interdisciplinary and subject-specific items. The interdisciplinary items would be constructed by experts in the field of critical thinking, who would collaborate with subject matter experts on the subject-specific items. Students would choose the subject matter area in which they would be examined. All students at grades 6, 9, and 12 would take the objective parts of the exam. For economic reasons, the essay assessment would be administered only to representative samples of the student populations.

The Florida Department of Education

The Florida Department of Education (1997a–g) created the Florida

Comprehensive Assessment Test (FCAT), which measures achievement in mathematics at grades 5, 8, and 10 and reading at grades 4, 8, and 10. Both mathematics and reading contain items at two cognitive levels based on Bloom's taxonomy. Level I items are intended to measure knowledge, comprehension, and application, where application is similar to that encountered in the classroom. Level II items are intended to measure application, analysis, synthesis, and evaluation, where application is unique to the situation described in the item. Level II items comprise 50%, 60%, and 70% of the 4th-, 8th-, and 10th-grade reading exams, respectively. They make up 50%, 60%, and 65% of the mathematics exam for the three grades. The mathematics assessment contains multiple-choice, gridded response, short response, and extended response items. The reading assessment contains multiple-choice, short response, and extended response items. The Sunshine State Standards define the content knowledge and skills for item development in both reading and mathematics. Higher order thinking skills are required by many test items as specified by Standard 4 of Goal 3 of Blueprint 2000: "Florida students use creative thinking skills to generate new ideas, make the best decision, recognize and solve problems through reasoning, interpret symbolic data, and develop efficient techniques for lifelong learning".

A separate assessment, *Florida Writes!,* is administered in grades 4, 8, and 10. *Florida Writes!* is a holistically scored direct writing measure in which students at grade 4 write on narrative or expository topics, and students at grades 8 and 10 write on expository or persuasive topics. Scoring is based on focus, organization, support, and use conventions. Examples of mathematics, reading items, writing prompts, and rubrics may be obtained from the Florida Department of Education.

Pennsylvania Department of Education

In 1997, the Pennsylvania Department of Education began to employ statewide mathematics tests at grades 5, 8, and 11 that contain both open-ended (performance) tasks and enhanced multiple-choice questions. Open-ended tasks

> require students to read a problem or task description and to write out their answers. Major components of such answers are both students' clear presentations of their computations and their explanations of the steps they followed in solving the problem. The types of tasks utilized do not always require solving a problem involving computations.

Enhanced multiple-choice questions generally involve higher order thinking skills and refer to situations in real life or the classroom, give information to the teacher about the processes involved in problem solutions, and integrate process and knowledge. The five content areas involved in the test are (1) number sense, properties, and operations; (2) measurement; (3) geometry; (4) data analysis, statistics, and probability; and (5) algebra and functions. A general rubric is used for scoring open-ended tasks. The five-point rubric contains levels ranging from "Advanced Understanding" to "Excellent" to "Incorrect Response." Detailed scoring explanations and sample student responses are provided. The intermediate levels can accept incorrect answers if the student provides the necessary information for solving the problem.

Pennsylvania also administers a direct writing assessment to students in grades 6 and 9. Three kinds of writing are assessed:

1. narrative/imaginative, which encourages creativity and speculation;
2. informational, whose function is "to present information through reporting, explaining, directing, summarizing and defining; to organize and analyze information through explaining, comparing, contrasting, and relaying cause/effect; or to evaluate information through judging, ranking or deciding"; and
3. persuasive, because "(a) it requires thinking skills such as analysis, synthesis, and evaluation; (b) it requires writers to choose from a variety of situations and to take a stand; and (c) it is a skill frequently used in school and the workplace".

Students randomly receive one of nine prompts on which to write. The assessment is administered in two 40-minute sessions on two consecutive days. In the first session, students think about the topic, make notes, and write a first draft; in the second, they reread the prompt, review their drafts, and produce a final copy. Each paper is holistically scored on a six-point scale by two trained raters.

King, Rohani, and Goodson investigated the feasibility of assessing the real-world problem-solving skills of samples of Florida's elementary, middle, and high school students. They identified 31 problem-solving skills that almost completely overlap with the skills listed by various authors previously cited in this report. Also, in agreement with previously cited investigators, they recommended that the proposed assessments should contain multiple-choice (select) and constructed-response (generate) items and possibly computer-administered performance tasks (generate). Explanation of solutions could be required with all three kinds of items or tasks. Items would be constructed to measure the 31 skills in ways consistent with the Sunshine State Standards.

King, Rohani, and Goodson suggested that the administration of a multiple-choice and constructed-response instrument to a Florida statewide sample of about 3,500 students at each of three chosen grade levels would be feasible. Activities involved in the assessment would include formation and training of item writing and review committees; preparation of test booklets, answer documents, answer keys, and rubrics; conducting a pilot study and validation committee meeting; and producing final editions of all materials.

The measurement of higher order thinking skills requires that students be unfamiliar with the questions or tasks they are asked to answer or perform and that they have sufficient prior knowledge to enable them to apply their higher order thinking skills to answer the question or solve the problem. Meeting these requirements is problematic in dealing with either real-life orsubject-matter domain problems. A recommended solution is to examine students using multiple-item formats to measure multiple aspects of a domain. Student profiles of correct answers can help to determine the extent to which the overall assessment is novel for individual students.

Psychological studies of transfer of higher order thinking skills suggest that skills taught in one context generalize to other contexts if explicit teaching for transfer and self-monitoring is included in the instruction. Other studies suggest that over long periods of time individuals, as a result of educational and other personal experiences, develop higher order skills (intellectual abilities) that apply to the solutions of a broad spectrum of complex problems. Conversely, psychometric studies of the generalizability of higher order thinking skills when measured by hands-on performance tasks show great method and task variability in student performance; that is, individual student achievement is highly dependent on the tasks and methods used in the assessment. Estimates of the number of tasks needed in an assessment to achieve generalizable (reliable) results range from 8 to 23.

Published tests of higher order thinking skills have been found to be sensitive to instruction. Three studies of such tests involved single group pre- and posttest comparisons and two used quasi-experimental treatment and control groups. In all studies, results were statistically significant, but treatment effects were small. A recommended procedure for those who might want to use a published test to assess student levels of critical thinking or for evaluating programs or courses is to examine the test items for content validity, then to take the test themselves and examine their own performance critically.

Three item/task formats have been identified for use in assessing higher order thinking skills:

(1) selection, which includes multiple-choice, matching, and rank order items;

(2) generation, which includes short answer, essay, and performance items or tasks; and

(3) explanation, which involves giving reasons for selection or generation responses. All three formats are valid for measuring some aspects of higher order thinking, but all three have some disadvantages. Multiple-choice and constructed-response items can be used for separately measuring many specific higher order skills such as deduction, inference, and prediction but are less successful for measuring synthesis and evaluation. Some validity problems can be avoided by using answer justification, where subjects select responses and then justify in writing their reasons for the choices they made. Multiple-choice items can sample many aspects of the subject matter, and performance tasks and essays can deal with complex real-life problems that require students to employ a number of higher order skills in solving them. However, final solutions to performance tasks and essays may not reveal the application of many higher order skills.

Even though classroom teachers recognize the importance of having students develop higher order thinking skills, teacher-made tests are often heavily weighted with recall questions. Teachers who have received training in teaching and testing higher order thinking skills use fewer recall questions than those who have not received such training.

Three comprehensive performance based models for assessing higher order skills have been constructed. They contain detailed procedures for constructing performance assessments in specific content domains. Two international curricula and assessment systems are available to instruct advanced students in both subject matter content and higher order thinking skills. Students are assessed by both local school personnel and external examiners.Statewide assessment systems for elementary, middle, and high school students may contain measures of higher order thinking skills. Two states, Florida and Pennsylvania, include select, generate, and select and explain items or tasks in their mathematics, reading, and writing assessments. In Florida, higher order skills comprise at least 50% of the items or tasks, and the Pennsylvania assessments also emphasize higher order skills.

A proposal for a nationwide test of higher order thinking skills and a report of a statewide pilot project for measuring such skills both emphasized the need for collaboration of subject matter experts and cognitive psychologists and/or critical thinking experts in preparing such assessments. The nationwide proposal contained a provision for multiple-choice and multiple-rating items to be administered to all students and essay items to be given to representative samples of students. The pilot project contained only multiple-choice items.

One study for the Florida Department of Education demonstrated the feasibility of statewide assessment of the real-world problem-solving skills of samples of students. Instruments for implementing the proposed assessments of the skills of elementary, middle, and high school students would consist of multiple-choice, constructed-response, and possibly computer-administered performance tasks. Example items and tasks reveal a wide variety of ways that have been used to measure higher order skills. They also demonstrate the difficulties inherent in the construction of instruments to assess these skills for students at all educational levels. It should be possible to construct measures for them through the use of carefully developed item/test specifications and adequate pilot testing and analysis.

References

Fisher, A (2002) *Thinking Skills for the 21st Century.* Cambridge: Cambridge International Examinations.

Gardner, H (1993) *Multiple Intelligences: the Theory in Practice.* New York: Basic Books.

Glaser, E (1941) *An Experiment in the Development of Critical Thinking* New York: Teachers College, Columbia University

Hamers, J.H.M and Overtoom, M.Th. (Eds.) (1997) *Teaching thinking in Europe. Inventory of European programmes.* Utrecht: SARDES

Lipman, M (1991) *Thinking in Education* Cambridge: Cambridge University Press.

5

Teaching Critical Thinking

Educators have long been aware of the importance of critical thinking skills as an outcome of student learning. More recently, the Partnership for 21st Century Skills has identified critical thinking as one of several learning and innovation skills necessary to prepare students for post-secondary education and the workforce. In addition, the newly created Common Core State Standards reflect critical thinking as a cross-disciplinary skill vital for college and employment. Despite widespread recognition of its importance, there is a notable lack of consensus regarding the definition of critical thinking.

Theoretical Background of Critical Thinking

The literature on critical thinking has roots in two primary academic disciplines: philosophy and psychology. Sternberg has also noted a third critical thinking strand within the field of education. These separate academic strands have developed different approaches to defining critical thinking that reflect their respective concerns. Each of these approaches is explored more fully below.

The Philosophical Approach

The writings of Socrates, Plato, Aristotle, and more recently, Matthew Lipman and Richard Paul, exemplify the philosophical approach. This approach focuses on the hypothetical critical thinker, enumerating the qualities and characteristics of this person rather than the behaviors or actions the critical thinker can perform. Sternberg has noted that this school of thought approaches the critical thinker as an ideal type, focusing on what people are capable of doing under the best of circumstances. Accordingly, Richard Paul discusses critical thinking in the context of "perfections of thought". This preoccupation with the ideal critical thinker is evident in the American Philosophical Association's consensus portrait of the ideal critical thinker as someone who is inquisitive in nature, open-minded, flexible, fair-minded, has a desire to be well-informed, understands diverse viewpoints, and is willing to both suspend judgment and to consider other perspectives.

Those working within the philosophical tradition also emphasize qualities or standards of thought. For example, Bailin defines critical thinking as thinking of a particular quality— essentially good thinking that meets specified criteria or standards of adequacy and accuracy. Further, the philosophical approach has traditionally focused on the application of formal rules of logic. One limitation of this approach to defining critical thinking is that it does not always correspond to reality. By emphasizing the ideal critical thinker and what people have the capacity to do, this approach may have less to contribute to discussions about how people actually think.

Definitions of critical thinking emerging from the philosophical tradition include

- the propensity and skill to engage in an activity with reflective skepticism";
- reflective and reasonable thinking that is focused on deciding what to believe or do";
- killful, responsible thinking that facilitates good judgment because it 1) relies upon criteria, 2) is self-correcting, and 3) is sensitive to context";
- "purposeful, self-regulatory judgment which results in interpretation, analysis, evaluation, and inference, as well as explanation of the evidential, conceptual, methodological, criteriological, or conceptual considerations upon which that judgment is based";
- "disciplined, self-directed thinking that exemplifies the perfections of thinking appropriate to a particular mode or domain of thought";
- thinking that is goal-directed and purposive, "thinking aimed at forming a judgment," where the thinking itself meets standards of adequacy and accuracy; and
- "judging in a reflective way what to do or what to believe".

The Cognitive Psychological Approach

The cognitive psychological approach contrasts with the philosophical perspective in two ways. First, cognitive psychologists, particularly those immersed in the behaviorist tradition and the experimental research paradigm, tend to focus on how people actually think versus how they could or should think under ideal conditions. Second, rather than defining critical thinking by pointing to characteristics of the ideal critical thinker or enumerating criteria or standards of "good" thought, those working in cognitive psychology tend to define critical thinking by the types of actions or behaviors critical thinkers can do. Typically, this approach to defining critical thinking includes a list of skills or procedures performed by critical thinkers.

Philosophers have often criticized this latter aspect of the cognitive psychological approach as being reductionist—reducing a complex orchestration of knowledge and skills into a collection of disconnected steps or procedures. For example, Bailin argues that it is a fundamental misconception to view critical thinking as a series of discrete steps or skills, and that this misconception stems from the behaviorist's need to define constructs in ways that are directly observable. According to this argument, because the actual process of thought is unobservable, cognitive psychologists have tended to focus on the products of such thought—behaviors or overt skills (e.g., analysis, interpretation, formulating good questions). Other philosophers have also cautioned against confusing the activity of critical thinking with its component skills, arguing that critical thinking is more than simply the sum of its parts. Indeed, a few proponents of the philosophical tradition have pointed out that it is possible to simply "go through the motions," or proceed through the "steps" of critical thinking without actually engaging in critical thought.

Definitions of critical thinking that have emerged from the cognitive psychological approach include

- "the mental processes, strategies, and representations people use to solve problems, make decisions, and learn new concepts";
- the use of those cognitive skills or strategies that increase the probability of a desirable outcome"; and
- "seeing both sides of an issue, being open to new evidence that disconfirms your ideas, reasoning dispassionately, demanding that

claims be backed by evidence, deducing and inferring conclusions from available facts, solving problems, and so forth".

The Educational Approach

Finally, those working in the field of education have also participated in discussions about critical thinking. Benjamin Bloom and his associates are included in this category. Their taxonomy for information processing skills is one of the most widely cited sources for educational practitioners when it comes to teaching and assessing higher-order thinking skills. Bloom's taxonomy is hierarchical, with "comprehension" at the bottom and "evaluation" at the top. The three highest levels (analysis, synthesis, and evaluation) are frequently said to represent critical thinking.

The benefit of the educational approach is that it is based on years of classroom experience and observations of student learning, unlike both the philosophical and the psychological traditions. However, some have noted that the educational approach is limited in its vagueness. Concepts within the taxonomy lack the clarity necessary to guide instruction and assessment in a useful way. Furthermore, the frameworks developed in education have not been tested as vigorously as those developed within either philosophy or psychology.

Areas for Agreement

Abilities Included

Despite differences among the three schools of thought and their approaches to defining critical thinking, there exist areas for agreement. First, researchers of critical thinking typically agree on the specific abilities encompassed by the definition, which include

- analyzing arguments, claims, or evidence;
- making inferences using inductive or deductive reasoning;
- judging or evaluating; and
- making decisions or solving problems.

Other abilities or behaviors identified as relevant to critical thinking include asking and answering questions for clarification; defining terms; identifying assumptions; interpreting and explaining; reasoning verbally, especially in relation to concepts of likelihood and uncertainty; predicting; and seeing both sides of an issue.

Dispositions

Most researchers also agree that in addition to skills or abilities, critical thinking also involves dispositions. As early as 1985, researchers working in the area of critical thinking recognized that the *ability* to think critically is distinct from the *disposition* to do so. Empirical evidence appears to confirm the notion that critical thinking abilities and dispositions are, in fact, separate entities. These dispositions have variously been cast as attitudes or habits of mind. Facione defines critical thinking dispositions as "consistent internal motivations to act toward or respond to persons, events, or circumstances in habitual, yet potentially malleable ways". Researchers tend to identify similar sets of dispositions as relevant to critical thinking. For example, the most commonly cited critical thinking dispositions include

- open-mindedness;
- fair-mindedness;
- the propensity to seek reason;
- inquisitiveness;
- the desire to be well-informed;
- flexibility; and
- respect for, and willingness to entertain, others' viewpoints.

Importance of Background Knowledge.

Finally, most researchers working in the area of critical thinking agree on the important role of background knowledge. In particular, most researchers see background knowledge as essential if students are to demonstrate their critical thinking skills. As McPeck has noted, to think critically, students need something to think critically about. Similarly, Bailin et al. argue that domain-specific knowledge is indispensable to critical thinking because the kinds of explanations, evaluations, and evidence that are most highly valued vary from one domain to another. Facione notes the following:

> Although the identification and analysis of critical thinking skills transcend, in significant ways, specific subjects or disciplines, learning and applying these skills in many contexts requires domain-specific knowledge. This domain-specific knowledge includes understanding methodological principles and competence to engage in norm-regulated practices that are at the core of reasonable judgments in those specific contexts... Too much of value is lost if critical thinking is conceived of simply as a list of logical

operations and domain-specific knowledge is conceived of simply as an aggregation of information.

AREAS FOR DISAGREEMENT

Role of Dispositions.

Much remains to be resolved regarding the definition of critical thinking. Although most researchers agree that critical thinking involves both skills and dispositions, there remains disagreement as to whether the disposition to think critically should be viewed in its normative sense in addition to its laudatory sense. In 1990, the American Philosophical Association (APA) formed a panel of critical thinking researchers for the purpose of coming to a consensus on a definition of critical thinking that could support future research efforts. Although most experts agreed that dispositions were an important component, they disagreed on the particular role of dispositions within the definition of critical thinking, with some arguing that dispositions have merely a laudatory role, and others maintaining that dispositions also have a normative role. In other words, most researchers agreed that critical thinking is synonymous with "good thinking," in the sense that truly critical thought can only be exhibited by those with both the ability and the disposition to think critically. By this standard, a person who is capable of thinking critically and chooses not to do so is not a critical thinker. However, a small minority of experts also argued that critical thinking must fulfill ethical standards to be truly critical. According to this argument, a defense attorney using critical thinking abilities and dispositions to get her guilty client acquitted would not be a critical thinker.

Domain Specificity.

Another area for disagreement is the extent to which critical thinking skills are domain-specific. On one hand, some researchers argue that critical thinking skills can be generalized across different contexts and domains and can thus be taught in a generic way. On the other side of the debate are those who argue that general critical thinking skills that transcend specific subjects do not exist. According to this argument, critical thinking skills can only be taught in the context of a specific domain. Ennis identifies a range of assumptions regarding domain specificity held by various theorists. For example, most researchers view background knowledge as a necessary but not sufficient condition for critical thinking. In addition, some researchers see the transfer of critical thinking skills across domains as unlikely unless students are provided with sufficient opportunities to practice these skills in a variety of domains and the students are explicitly taught to transfer. Finally, an even smaller number of researchers hold the view that general instruction in critical thinking skills is unlikely to be successful because critical thinking skills are inherently domain-specific.

Proponents of domain specificity include Willingham, who argues that it is easier to learn to think critically within a given domain than it is to learn to think critically in a generic sense. Similarly, Bailin argues that domain-specific knowledge is necessary for critical thinking because what constitutes valid evidence, arguments, and standards tends to vary across domains:

> For example, it makes no sense to refer to a process of interpreting which remains constant regardless of subject matter. Rather, what is involved in and even meant by interpreting varies with the context, and this difference is connected with the different kinds of knowledge and understanding necessary for successful completion of a particular task.

Although McPeck concedes that there are a limited number of general thinking skills, he argues that the most useful thinking skills are those that are domain-specific. According to McPeck, the more general the thinking skill, the less helpful it is. Bailin concurs, arguing that what is common and general to the concept of critical thinking is so generic that it is not useful.

Those who maintain that critical thinking skills and abilities are not domain-specific include Halpern, who reviews evidence on the success of general instruction in critical thinking skills and concludes that such instruction has great potential. Lipman notes that critical thinking facilitates good judgment because it relies on criteria. These criteria may differ across domains, but the fundamental meaning of critical thinking remains the same. Van Gelder (2005, p. 43) argues that critical thinking is "intrinsically general in nature," which, paradoxically, is why critical thinking skills and abilities are notoriously difficult to transfer to new contexts.

There are also those who maintain that critical thinking includes both general and domain-specific elements. As Ennis notes, in math, deductive proof is the gold standard for reason, whereas in the social sciences statistical significance is most highly regarded, and in art subjectivity is usually acceptable. On the other hand, Ennis acknowledges that there appear to be aspects of critical thinking that are common across disciplines, such as the notion that a conflict of interest detracts from the credibility of a source. Facione has designed the California Critical Thinking Skills Test as a general test of critical thinking rather than one embedded within the context of a specific domain. Yet Facione also notes the importance of domain-specific knowledge in any application of critical thinking skills and abilities. Thus, Facione also falls into the category of researchers who acknowledge both general and domain-specific elements of critical thinking. Finally, Paul identifies critical thinking as learning to think within one's discipline by appropriating the standards and values embodied in that discipline. At the same time, however, Paul points out that critical thinking skills and abilities can be taught using both general critical thinking courses and infusing critical thinking instruction into discipline-specific courses.

Transferability.

Another area of disagreement among critical thinking researchers is the extent to which critical thinking skills and abilities can be transferred to new contexts. For example, researchers have noted that students may exhibit critical thinking skills and abilities in one context, or domain, but fail to do so in another. This issue is closely related to that of the domain-specificity of critical thinking. For example, those maintaining that critical thinking is completely domain-specific are more likely to be skeptical of students' abilities to transfer critical thinking skills from one domain to another. Accepted wisdom within cognitive psychology holds that spontaneous transfer to new contexts is rare. Others, however, are more sanguine about the possibility of student transfer, particularly if students are given opportunities to practice critical thinking skills in multiple domains and contexts and if students are taught specifically to transfer those skills. McPeck, a staunch proponent of domain specificity, notes that his approach does not preclude the transfer of critical thinking skills and abilities to real-world contexts, particularly when instruction emphasizes authentic learning activities that represent problems encountered in daily life.

Empirical evidence on transfer documents both successes and failures. Halpern describes the results of one study that sought to determine whether college students would transfer critical thinking skills acquired in the context of a specific discipline to an entirely new context several months after the course had ended. Most students in this study did indeed appl the reasoning they had previously learned to a non-academic topic several months later. However, in his review of the research, Nickerson finds the empirical evidence on transfer to be mixed. He concludes that the success of any transfer method appears to depend on what is being taught and how it is being taught. For example, instructional programs aimed at improving students' metacognitive skills have demonstrated more successful transfer than training programs for basic cognitive processes, such as observing, measuring, and classifying. Moreover, stand-alone approaches to instruction in general critical thinking appear to be less successful than approaches in which critical thinking instruction is infused into discipline-specific courses alongside traditional academic content.

One problem with attempting to investigate the degree of transfer is the ambiguity surrounding the "distance" of such transfer. In other words, is transfer near or far? On one end of the spectrum, students may be asked to transfer skills to a new but similar task. On the opposite end of the spectrum, transfer could refer to application within an entirely new discipline. In addition, some have used the term "transfer" to describe the process of applying skills learned within an academic school setting to problems encountered in everyday life. Clearly, the particular meaning a person imparts to the word "transfer" tends to affect the level of optimism regarding the potential for transfer. Transfer to new problems within the same domain is more likely to occur than transfer to new disciplines.

Role of Criteria.

Another area for disagreement among critical thinking researchers is the role of criteria. This debate occurs primarily between the philosophical and psychological approaches, with most of the philosophers maintaining the importance of attending to criteria and most of the psychologists ignoring the issue. From a philosophical perspective, critical thinking involves using criteria to make judgments or to support decisions. Criteria are needed for evaluating the arguments and positions of others, for evaluating evidence, and for evaluating one's own thoughts. These criteria may come in the form of standards—"standards for judging the adequacy of claims about meaning; the credibility of statements made by authorities; the strength of inductive arguments; and the adequacy of moral, legal, and aesthetic reasons". The criteria may also come in the form of laws, regulations, norms, or ideals. The particular criteria that are relevant in a given situation will depend on the domain of interest. For example, as Lipman points out, the criteria needed to evaluate a piece of architecture are different from those needed to assess the strength of a legal argument.

Criteria are also needed for evaluating one's own thought. As evidenced in Paul's "perfections of thought," these criteria communicate to students the qualities of thought they should strive to achieve: clarity, accuracy, precision, specificity, relevance, consistency, logic, depth, completeness, significance, fairness, and adequacy. Given the important role of criteria in critical thinking, philosophers tend to emphasize the need to communicate these criteria to students. Thus, Paul recommends being explicit about the intellectual standards used for evaluating student work. Similarly, Bailin et al. and Case include knowledge of criteria for judging the quality of thinking as one of five resources students need to think critically.

Relationships to Other Concepts

As a way of defining the concept of critical thinking, many researchers have drawn connections to other skills commonly identified as twenty-first century skills, including metacognition, motivation, and creativity. Each of these related concepts will be discussed separately.

Metacognition.

Metacognition has been defined most simply as "thinking about thinking." Other definitions include

- "the knowledge and control children have over their own thinking and learning activities"
- "awareness of one's own thinking, awareness of the content of one's conceptions, an active monitoring of one's cognitive processes, an attempt to regulate one's cognitive processes in relationship to further learning, and an application of a set of heuristics as an effective device for helping people organize their methods of attack on problems in general"; and
- "the monitoring and control of thought".

What is the relationship between critical thinking and metacognition? Kuhn sees critical thinking as being a form of metacognition, which includes metacognitive knowing (thinking that operates on declarative knowledge), meta-strategic knowing (thinking that operates on procedural knowledge), and epistemological knowing (encompassing how knowledge is produced). Likewise, Flavell sees critical thinking as forming part of the construct of metacognition when he argues that "critical appraisal of message source, quality of appeal, and probable consequences needed to cope with these inputs sensibly" can lead to "wise and thoughtful life decisions". On the other hand, Van Gelder and Willingham appear to perceive metacognition as being subsumed under critical thinking when they argue that a component critical thinking skill is the ability to deploy the right strategies and skills at the right time, typically referred to as conditional or strategic knowledge and considered part of the construct of metacognition. Halonen identifies metacognition as the ability to monitor the quality of critical thinking. Similarly, Halpern casts metacognition as monitoring thinking and strategy use by asking the following kinds of questions: What do I already know? What is my goal? How will I know when I get there? Am I making progress?

Some researchers have argued that the link between critical thinking and metacognition is self-regulation. For example, the APA Delphi report includes self-regulation as one component skill of critical thinking. Schraw et al. draw connections between metacognition, critical thinking, and motivation under the umbrella of self-regulated learning, which they define as "our ability to understand and control our learning environments". Self-regulated learning, in turn, is seen as comprising three components: cognition, metacognition, and motivation. The cognitive component includes critical thinking, which Schraw and associates explain consists of identifying and analyzing sources and drawing conclusions.

However, others have argued that critical thinking and metacognition are distinct constructs. For example, Lipman has pointed out that metacognition is not necessarily critical, because one can think about one's thought in an unreflective manner. McPeck, on the other hand, argues that the ability to recognize when a particular skill is relevant and to deploy that skill is not properly a part of critical thinking but actually represents general intelligence. At the very least, metacognition can be seen as a supporting condition for critical thinking, in that monitoring the quality of one's thought makes it more likely that one will engage in high-quality thinking.

Motivation.

Critical thinking is also related to motivation. For example, most researchers view critical thinking as including both skills, or abilities, and dispositions.

The disposition to think critically has been defined as the "consistent internal motivation to engage problems and make decisions by using critical thinking". Thus, student motivation is viewed as a necessary precondition for critical thinking skills and abilities. Similarly, Halonen notes that a person's propensity, or disposition, to demonstrate higher-order thinking relates to their motivation. Halpern argues that effort and persistence are two of the principal dispositions that support critical thinking, and Paul maintains that perseverance is one of the "traits of mind" that renders someone a critical thinker. Thus, like metacognition, motivation appears to be a supporting condition for critical thinking in that unmotivated individuals are unlikely to exhibit critical thinking. On the other hand, several motivation researchers have suggested that the causal link goes the other way. In particular, some motivation research suggests that difficult or challenging tasks, particularly those emphasizing higher-order thinking skills, may be more motivating to students than easy tasks that can be solved through the rote application of a pre-determined algorithm.

Creativity

Finally, many researchers have made connections between critical thinking and creativity. At first glance, critical thinking and creativity might seem to have little in common, or even to be mutually exclusive constructs. However, Bailin argues that a certain amount of creativity is necessary for critical thought. Paul and Elder note that both creativity and critical thinking are aspects of "good," purposeful thinking. As such, critical thinking and creativity are two sides of the same coin. Good thinking requires the ability to generate intellectual products, which is associated with creativity. However, good thinking also requires the individual to be aware, strategic, and critical about the quality of those intellectual products. As the authors note, "critical thinking without creativity reduces to mere skepticism and negativity, and creativity without critical thought reduces to mere novelty" Paul and Elder point out that, in practice, the two concepts are inextricably linked and develop in parallel. Accordingly, the authors believe both creative and critical thinking ought to be integrated during instruction.

Development of Critical Thinking

This section reviews the empirical literature on the critical thinking capacities of the average person, followed by an investigation of critical thinking in young children. Finally, we review one theoretical approach to understanding how critical thinking might appear and develop over time.

Critical Thinking in the Average Person

Many researchers working in the area of critical thinking lament the poor state of critical thinking in most educated adults and children. For example, Halpern points to research from the field of psychology, concluding that many, if not most, adults fail to think critically in many situations. Kennedy et al., and Van Gelder have likewise concluded that many adults lack basic reasoning skills. Halpern cites the example that large numbers of people profess to believe in paranormal phenomena, despite a lack of evidence in support of such things. Halpern attributes such failures not to the inability to reason well but to simple "bugs" in reasoning. She argues that human beings are programmed to look for patterns, particularly in the form of cause-and-effect relationships, even when none exist. Van Gelder echoes this sentiment, characterizing humans as "pattern-seekers and story-tellers". This inclination results in a tendency to jump to the first explanation that makes intuitive sense without carefully scrutinizing alternative possibilities, a phenomenon that Perkins, Allen, & Hafner have termed "makes-sense epistemology". Moreover, the general public often finds "personal experience" to be more compelling evidence than a carefully conducted, scientific study. Given these natural tendencies toward deficient reasoning, Halpern warns that we should not expect to see dramatic improvements in critical thinking over time as a result of instructional interventions. Improvements in critical thinking, when they do occur, are slow and incremental.

One reason for this gap in basic reasoning skills may be deficient educational experiences. Paul argues that typical school instruction does not encourage the development of higher-order thinking skills like critical thinking. Paul explains that knowledge is coterminous with thinking, especially good or critical thinking. However, typical school instruction, with its emphasis on the coverage of content, is designed as though recall were equivalent to knowledge. This type of lower-order learning is simply learning by rote or association, with the end result that students memorize material without understanding the logic of it. Students tend not to recognize that their assertions, beliefs, and statements have implications, and thus require evidence to support them. For most students, believing, not thinking, is knowing.

Despite evidence suggesting that the average person struggles to think critically, many researchers are sanguine about the capacity of humans to become critical thinkers with appropriate instruction. Kennedy et al. point out that empirical research suggests that students of all intellectual ability levels can benefit from critical thinking instruction. Similarly, Lewis and Smith argue that critical thinking skills are for everyone, not just the gifted.

Critical Thinking in Children

Early research in the Piagetian tradition tended to view the cognitive processes of young children as being deficient in relation to those of older individuals. Many following this tradition interpret Piaget's stages of development to mean that young children are incapable of formal operations (abstract reasoning), which are required for critical thought. However, more recent research has found that young children engage in many of the same cognitive processes that adults do, concluding that there is a place for critical thinking in the lower elementary curriculum. Silva argues that there is no single age when children are developmentally ready to learn more complex ways of thinking. Furthermore, Willingham indicates that very young children have been observed thinking critically, whereas trained scientists occasionally fall prey to errors in reasoning. Kennedy, et al. surveyed the research literature and concluded that, although critical thinking ability appears to improve with age, even young children can benefit from critical thinking instruction. The authors speculate that many of the earlier gloomy conclusions, vis-à-vis the limited critical thinking skills of young children, were spurious-due to a lack of relevant background or content knowledge needed to engage in a task.

Bailin et al. argue that critical thinking instruction at the primary grade levels can include teaching students to

- value reason and truth;
- respect others during discussion;
- be open-minded;
- be willing to see things from another's perspective;
- perceive the difference between definitions and empirical statements;
- use cognitive strategies, such as asking for examples when something is unclear; and

- use principles of critical thinking, such as considering alternatives before making a decision.

Similarly, the APA Delphi report recommends that "from early childhood, people should be taught, for example, to reason, to seek relevant facts, to consider options, and to understand the views of others". Moreover, the report maintains that explicit instruction dedicated to critical thinking skills, abilities, and dispositions should be built into all levels of the K-12 curriculum, rather than being limited to junior high or high school students.

Empirical evidence supports the notion that young children are capable of thinking critically. For example, Koenig and Harris have demonstrated that 3- and 4-year-old children will differentiate the credibility of various sources of information. In particular, 4-year-old children appeared to prefer the judgments of adult participants who had a history of being correct over those who were purposefully inaccurate. This finding was replicated in a number of other studies. Similarly, Lutz and Keil found that children as young as 4 years appeared to be aware that different people may possess differing domains of expertise and that these areas of expertise might be related to their credibility on certain topics. For example, a car mechanic's diagnosis of car trouble was found to be more credible than a doctor's. Finally, Heyman and Legare found that children between the ages of 7 and 10 became increasingly aware that people may have motives to distort the truth, whereas children younger than this were not consistently critical of the credibility of people with such motives.

Critical Thinking Over Time

Little is known about the development of critical thinking skills and dispositions over time. The APA, for example, has specifically cautioned that its framework for critical thinking should not be interpreted as implying any kind of developmental progression or hierarchical taxonomy. A few empirical studies have investigated the evolution of critical thinking skills and abilities as students proceed through college. O'Hare and McGuinness found that the critical thinking scores of third-year university students in Ireland were significantly higher than the corresponding scores of first-year students. The authors speculated that attending university exerts an independent effect on the development of critical thinking. In a meta-analysis of eight studies from 1991 to 2000, Gellin concluded that college students who engaged in activities such as interacting with faculty and peers, living on campus, and participating in college clubs or organizations increased their measured critical thinking skills by 0.14 standard deviations as compared to college students who did not participate in such activities.

One of the only researchers to postulate a developmental progression of critical thinking skills and abilities is Kuhn, who synthesized a wealth of empirical research on cognitive development to construct such a progression. Kuhn's definition of critical thinking draws from the literature on metacognition, which she views as being related to critical thinking. She distinguishes three forms of metacognition, which represent successively more sophisticated ways of thinking. Metacognitive understanding is thinking that operates on declarative knowledge. In other words, it is concerned with cataloging what an individual knows and how that individual comes to know it. Meta-strategic knowing is thinking that operates on procedural knowledge. Thus, this type of cognition is concerned with monitoring and evaluating strategy use, as well as answering questions such as, "Am I making progress?" and "Is this strategy working?" Finally, epistemological understanding is concerned with philosophical questions, such as, "How does anyone know anything?"

According to Kuhn's theoretical framework, metacognitive knowing characterizes the first stirrings of critical thought in very young children. There are two distinct stages within metacognitive knowing. The first stage is called Realism and is typically achieved between the ages of 3 and 5. This stage is characterized by the belief that assertions are expressions of someone's belief, and as such, may depart from reality. Thus, the child is able to identify true and false statements. Prior to reaching this stage, children regard beliefs and assertions as isomorphic with reality. "In other words, the world is a simple one in which things happen and we can tell about them. There are no inaccurate renderings of events".

According to Kuhn's framework, the second stage of metacognitive knowing, typically achieved by 6 years of age, allows the child to be aware of sources of knowledge and further, to distinguish between theory and evidence. In other words, prior to reaching this second stage, the child has difficulty distinguishing evidence for the claim that an event has occurred from the causal theory that makes occurrence of the event plausible. In other words, is something true because it makes intuitive sense or because there is empirical evidence for it? Kuhn describes a study in which children were shown a series of pictures depicting two runners competing in a race. The last picture shows one of the runners holding up a trophy and smiling. When children were asked who won the race, most children correctly indicated that the runner represented in the final photo was the winner. However, when asked to justify this claim, younger children tended to cite causal theories ("because he is wearing fast shoes") rather than evidence in support of the claim ("because he is holding a trophy"). According to Kuhn, by the second stage of metacognitive knowing children are able to make this distinction.

Based on the empirical research in meta-memory, Kuhn's framework also portrays meta-strategic knowing in two stages. According to Kuhn, during the first stage, typically achieved during middle childhood, children begin to understand the value of cognitive strategies in aiding cognition. A child who has reached this stage recognizes that a memory strategy such as categorization will aid recall and tends to effectively manage and deploy cognitive resources during problem solving. The second stage of meta-strategic knowing may not be achieved at all. If it is attained, it is typically reached during adolescence and adulthood. According to Kuhn, this stage is characterized by consistent and appropriate strategy selection from a repertoire of available strategies. Thus, the individual monitors strategy use, evaluates the success of strategies, and moderates use of such strategies accordingly. Individuals at this stage also tend to justify their knowledge claims.

Finally, Kuhn's framework posits epistemological understanding as the most sophisticated level of critical thought. According to Kuhn, this level is characterized by three distinct stages. The first stage, called the Absolutist position, is the norm during childhood and is common during adolescence, and can even persist into adulthood for some individuals. People who have reached this stage believe that absolute truth is either "known or potentially knowable, either through direct apprehension or the opinion of experts". All belief states can be evaluated in relation to this objective truth. In other words, all disagreements are ultimately resolvable.

According to Kuhn, the second stage in epistemological understanding, labeled the Multiplist Epistemological position, tends to be prevalent during adolescence. During this stage, the individual acknowledges that experts can disagree and actually relinquishes the idea of certainty. A person in this stage moves to the opposite end of the subjectivity-objectivity continuum, vis-à-vis those in the Absolutist stance. Instead of viewing the world as inherently and objectively knowable, individuals in this stage perceive the world as a completely subjective place. In other words, "because all people have a right to their opinions, all opinions are equally right". Kuhn points out that many people become permanently stuck in this phase.

Finally, Kuhn argues that the last stage in epistemological understanding (and critical thinking), to which only a minority of people will ever progress, is known as Epistemological Metaknowing. According to Kuhn's framework, at this stage the individual is able to balance the subjective and objective, recognizing a multiplicity of valid representations of reality. This person uses judgment, evaluation, and argumentation to sift through opinions and arrive at those that are most valid. Not all opinions are valued equally; rather, reason, logic, and empirical evidence can be used to privilege certain positions over others.

Teachability of Critical Thinking

This section explores the teachability of critical thinking, as well as the instructional implications of the empirical literature on critical thinking skills. Specific instructional recommendations for fostering the development of critical thinking will be summarized, as well.

Fortunately, many critical thinking researchers maintain that critical thinking skills and abilities can be taught. Halpern offers evidence of two instructional programs aimed at improving the critical thinking skills and abilities of college students. In one study, students who were taught general problem-solving skills improved on Piagetian-inspired measures of cognitive development. In the other study, college students instructed in a specific type of problem-solving strategy produced mental math representations that were more like those of experts than of novices.

In their review of the literature, Kennedy et al. concluded that instructional interventions aimed at improving students' critical thinking skills have generally shown positive results. In a meta-analysis of 117 empirical studies examining the impact of instructional interventions on students' critical thinking skills and dispositions, Abrami et al. found that these interventions, in general, have a positive impact, with a mean effect size of 0.34. However, the distribution of effect sizes was highly homogeneous, with effect sizes varying dramatically by type of intervention and sample characteristics. For example, effect sizes for students in K–12 settings were higher than those observed among undergraduates.

Domain Specificity

The debate about domain specificity has implications for critical thinking instruction. Ennis described four instructional approaches that vary in terms of the extent to which critical thinking skills are taught as a stand-alone course versus integrated into regular instruction. The general approach entails direct and explicit instruction in critical thinking skills as a separate course, where critical thinking skills and abilities are emphasized outside the context of specific subject matter. Typically, some content is involved to contextualize examples and tasks. However, the content is not related to discipline-specific knowledge, but tends to be drawn from problems that students are likely to encounter in their daily lives. Van Gelder appears to advocate for the general approach to critical thinking instruction. Drawing from the literature on expertise, Van Gelder argues that students need "deliberate practice" in exercising critical thinking skills and abilities. This type of practice can only occur when critical thinking is taught as a separate and explicit part of the curriculum. However, students must be taught to transfer critical thinking to a variety of contexts by providing them opportunities to practice applying critical thinking skills in diverse contexts. Similarly, Halpern argues that instruction in general thinking skills, taught as a "broad-based, cross-disciplinary" course, is the most effective way of teaching critical thinking.

The infusion approach entails in-depth instruction in the subject matter plus explicit instruction on general critical thinking principles. This critical thinking instruction is provided in the context of specific subject matter. Ennis indicates that this approach is commonly seen in the "across the curriculum" movements. Somewhat related to the infusion approach is immersion. In immersion instruction, students are engaged in deep subject-matter instruction. Although critical thinking skills and abilities are part of the content to be learned, critical thinking instruction is not made explicit. In other words, critical thinking skills and abilities are not the focus of direct and explicit instruction. Rather, students are expected to acquire these skills as a natural consequence of engaging with the subject matter. Proponents of the infusion and immersion approaches appear to include both Bailin et al., who vigorously defend the domain specificity of critical thinking, and Lipman, who views critical thinking skills as being somewhat general but who argues, nonetheless, that instruction in critical thinking must go hand-in-hand with instruction in basic skills, such as reading, writing, listening, and speaking. Silva echoes this viewpoint, maintaining that knowledge and thinking have to be taught simultaneously. Likewise, Case argues that critical thinking is a lens through which to teach the content and skills embedded in the curriculum; and Pithers and Soden reject the view that critical thinking could be taught as a separate subject. Rather, critical thinking should be viewed as a way of teaching and learning in any domain.

Finally, the mixed approach combines elements of both the general and subject-specific approaches. Teachers pair stand-alone instruction in general critical thinking principles with application of critical thinking skills in the context of specific subject matter. Explicit instruction in critical thinking skills can be incorporated into both the general and the specific components. Facione appears to advocate for this approach when he notes that critical thinking can be taught in the context of domain-specific content, or content drawn from "events in everyday life". Paul recommends basic critical thinking skills courses, as well as including critical thinking within discipline-specific courses. Kennedy et al., after reviewing extant research on the various approaches, conclude that the evidence does not support the superiority of any particular approach. Accordingly, they recommend using the mixed approach.

In their meta-analysis of 117 empirical studies on the effects of instructional interventions on students' critical thinking skills and dispositions, Abrami et al. found that a substantial amount of the variation in effect sizes across studies was driven by pedagogical grounding and by type of intervention. In other words, when instructional approach was categorized as general, immersion, infusion, or mixed, the mixed approach had the largest effect-sizes and the immersion approach had the smallest. This finding suggests that educators should approach critical thinking instruction both by integrating critical thinking into regular academic content and,by teaching general critical thinking skills as a stand-alone component. This finding reinforces the importance of providing explicit instruction in critical thinking rather than simply viewing critical thinking as an implicit goal of a course. The authors also found that interventions in which educators received special training in teaching critical thinking had the largest effect-sizes, compared to studies in which course curricula were simply aligned to critical thinking standards or critical thinking was simply included as an instructional objective. Thus, successful interventions may require professional development for teachers specifically focused on teaching critical thinking.

Teaching for Transfer

As noted before, researchers disagree on the extent to which critical thinking skills learned in one context are transferrable to new contexts, domains, and disciplines. Most researchers tend to agree, however, that transfer is unlikely to occur unless students are taught specifically to transfer. What does this mean from an instructional standpoint? First, students must be given opportunities to apply critical thinking skills and abilities in a wide range of contexts and subject areas. Second, instruction should emphasize executive functioning or metacognitive skills, such as setting goals, planning, and monitoring progress toward goals. Third, students should be sensitized to deep problem structure, because most students' thinking tends to focus on the surface structure of problems, or the superficial aspects of tasks. Hummel and Holyoak define structure sensitivity as the ability to "code and manipulate relational knowledge". The goal of structure training is to enable students to recognize a particular problem structure whenever they see it— whether it appears in math, science, or social studies— so that they may deploy appropriate strategies. Structure training involves distributing practice in a variety of contexts and settings. Halpern points out that use of "authentic" or real-world learning activities helps to promote the transfer of critical thinking skills. Brown argues that domain-specific knowledge may also be necessary for young children to successfully transfer skills to new problems that display the same deep structure. She observes, "We conclude that even young children show insightful learning and transfer on the basis of deep structural principles, rather than mere reliance on salient perceptual features, when they have access to the requisite domain-specific knowledge to mediate that learning". Thus, teaching for transfer may also entail providing adequate instruction on relevant background information.

Specific Instructional Strategies

A number of researchers have recommended using particular instructional strategies to encourage the development of critical thinking skills and abilities, such as explicit instruction, collaborative or cooperative learning, modeling, and constructivist techniques. For example, many researchers have noted that critical thinking skills and abilities are unlikely to develop in the absence of explicit instruction. Facione points out that this explicit instruction should also attend to the dispositional or affective component of critical thinking.

Another method recommended by several critical thinking researchers is a collaborative or cooperative approach to instruction. This recommendation appears to be rooted in Piagetian and Vygotskyian traditions that emphasize the value of social interactions for promoting cognitive development. Piaget touted the instructional value of cognitive conflict for catalyzing growth, typically achieved by interacting with another person at a higher developmental stage. Along similar lines, Vygotsky identified the zone of proximal development as the distance between what an individual can accomplish alone and what he/she can accomplish with the help of a more capable other (either a peer or an adult). Each of these approaches highlights the potential for cognitive improvement when students interact with one another.

Proponents of collaborative or cooperative learning include Thayer-Bacon, who emphasizes the importance of students' relationships with others in developing critical thinking skills. Supporters also include Bailin et al., who argue that critical thinking involves the ability to respond constructively to others during group discussion, which implies interacting in pro-social ways by encouraging and respecting the contributions of others. Similarly, Heyman indicates that social experiences can shape children's reasoning about the credibility of claims. In their meta-analysis of 117 empirical studies on the effects of instructional interventions for improving students' critical thinking skills and dispositions, Abrami et al. found a small but positive and significant effect of collaborative learning approaches on critical thinking.

Nelson provides some clues as to how collaboration can prompt cognitive development among college students. According to Nelson, students' misconceptions interfere with their ability to acquire new knowledge, despite appropriate instruction. Collaborations create opportunities for disagreements and misconceptions to surface and to be corrected. Collaboration also provides a vehicle for students to attain necessary acculturation to the college learning environment and helps to make tacit disciplinary expectations more explicit for students.

Nelson points out that collaboration must be scaffolded, arguing that this scaffolding process has three stages. First, students must be prepared for collaboration by providing them with a common background on which to collaborate, such as common assigned readings. Second, student groups should be provided with questions or analytical frameworks that are more sophisticated than they would tend to use on their own. Finally, collaborative activities should be structured by specifying student roles and by creating incentives for all group members to actively participate. Bonk and Smith identify a number of classroom activities that build on the potential for collaboration to enhance learning. These activities include think-pair-share, round-robin discussions, student interviews, roundtables, gallery walks, and "jigsawing."

In addition to explicit instruction and collaboration, several other strategies have been identified as helpful in promoting critical thinking. For example, teachers are urged to use constructivist learning methods, characterized as more student-centered than teacher-centered. Constructivist instruction is less structured than traditional instruction, amplifying students' roles in their own learning and de-emphasizing the role of the teacher. Educators should model critical thinking in their own instruction by making their reasoning visible to students. This could be accomplished by "thinking aloud" so that students can observe the teacher using evidence and logic to support arguments and assertions. Educators are also urged to use concrete examples that will be salient to students to illustrate abstract concepts like "conflict of interest". For example, Heyman found that children were more likely to be skeptical of another child's claim of illness when they learned that the child did not want to attend camp that day. Examples that rely upon common experiences are more likely to be intuitively obvious to students. Specific classroom learning activities believed to promote critical thinking include the creation of graphic organizers, such as concept maps and argument diagrams; KWL charts, which require students to identify what they already know about a topic, what they want to know, and what they have learned upon completing instruction; "in a nutshell" writings, which entail summaries of arguments; exit slips, which identify the most important thing learned and the areas of needed clarity; problem-based learning, particularly the use of ill-structured problem contexts; and mock trials.

Assessment Implications

This section reviews challenges in assessing critical thinking and identifies specific recommendations from the literature for measuring critical thinking.

Challenges in Assessing Critical Thinking

There are a number of challenges in assessing critical thinking skills and dispositions in students. Researchers have pointed out problems associated with both reliability and validity of existing measures. For example, Moss and Koziol factor analyzed scores from a set of writing tasks intended to measure the critical thinking skills of students in grades 5, 8, and 11 in the context of social studies. Students who read a social studies passage either supported an inference with argumentation or evaluated an argument from the passage. The authors found no clear, common factor underlying performance across tasks that were designed to be parallel. Furthermore, students' abilities to use topic statements, evidence, explanations, conclusions, and logical organization did not generalize across tasks, suggesting that idiosyncratic and perhaps construct-irrelevant features of each passage or task were more salient aspects of student performance than any general ability to think critically. Silva has noted that performance-based assessments of creativity introduce, rather, subjectivity and error. Moreover, use of such performance tasks to assess the growth of critical thinking skills over time remains fraught with difficulties as long as individual tasks communicate more noise than signal.

Norris argues that the fact that the degree of domain specificity in critical thinking remains unresolved makes assessment of critical thinking difficult. First, the type of inferences one is trying to make remains unclear to the extent that researchers cannot agree whether critical thinking is general or subject-specific. Second, it is difficult to assess critical thinking transfer, because transfer to other contexts is confounded with subject-specific knowledge that is necessary for exercising critical thinking. Thus, a student who fails to transfer to another subject either requires additional instruction in critical thinking or additional instruction in the subject matter. Similarly, the disposition to think critically is confounded with the ability to do so. Thus, despite the fact that researchers have identified critical thinking skills and dispositions as distinct from one another, delineating their separate effects using an assessment is difficult in practice. Finally, Norris argues that traditional assessment formats are ill-suited for testing even limited aspects of the construct. Standardized instruments using multiple-choice formats to assess credibility judgment or deductive reasoning are as likely to reflect extraneous constructs—such as test-makers' empirical, religious, or political beliefs and judgments—as they are to reflect critical thinking.

Existing published assessments of critical thinking are numerous, and include the California Critical Thinking Skills Test, the Cornell Critical

Thinking Tests, the Ennis-Weir Critical Thinking Essay Test, and the Watson-Glaser Critical Thinking Appraisal. As Ku points out, these instruments vary widely in both purpose and item format. However, as Kennedy et al. note, none of these tests are intended for use with students below the fourth-grade level. Moreover, these assessments tend to be general critical thinking assessments rather than subject-specific.

Assessment Recommendations

Researchers have made several suggestions for designing assessments ideally suited to assess critical thinking skills. First, open-ended problem types may be more appropriate for assessing critical thinking than traditional multiple-choice formats. As Ku argues, available empirical evidence suggests that open-ended measures better capture the construct of critical thinking because they are more sensitive to the dispositional aspects of critical thinking than are multiple-choice measures. For this reason, Ku recommends using tests of mixed item format, both multiple-choice and open-ended, to more completely represent both the cognitive and dispositional aspects of critical thinking. As Ku argues, "teachers should adopt different assessment methods, such as exercises that allow students to self-construct answers, assignments that facilitate the practice of strategic use of thinking skills in everyday contexts, and when adopting multiple-choice exercises, follow-up questions should be given to probe students' underlying reasoning".

Assessment tasks should also reflect "authentic" problem contexts and performances. This means that assessments should be based on simulations that approximate real-world problems and issues. Assessments should also use ill-structured problems, which Moss and Koziol explain to mean that test questions should require students to go beyond the available information in the task to draw inferences or make evaluations. In addition, problems should have more than one plausible or defensible solution, and there should be sufficient information and evidence within the task to enable students to support multiple views.

Fischer, Spiker, and Riedel argue that critical thinking is a "stimulus-bound phenomenon," meaning that certain external task features may impact whether critical thinking is elicited in a given assessment context. The authors identify a number of context variables that affect one's use of critical thinking. For example, stimulus characteristics focus on whether the stimuli present a set of materials that is orderly, well-organized, and coherent, or a set of materials that is uncertain, ambiguous, disorganized, and contradictory. In experimental studies that attempted to validate their model of critical thinking, Fischer et al. demonstrated that some contextual stimulus variables do seem to matter, whereas others do not. For example, the level of substance of stimulus text—in terms of the number of unique propositions contained in that text—had no main effect on the subjects' propensity to use critical thinking, operationalized in this study as the number of questions of belief and checks on thinking observed during "think-aloud" procedures. However, the level of consistency, or lack of contradictions, within stimulus materials did have a main effect, with inconsistent or contradictory materials more likely to prompt critical thinking than consistent and coherent stimulus materials.

Moreover, Fischer et al. demonstrated that certain types of tasks are more likely to elicit critical thinking than others. For example, tasks requiring the exercise of judgment were better for assessing critical thinking than tasks focused on simply understanding material presented in stimulus text. In particular, a task requiring examinees to either accept or reject a manuscript for publication elicited more questions of belief and checks on thinking than a task asking examinees to identify the main topic of a set of materials or to explain a scientific study described in stimulus materials.

Moss and Koziol advocate for evaluating students on the basis of the quality of the arguments underlying their position, rather than the "correctness" of the answer. Lewis and Smith point out that assessment tasks must go beyond requiring simple recall of learned information. Rather, tasks should require students to manipulate what they learned in new or novel contexts. Another suggestion is that critical thinking assessments should make student reasoning visible. For example, Norris argues that testing validly for critical thinking requires that we observe an examinee's process of thinking. One recommendation for accomplishing this in the context of a multiple-choice test is to require students to provide a rationale or justification for their choice, an idea that was repeated by Kennedy et al..

Silva argued that new assessment modes are needed to measure higher-order skills, identifying several examples of recent critical thinking assessments that use novel item formats. For example, the College and Work Readiness Assessment (developed by the Council for Aid and the RAND Corporation) presents students with a 90-minute task and access to a variety of written materials on the topic, which typically represents a real-world problem. Students are then asked to make judgments and formulate a solution. River City Research Project (developed within Harvard's graduate school of education with National Science Foundation funding) is an assessment and instruction program that uses an interactive, virtual environment to present middle-school students with simulated, real-world problems that they must solve through the application of the scientific process: generating hypotheses, testing hypotheses, analyzing results, and drawing inferences and conclusions. Finally, PowerSource—developed by researchers at the National Center for Research on Evaluation, Standards & Student Testing (CRESST)—is a middle-school math assessment that combines higher-order thinking skills with mastery of basic math content in the form of narrative themes or graphic novels. Students are asked to apply math principles and to explain their reasoning.

Educators have long seen critical thinking as a desirable educational outcome. More recently, the Partnership for 21st Century Skills has identified critical thinking as one of several skills necessary to prepare students for post-secondary education and the workforce. Furthermore, the newly created Common Core State Standards reflect critical thinking skills. Although a concrete definition of critical thinking on which most researchers can agree remains elusive, common areas of overlap exist among the various approaches. Typically, critical thinking is believed to include the component skills of analyzing arguments, making inferences by using inductive or deductive reasoning, judging or evaluating, and making decisions or solving problems. Background knowledge is believed to be a necessary, though not sufficient, condition for enabling critical thought within a given subject. Critical thinking entails cognitive skills, or abilities, and dispositions. These dispositions, which can be seen as attitudes, or habits of mind, include open- and fair-mindedness, inquisitiveness, flexibility, a propensity to seek reason, a desire to be well-informed, and a respect for and willingness to entertain diverse viewpoints. There appear to be both general and domain-specific aspects of critical thinking, which suggests two main conclusions. First, instruction should represent a fusion of preparation in general critical thinking principles, as well as practice in applying critical thinking skills within the context of specific domains. Second, transfer of critical thinking skills to new contexts is unlikely to occur unless students are specifically taught to transfer by sensitizing them to deep problem structures and are given adequate opportunities to rehearse critical thinking skills in a variety of domains.

Critical thinking skills relate to several other important student learning outcomes, such as metacognition, motivation, collaboration, and creativity. Metacognition (or thinking about thinking) supports critical thinking in that students who can monitor and evaluate their own thought processes are more likely to demonstrate high-quality thinking. In addition, the ability to critically evaluate one's own arguments and reasoning is necessary for self-regulated learning. Motivation supports critical thinking in that students who are motivated to learn are more likely to persist at tasks that call for critical thinking. In turn, learning activities and assessment tasks that call for critical thinking may spark student motivation because they are more challenging, novel, or interesting. Students possessing critical thinking dispositions, such as willingness to consider diverse perspectives, may make better collaborators, and opportunities for collaboration may promote higher-order thinking. Finally, creativity requires the ability to critically evaluate intellectual products, and critical thinking requires the open-mindedness and flexibility that is characteristic of creative thinking.

Although learning progressions of critical thinking skills and dispositions do not yet (and may never) exist, at least one researcher has tied the progression of critical thinking skills to cognitive development in general and metacognition in particular. Empirical research in the area of metacognition suggests that people begin developing critical thinking competencies at a very young age and continue to improve them (or not) over the course of a lifetime. Many adults exhibit deficient reasoning and fail to think critically. However, in theory, all people—from all intellectual ability levels and from the very young to the very old—can be taught to think critically. Empirical evidence suggests that children are, in fact, much more capable of critical thought than once predicted.

If teachers are to be successful in encouraging the development of critical thinking skills, explicit instruction in critical thinking needs to be included in the curriculum, whether that instruction occurs as a stand-alone course, is infused into subject-matter content, or both. Cooperative or collaborative learning methods hold promise as a way of stimulating cognitive development, along with constructivist approaches that place students at the center of the learning process. Teachers should model critical thinking in their instruction and provide concrete examples for illustrating abstract concepts that students will find salient.

Assessing critical thinking skills poses challenges that are similar to those in other measurement contexts. Standardized instruments that use multiple-choice items to measure limited aspects of critical thinking may meet reliability standards, but these standardized instruments are vulnerable to criticisms of construct underrepresentation. Performance-based assessments (PBAs), which are seen as more valid representations of the construct, are susceptible to low reliability and a lack of generalizability across tasks when task development and administration cannot be standardized. When such standardization cannot be assured, PBAs should not be used to compare students to one another or to track student progress or growth over time. On the other hand, when PBAs are used for low-stakes, classroom assessment purposes, the need for strict standardization can be relaxed.

Educators are urged to use open-ended problem types and to consider learning activities and assessment tasks that make use of authentic, real-world problem contexts. In addition, critical thinking assessments should use ill-structured problems that require students to go beyond recalling or restating learned information and also require students to manipulate the information in new or novel contexts. Such ill-structured problems should also have more than one defensible solution and should provide adequate collateral materials to support multiple perspectives. Stimulus materials should attempt to embed contradictions or inconsistencies that are likely to activate critical thinking. Finally, such assessment tasks should make student reasoning visible by requiring students to provide evidence or logical arguments in support of judgments, choices, claims, or assertions.

References

McGuinness, C (1999) *From Thinking Skills to Thinking Classrooms; A Review and Evaluation of approaches for developing pupils' thinking* Research report No 115; Nottingham: DfEE Publications.

McPeck, J (1981) *Critical Thinking and Education* Oxford: Martin Robertson

Marzano, R.J., Pickering, D.J., and Pollock, J.E (2001) *Classroom instruction that works: Research-based strategies for increasing student achievement.* Alexandria, VA: Association for Supervision and Curriculum Development

Swartz, R, Fischer, S., and Parks, S (1998) *Infusing the Teaching of Critical and Creative Thinking Into Secondary Science* Pacific Grove, CA: Critical Thinking Books and Software.

Watson, G and Glaser, E.M. (1980) *Watson Glaser Critical Thinking Appraisal,* Cleveland, Ohio: The Psychological Corporation

6

The Thinking Classroom

In an elementary school, the classroom buzzes with activity. Children work in small research and discussion groups, intent on discovering the answer to a question posed by the teacher: "How do simple machines increase work efficiency?" Students collaborate as they hypothesize and design and carry out experiments using levers, pulleys, and ramps. The teacher asks the students to use the concepts of *force* and *energy* to describe the results of their experiments. Students express ideas, question each other, and extend their thinking. New understandings emerge and are recorded in sentences next to drawings of their simple machines. A visual scan of the classroom confirms an active learning environment. Student work lines the walls, and books, art prints, science materials, mathematics manipulatives, and computers are evident in the plentiful workspace.

In a secondary school, students use desktop computers and access databases to find relevant material on global pollution. They process the information through the conceptual lens of *environmental sustainability* as they think beyond the facts. They compare notes with students around the world, and design PowerPoint programs to display their research and deepening understanding of global pollution and sustainability. They scan in pictures to enhance the graphic appeal. These are the students of the computer age, and they produce a score of intellectual, artistic, and informative products.

Down the hall in another classroom, students sit placidly in rows and stare at their textbooks while child after child reads a paragraph. Behind the vacant eyes, minds are playing—outside. The teacher controls the scene from a stool in the front of the room and questions the facts just read. Posters hang on the wall like soldiers at attention, and books sit in tidy positions on the shelves, sorted by size. The room is quiet except for the bored drone of the student reading and the interminable tick of a clock on the teacher's desk.

The art and science of teaching go beyond the presentation of information. Artful teachers engage students emotionally, creatively, and intellectually to instill deep and passionate curiosity in learning. They know how to effectively use the structures offered by the science of teaching to facilitate the personal construction of knowledge. But the personal construction of knowledge is not "whatever." The teachers are clear on what they want their students to know factually, understand conceptually, and be able to do in skills and processes.

What may appear to the casual observer as ill-structured activity in a classroom is actually goal-oriented learning. The teacher has artfully designed the lesson with questions and experiences so that students are building and sharing disciplinary knowledge and understanding aligned to academic standards. The learning is purposeful. But the teacher also designs for learning to encourage the discovery of unintended insights and understandings. The discussion of essential questions, inquiry-based learning, and the encouragement to make meaning and express ideas through art supports this extension. Intellectual development, mindful learning, and creative expression are key instructional goals.

Mr. Howe is a middle school social studies teacher. He has been teaching about early American colonization and wants his students to internalize an enduring understanding of history—that *developing nations may resist or revolt against a ruling country's social, economic, and political policies if they are perceived as unjust.* He developed the following lesson to help students internalize facts supporting this understanding.

You are a creative designer for Gameboards USA. You have been charged by the president of the company with designing a game to teach fifth graders about the reasons leading up to the American Revolution. Your game must have questions that address the social, political, and economic conflicts between England and the settled colonies.

To assess the students' factual knowledge on reasons for the American Revolution, Mr. Howe gave a selected response test. As an extension assignment, Mr. Howe asked students to research the causes of two other political revolutions in history (students chose their revolutions from a teacher-supplied list). Then he assessed their conceptual understanding that *people may revolt against governmental policies that are perceived as oppressive or unjust* through the following task:

You have studied the causes of the American Revolution and two other political revolutions in history. Working in a cooperative group, create a graphic organizer that compares the causes of the three revolutions. As a group, determine one common factor that led to revolution across the three examples. Individually, choose one of the following formats and illustrate that common factor:

- Political cartoon
- Newspaper article
- Poster
- Poem

Thinking classrooms employ concept-based curriculum and instruction design models. These models are inherently more sophisticated than traditional models because they are as concerned with intellectual development as they are with gaining knowledge.

Concept-based curricular and instructional designs are *three-dimensional*— that is, curriculum and instruction is focused on what students will...

- *K* now (factually),
- *U*nderstand (conceptually), and
- be able to *Do* (skillfully).

Traditionally, curriculum and instruction has been more *two-dimensional* in design (know and able to do)—resting on a misguided assumption that knowing facts is evidence of deeper, conceptual understanding.

The following performance indicators, for example, are typical expectations across state history standards:

- Identify economic differences among different regions of the United States.
- Compare changes in technology (past to present).

These performance indicators are written in the traditional format of content "objectives," with a verb followed by the topic. It is assumed that the ability to carry out these objectives is evidence of understanding; but, as written, they fail to take students to the third dimension of *conceptual understanding* where the deeper lessons of history reside. Students will research and memorize facts about the economic differences in regions of the United States, but the thinking stops there. Try this task to reach the third dimension. Complete the sentences by extrapolating transferable understandings (timeless ideas supported by the factual content):

- Identify economic differences among different regions of the United States *in order to understand that...*
- Compare changes in technology (past to present) *in order to understand* that...

What do you think the writers of these performance indicators for middle school expected students to understand at a level beyond the facts? Below are some possible endings:

- Identify economic differences among different regions of the United States *in order to understand that the geography and natural resources of a region shape the economy.*
- Compare changes in technology *in order to understand that advancing technologies change the social and economic patterns of a society.*

We cannot just assume that teachers reach the conceptual level of understanding with students. In fact, years of work facilitating the writing of these essential, enduring understandings with teachers has shown me that it is a skill that takes practice. Extrapolating deeper understandings from factual knowledge is not easy work. It involves thinking beyond the facts to the "So what?"—the significant and transferable understandings. It involves mentally manipulating language and syntax so that conceptual understandings are expressed with clarity, brevity, and power. Teachers across the board say, "This is hard work!" when they begin this writing process. The learning curve is steep, but with a little practice, teachers take pride in their finely honed understandings.

Becoming a three-dimensional, concept-based teacher is a journey that merges best practices in teaching and learning with a developing understanding of brain-based pedagogy. But we have much to learn. So let's get on with the journey.

The Brain at Work

The cognitive sciences have produced prolific writers on the anatomy and functioning of the brain and on the implications for teaching and learning.

At the cellular level, the brain is composed of billions of neurons and trillions of glial support cells. Robert Sylwester These describes the brain's macrocompo-sition as a subcortical area consisting of the brain stem and surrounding systems with "pea- to walnut-shaped modular structures" that control basic brain processes governing survival and emotional needs. Above the subcortical area is the cortex. Sylwester describes the cortex as a "six layer sheet of deeply folded neural tissue... that encompasses 85% of our brain, and processes learned rational logical behaviors."

The sensory lobes process relevant incoming sensory information and integrate it into a unified perceptual field. This analysis is then relayed to the frontal lobes for evaluation and action. Pat Wolfe, in *Brain Matters*, states, "Our human cortex allows us to build cathedrals, compose symphonies, dream and plan for a better future, love, hate, and experience emotional pain, because it is in the cortex that consciousness—our ability to be aware of what we are thinking, feeling, and doing—emerges."

Other books devoted to the structure and function of the brain provide detailed information related to other parts of the brain, such as the thalamus and hypothalamus, and describe the neural communication process across synaptic divides. But since the focus of this book is developing intelligence through conceptual thinking, a primary function of the cerebral cortex, we will leave the remaining details on the structure and function of the brain to other authors.

It is important to this book, however, to share and affirm an observation by Sylwester: "We're used to thinking of intelligence as something that occurs entirely within our brain, but this is now seen as a very narrow view of a complex process that also involves our body and the environment in which our body-brain functions." How true! Intelligence does not operate in a vacuum. Our senses, emotions, physical involvement, and environmental context all play a critical role in the development of intelligence.

Synergistic Thinking

As a career educator who has climbed peaks and fallen into valleys in my work over the years, I now realize some of the major reasons that children do not retain, transfer, and understand knowledge as well as they should—in spite of the dedicated and tireless efforts of teachers to teach and reteach year after year. Perhaps the most significant reason that children overall are not performing as well as they should academically is that we provide teachers with intellectually shallow curriculum materials that fail to engage higher-order thinking. Let me explain.

To memorize information is lower-level cognitive work. To stimulate more sophisticated, complex thinking, we need to create a *synergy* between the simpler and more complex processing centers in the brain. This interactive synergy requires the mind to process information on two cognitive levels—the factual and the conceptual. The conceptual mind uses facts as a tool to discern patterns, connections, and deeper, transferable understandings.

But curriculum materials are seldom designed to systematically set up this intellectual synergy between the factual and conceptual levels of thinking. Though concepts are mentioned, and often defined, they appear to be "Oh, by the way..." afterthoughts that one might want to consider. To provide teachers with a specific strategy for creating this intellectual synergy, the next section discusses and demonstrates the use of a *conceptual lens* in curriculum design and instruction.

The Power of a Conceptual Lens

Concept-based teachers know how to adapt lower-level curriculum materials to teach for deeper understanding. For example, they may use a conceptual lens to invite students to bring their own thinking to the study at hand. Janet Kaduce is teaching a unit on the Holocaust in her high school class. She invites students to consider the events in terms of the dual conceptual lens of *humanity/inhumanity*.

This lens is the vehicle that sets up a synergy between the factual and conceptual processing centers in the brain. Students think deeply because they must process the facts in terms of their relationship to the ideas of *humanity* and *inhumanity*.

The teacher uses different types of questions to extend student thinking and deepen understanding:

Factual Questions:

— Why was the Holocaust a significant event in world history?

- — What beliefs did Hitler hold that drove his actions?
- — Why is Hitler's persecution of the Jewish people considered inhumane?

Conceptual Questions:

- — What examples of inhumanity can you cite from our world today?
- — What acts of humanity can you cite from our present-day world?
- — How are beliefs, values, and perspectives related to views of humanity and inhumanity?

Provocative (Debate, or Essential) Question:

- — Can one be inhumane and civilized at the same time? (Explain your answer.)

Students retain the factual information longer because the use of the conceptual lens requires them to intellectually process at a deeper level. Furthermore, because students are invited to bring their own thinking to the factual study, they are better able to make personal meaning. This invitation involves them emotionally—they are personally invested—and the motivation for learning increases.

Conflict	*Complexity*
Beliefs/Values	Paradox
Interdependence	Interactions
Freedom	Transformations
Identity	Patterns
Relationships	Origins
Change	Revolution
Perspective	Reform
Power	Influence
System	Balance
Structure/Function	Innovation
Design	Genius
Heroes	Utility
Force	*Creativity*

Figure 1. Sample Conceptual Lenses

Figure 1 provides a list of potential conceptual lenses that teachers could use to engage a student's conceptual mind. The focus a teacher wishes to bring to a study suggests a particular lens, so it is best to start with the topic and then select the lens. There are times, however, such as in literature study, when a teacher might begin with a lens, such as *tragedy* or *archetypes,* and then select the support material, but generally the link is stronger if the topic is considered first. Notice that some of the lenses in Figure 1 are very broad (macroconcepts), such as *system* or *change;* while others are more specific (microconcepts), such as *identity* or *heroes.*

A more specific lens reflects the teacher's particular conceptual focus. As a general rule, discipline-based studies (e.g., a literature unit) draw more on the specific lenses; interdisciplinary studies draw on the broader lenses because they can then be accessed by a variety of disciplines involved in the study.

The Integration of Thinking

When we can rise above the facts and see the patterns and connections between the facts and related concepts, principles, and generalizations—and when we can understand the deeper, transferable significance of knowledge—then we can say our thinking is *integrated* at a conceptual level. This factual/conceptual integration of thinking should be a conscious design goal for curriculum and instruction.

We view integration as a cognitive process rather than what we do with subjects. Under this view, integration can occur in inter- and intradisciplinary contexts as long as there is a conceptual lens or focus that pulls thinking to the integration level—where patterns and connections are made between the factual and conceptual levels of knowledge.

This integration of thinking allows knowledge to be transferred. For example, the lens of *beliefs and values* can provide intellectual focus to a unit on "The Iraq War" and be the invitation for students to use their own minds to think more deeply. The deeper thinking on the complexities of war leads to lessons of history that can be transferred through time and across situations.

In addition to using a conceptual lens to integrate thinking, teaching inductively to conceptual ideas (generalizations and principles) also facilitates the integration of thinking. These conceptual ideas are commonly referred to as "enduring understandings", "essential understandings", or "big ideas" in today's education jargon.

The enduring understanding that "artists often use a combination of color harmonies to create emotional complexity" is not just an empty idea in art education. It is a synthesis of thought and conceptual understanding supported by concrete examples—from the bold and vibrant colors of a Matisse still life, which reflect assertiveness and joy, to the muted tones of a Picasso blue period.

The Transfer of Knowledge

The ability to transfer knowledge and skills to new or similar contexts is evidence of deeper understanding and higher-order thinking. Because the coverage model of curriculum design values memorization over the integration of thinking and the transfer of knowledge, these higher-order processes may appear to teachers as serendipitous displays of student genius when they bolt out of the classroom blue. Teachers eagerly e-mail a colleague, "You wouldn't believe the insight and thinking that came out of Robert and Kim today when we were discussing the global issue of overpopulation!"

Yet integrated thinking and the transfer of knowledge should be daily fare in classrooms. *Making meaning* is not simply doing hands-on activities related to a topic, or learning the meaning of vocabulary words. Making meaning includes the interplay of lower- and higher-order thinking. This means that the design of curriculum and instruction needs to set up this interplay.

Curriculum and instruction models that set up a synergistic interplay between the factual and conceptual levels of thinking are critical to intellectual development. The sophistication of the intellectual dance across synaptic divides in the brain determines the quality of the performance. As educators, we are responsible for the design of the dance.

Richard Paul (Foundation for Critical Thinking) wrote a paper titled "Making Critical Thinking Intuitive" and stated that "intuitive understanding enables [us] to insightfully bridge the gap between an abstract concept and concrete applications". He calls on all levels of education to teach in a way that fosters intuitive understanding. Paul states,

If we focused attention, as we should, on the ability of students to move back and forth comfortably and insightfully between the abstract and the concrete, they would soon develop and discipline their imaginations... to generate cases that exemplify abstractions. All students have, as a matter of fact, experienced hundreds of situations that exemplify any number of important abstract truths and principles. But they are virtually never asked to dig into their experience to find examples, to imagine cases, which illustrate this or that principle, this or that abstract concept. The result is an undisciplined and underdeveloped imagination combined with vague, indeed muddled, concepts and principles.... What is missing is the intuitive synthesis between concept and percept, between idea and experience, between image and reality.

Developing The Intellect

Intellectual Character

Schools play a critical role in the development of the intellect. But as Ron Ritchart, in *Intellectual Character* These, so aptly observes, School... [is more about] style than substance, breadth than depth, and speed above all else We've come to mistake curriculums, textbooks, standards, objectives, and tests as ends in themselves rather than as means to an end. These Ritchart cautions that we are teaching for the wrong thing—that we need to keep our focus on the development of "intellectual dispositions" that develop strong "intellectual character" Ritchart defines *intellectual character* as the "patterns" of behavior, thinking, and interaction that are shaped and exhibited over time These. He frames the idea of *intellectual dispositions* under the categories of creative thinking (open-minded, curious), critical thinking (seeking truth and understanding, strategic, skeptical), and reflective thinking (metacogni-tive) These.

Many educators feel that the pressure to meet academic standards necessitates coverage and speed, and that there is not enough time to develop "intellectual character." But let's not lose sight of the purpose of education. It has to be more than obtaining a fund of information or learning sets of discrete skills. Indeed, the survival of a society depends on its ability to respond intelligently and creatively to social, economic, political, and environmental problems. Information without intellect is meaningless.

We can meet the intent of standards and still keep our focus on intellectual development. The secret is in the design of curriculum and instruction—and in the willingness of the teacher to learn and practice strategies that develop intellectual dispositions. Three-dimensional, concept-based curriculum and instruction provide a powerful frame for the development of these intellectual dispositions.

Creative Thinking

Ritchart states that the dispositions of open-mindedness and curiosity are components of creative thinking. Open-mindedness depends on the ability to reflect critically on incoming information, consider and "play" with alternative points of view, and intuitively and flexibly look for patterns and connections between elements. Curiosity drives the development of intelligence. It is the "on" switch for learning, and the gateway to creative problem solving.

The role of emotional engagement in learning has been well documented in recent years. We retain knowledge longer and gain deeper understanding when there is an emotional response to learning. This, too, is an important point to remember when designing curriculum and instruction. Creative thinking and learning generate an emotional response because they tap the personal connection to experience.

It is interesting that Anderson and Krathwohl, in *A Taxonomy for Learning, Teaching, and Assessing: A Revision of Bloom's Taxonomy of Educational Objectives*, changed the term for Benjamin Bloom's cognitive process of "synthesis" to "creativity" and moved it to the highest level of intellectual functioning. This change makes sense—because the ability to create requires the production of an original or unique product or idea generated from the synthesis and creative extension of discrete elements.

The area of creative thinking fascinates me because it is the ultimate expression of reflective and critical thinking. Creative thinking becomes increasingly important in a world dealing with complex problems. Daniel H. Pink, a writer, lecturer, and international observer of economic and social trends, wrote an interesting book titled *A Whole New Mind: Moving From the Information Age to the Conceptual Age* These. His opening paragraph:

The last few decades have belonged to a certain kind of person with a certain kind of mind—computer programmers who could crack code, lawyers who could craft contracts, MBAs who could crunch numbers. But the keys to the kingdom are changing hands. The future belongs to a very different kind of person with a very different kind of mind—creators and empathizers, pattern recognizers, and meaning makers. These people—artists, inventors, designers, storytellers, caregivers, consolers, big picture thinkers—will now reap society's richest rewards and share its greatest joys. These

Hmmm. This is an interesting observation. Pink further states,

The wealth of nations and the well-being of individuals now depend on having artists in the room. In a world enriched by abundance but disrupted by the automation and outsourcing of white-collar work, everyone, regardless of profession, must cultivate an artistic sensibility.... Today we must all be designers. These

Pink is not implying that we no longer need linear, logical, and deductive thinkers; but he is highlighting the increasing importance of creative thinking to solve increasingly complex problems and to enhance daily lives.

The August 2005 report on "Getting Smarter, Becoming Fairer," by the Center for American Progress and the Institute for America's Future, reported that in 2001, 47 percent of U.S. patents went to foreign inventors. Though American citizens received the most patents, they were followed closely by Japanese citizens. Japan, China, and India have each more than tripled their U.S. patent awards since 1991. The innovative and creative edge that the United States has long relied on is facing strong competition today.

Though all disciplines benefit from the use of creative thinking in problem solving, it is a wellspring for the arts. It is alarming to see schools cutting out art programs to make more time for standards drill and kill. Science helps people understand and explain phenomena in the natural and constructed world. Art goes a step further and allows one to create and share a personal interpretation of the physical and sociocultural world.

Creative thinking is the personal construction of *meaning*. Creative thinking employs imagination and playful tinkering with shapes, sounds, colors, words, and ideas. Creative thinking is the birthplace for unique and innovative products, cultural expressions, and solutions to global problems.

Of all the disciplines, art is the most open-ended. Though it has a formal structure of concepts and principles that provide the language of the craft and critique, art stimulates the creative mind more than any other discipline. The creative mind develops cognitive flexibility; can examine situations, objects, and issues from multiple perspectives; and can propose novel solutions to persistent problems. So even though art has intrinsic value as a personal and social expression of culture and emotion, it has heightened importance today as a powerful vehicle for developing creative thinking. The future of our world depends on the marriage of creative, critical, conceptual, and reflective thinking. No doubt about it.

Critical Thinking

Ritchart includes the dispositions of "seeking truth and understanding, being strategic, and being skeptical" as components of critical thinking. Citizens today are inundated with multiple perspectives and opinions that may or may not be supported by facts. Critical thinkers open-mindedly evaluate incoming information by determining the basis and validity for the views being expressed. They maintain a healthy skepticism toward the information until all the facts are in. They are aware of the times when they are interjecting their personal bias into the evaluation of a situation, and attempt to hold their bias in check as they consider the evidence. Critical thinkers use logic to solve problems. They strategically plan for dealing with the issue by clarifying the problem and its components, by considering the viability of alternative solutions, and by laying out a time line and set of steps to achieve resolution.

Critical thinking is a process by which the thinker improves the quality of his or her thinking by skillfully taking charge of the structures inherent in thinking and imposing intellectual standards upon them. Critical thinking is, in short, self-directed, self-disciplined, self-monitored, and self-corrective thinking.

Reflective (Metacognitive) Thinking

One of the greatest contributions Paul and Elder have made to the area of critical thinking is a set of intellectual standards. The journey of conceptual thinking, as well as the other kinds of critical thinking, requires ongoing metacognitive work. Intellectual standards and questions provided by Paul and Elder in *The Thinker's Guide to the Nature and Function of Critical and Creative Thinking* aid this metacognitive work.

In *The Logic of Creative and Critical Thinking*, Richard Paul discusses the symbiotic relationship between critical and creative thinking. He suggests that excellent thinking results in creative ends—"designing or engendering, fashioning or originating, creating or producing...," but to achieve these ends there must be continual metacognitive assessment of our thinking—"is it on-track and sufficiently clear, accurate, precise, consistent, relevant, deep, or broad for the end goals? In other words, creativity and criticality [are] interwoven into one seamless fabric" These.

Metacognitive assessment of thinking needs intellectual standards. Teachers can use the work of Paul and Elder to help students reflect on the quality and progress of their thinking abilities. We have so much work to do in the area of metacognition. These intellectual standards are a solid starting point.

Conceptual Thinking

Though Ritchart and Paul do not single out the area of conceptual thinking in their discussions of intellectual work, it is a recognized form of thinking that includes aspects of critical, creative, and metacognitive thinking. Conceptual thinking requires the ability to critically examine factual information; relate to prior knowledge; see patterns and connections; draw out significant understandings at the conceptual level; evaluate the truth of the understandings based on the supporting evidence; transfer the understanding across time or situation; and, often, use the conceptual understanding to creatively solve a problem or create a new product, process, or idea.

Disciplinary Ways of Thinking and Doing

Lael advocates the design of curriculum and instruction that gives students the experience of being "practitioners" in a discipline. This means going beyond the teaching of content in a subject area. It means that the teacher becomes familiar with the disciplinary ways of knowing, understanding, and doing so they can design learning experiences that develop these unique approaches to problem solving and insight. This does not mean that students should always learn in disciplinary "boxes."

On the contrary, examining problems and issues through *interdisciplinary* perspectives gives breadth and depth to understanding. But the reality is that interdisciplinary work is only as strong as the content, concepts, and approaches of the various disciplines brought into the study. So our suggestion to curriculum developers and teachers is this—develop disciplinary ways of knowing, understanding, and doing systematically through the grades, but engage students in complex problems to solve, or issues to understand, that encourage the flexible use of disciplinary knowledge and processes in interdisciplinary studies.

Thinking Teachers and Students

If a major goal is the development of student intellect, then the importance of the teacher's ability to think critically, reflectively, creatively, and conceptually goes without question. It has been rewarding to observe teachers in concept-based workshops as they think beyond the facts in their subject area and grapple with the "so what" of why they teach particular content. The common refrain at the end of the workshop is, "My head hurts from thinking so hard!" But they also say they can hardly wait to get back to the classroom and apply what they have learned. At first, I wondered why teachers showed so much enthusiasm in workshops after expressing how hard it was to think. And then it struck me—humans are intellectual beings; we are made to think. And when we are successful in using our minds well, we feel intelligent—and are motivated to learn more. This important premise applies to students as well. They feel personal satisfaction from using their minds well.

Sometimes teachers enter the workshops eager to learn, and feel validated for the concept-based pedagogy they already practice. But they gain even deeper understandings and expand their skills as they journey forward. Other teachers may enter the workshop with negative preconceived notions; but when they see that facts are still valued as critical elements in the broader intellectual scheme, they relax and put their minds to work. Some teachers enter with trepidation because they fear they won't be able to grasp the ideas being presented. But these teachers usually leave with the comment, "I have to think more about concept-based teaching—but I know I can do this!"

References

Anderson, L. W. & Krathwohl, D. R. (Eds.). (2001). A taxonomy for learning, teaching and assessing: A revision of Bloom's Taxonomy of educational objectives: Complete edition, New York: Longman.

Angelo, T. A. & Cross, P. K. (1993). *Classroom assessment techniques* (2nd ed.). San Francisco: Jossey-Bass.

Bonwell, C. C. & Eison, J. A. (1991). Active Learning: Creating Excitement in the Classroom. *ASHE-ERIC Higher Education Report No. 1.* Washington, D.C.: George Washington University.

Clasen, D. R. & Bonk, C. (1990). *Teachers tackle thinking*. Madison, WI: Madison Education Extension Program.

Elder, L. & Paul, R. (Winter, 1997). "Critical thinking: Crucial distinctions for questioning," *Journal of Developmental Education 21*(2), p. 34.

Fink, L. D. (2003). A self-directed guide to designing courses for significant learning. Retrieved May 13.

7

Developing Problem-solving Skills

It is your role as an early childhood educator to provide opportunities for children to develop cognitive skills. Children's brains are wired for learning; they are the metaphorical 'sponge' waiting for information. But information alone does not provide learning. Children must be able to comprehend what they are hearing, seeing, touching, feeling or smelling in order to form experiences. Your role extends to the facilitation of these experiences to best suit the child's development.

Child's Stage of Development and Interests

As a child develops, their interests and abilities change. To encourage continued growth, you should provide opportunities that extend the child's skills and knowledge. Choosing resources and creating a positive environment sets a good foundation for the child's learning.

Awareness of the developmental stages of a child allows you to choose appropriate resources. The stages of childhood development as theorised and popularised by Jean Piaget are:

Stage of development	***Typical behaviours***
Stage 1: *The sensorimotor stage* (from birth to 2 years)	During this stage, a child experiences the world through touch, smell, movement, taste, sight and sound. They cannot view their situation from the perspective of other people nor can they consider complex meanings. Typical behaviours include:, basic reflexes, primary and secondary circular

	reactions (do this and feel what it's like – do this, enjoy it, and do it again), the coordination of circular reactions (I know how to get milk; I cry), tertiary circular reactions such as curiosity and the desire toexperience new things (these develop along with the beginnings of memory, knowledge and language).
Stage 2: *The pre-operational stage* (2 to 7 years)	During this stage the child's egocentric behaviour starts to decline. They begin to share and demonstrate care and concern for others. The child is engrossed in a magical world where reality and impossibility easily overlap. Logical thinking has not yet developed during this stage in most children. In children's services, this stage is broken into toddlers (1–3 years), preschool (3–5 years) and 5–7 years, with some crossover of cognitive skills between each group.
Stage 3:*The concrete operational stage*(7 to 12 years)	Children begin to think logically during this phase. This logic only extends to the real world. Conceptualisation is still developing at the end of this time, and the children tend to lose their egocentricity.
Stage 4:*Formal operational stage* (12 years onwards)	As the child enters a new level of education, they develop abstract thinking and conceptualisation skills. Logical thought is practised regularly by this time.

Types of Thinking Skills

Opportunities vary with the developmental stages of the child. At each level, you can observe and cater for the following types of thinking skills:

Thinking skills	***Opportunities to develop these skills***
Reasoning	At the infant level, reasoning means that the child can think coherently. If the child performs the same task differently each time, with no improvement, this demonstrates a lack of reasoning skills. At a toddler and preschool level, reasoning might also include logic (at its most basic level) where circular reactions are tested and improved upon.
Developing understanding and explanations	The child will necessarily develop understanding through doing activities in the natural world. Explanations can be provided to reinforce the learning, but up to the preschool stage, the explanations derived

	internally (by the child) are usually fanciful. As an educator you should try to pitch the explanation at the appropriate level but don't be too concerned if it doesn't appear to have meant anything to the child, as they're still processing the words you've said or the actions you've demonstrated.
Critical thinking	This level of thinking is not known to develop in children under 6 years. It involves analysing a subject from multiple perspectives and analysing the various aspects of it to acquire some higher level of understanding. It necessarily involves reflection. This technique *can* be used in an educator-led activity.
Use ofmathematicalconcepts	These include estimation of distances, times and weights as well as basic arithmetic. Thinking *mathematically* simply means thinking about the quantitative (or measurable) aspects of a subject.
Problem-solving	As a thinking skill, problem-solving is probably the most important and one of the easiest to develop. All ages experience some form of problem (something that requires a solution) almost every hour of every day, from getting food or a nappy changed, through to working out the use of a toy or play equipment.
Inventing, discovering and planning	These thinking skills involve activities where the child must communicate his or her intention. Inventing can mean scrunching paper into a ball then making a game with the ball. Discovering can mean learning to use a new word in the right context. Planning is the ability to think several steps ahead to solve a problem.

Applying Multiple Intelligences

There are several areas in which children require development to discover their potential.

According to Howard Gardner, people have seven areas of intelligence:

- *Linguistic* – the ability to use spoken or written words
- *Logical-mathematical* – reasoning abilities, logic, inductive and deductive thinking, the use of numbers and abstract pattern recognition
- *Visual-spatial* – the ability to visualise objects and spatial dimensions
- *Kinaesthetic* – knowledge of the body and the ability to control physical motion

- *Musical-rhythmic* – the ability to grasp the intricacies of music as well as rhythms, beats, tones and melodies
- *Interpersonal* – communicating efectively with other people and being able to develop relationships
- *Intrapersonal* – the ability to understand your own emotions, motivations, inner states of being, and self-refection.

In education, the creation of learning opportunities should embrace not only the linguistic and logical intelligences, but also those involved in social growth and emotional development. Let's see how these might be incorporated in learning opportunities.

Creating the Opportunities

Opportunities for children to develop cognitive skills will vary according to the child's age and abilities. In children's services, it is accepted that these opportunities must include age-appropriate stimuli and consistent support from the caregiver. Tey can incorporate a range of cognitive intelligences in some relatively simple activities.

Childcare workers can provide opportunities for cognitive development for diferent age groups as follows.

Infants (Birth to 12 Months)

- Carers must respond to the children promptly and consistently to reinforce positive behaviours and allow for the infant to consider the consequences.
- Provide routines that allow for multiple sensory experiences (taste, smell, touch, sounds and sight).
- Provide simple equipment and toys that stimulate *all* the senses for the child to investigate and use regularly.
- Provide opportunities for the child to perceive similarities and diferences between objects, occurrences and subjects.

Toddlers (1 to 3 years)

- Provide songs, rhymes and stories to aid in the development of memory. Encourage the child to recognise and repeat patterns, sounds, stories and words.

- Provide toys and equipment to explore the concepts of size, shape, number, volume, weight, temperature and time.
- Provide sensory stimuli such as posters, toys, equipment and food types.
- Provide opportunities to help with household duties and explore the built and natural environment (indoors/outdoors).

Preschoolers (3 to 5 years)

- Carers must make time for children to explore their surroundings undirected.
- Provide social opportunities that encourage interaction with real people and objects for children to gain an understanding of themselves, others and the world around them.
- Provide a variety of materials and resources to develop understanding, reasoning, planning ability, problem-solving and discovery.
- Carers should guide children to view or sense aspects of the environment they may have overlooked.
- Carers should respond to children's reasoning in a respectful manner.

In addition to these age-appropriate opportunities, mathematical concepts may be introduced as early as the infant stage by simple counting games, toys and videos. As the child develops this thinking skill, you should provide more complex examples for them to consider and work out. It is important to remember that as with physical skills or social skills, each child will develop this area of cognition at a diferent rate.

The opportunities you provide should also take into account each child's cultural background. Cultural expectations can dictate which activities a child can participate in; how the child responds to an activity; how the child comprehends their peers' responses to an activity. All of these factors may infuence the child's cognitive development.

Peer Group Interactions

Interacting with other children of the same age provides the opportunity to learn important skills and knowledge. Peers act as a normative reference in that they can refect a level of development to the child that indicates their own progress. For example, if all the child's friends are able to run and they are able to keep up, their sense of achievement is refected in the abilities of others. Alternatively, if the child cannot speak as well as their friends, they might try harder or feel frustrated; either way, the carer can support the child's learning.

Learning occurs during social interaction. That may mean the use of speech and language is afected by peer interaction as is the sharing of knowledge and demonstration of skills to support one another.

Development of cognitive functions such as problem solving, critical thinking and reasoning are greatly afected by observing and listening to others. The child's peers may get things right or wrong during any given activity, but learning is achieved by all who watch and consider the results of the activity. Social learning continues throughout life. It's therefore an important part of a child's development to be able to interact meaningfully and fairly with their peers.

Factors that May Affect Cognitive Development

An important part of caring for children is the development of practices that assist them to maintain a good level of health and ftness now and also in later in life. Children's health and physical needs must be met so that optimum learning and development can take place.

Ofering children a nutritious diet rich in vitamins and minerals provides them with the necessary nutrients to support healthy growth and development. In addition, encouraging active play and incorporating physical activity into daily life helps children build muscle, increase coordination and develop self-confdence.

Carers can do much to foster good health in children and parents should also be encouraged to model and sustain an active, healthy lifestyle. By including the child and their family in the process, you can work together to ensure healthy practices are the norm even when the child is away from the centre. Be aware of the fne line between promoting good health practices and becoming intrusive; you need to ensure you don't overstep your boundaries with parents and your role is one of assistance and advice. Your role is to promote healthy eating and physical activity to support the child's development.

Promoting Healthy Eating

Children's daily nutritional needs should be managed and met in conjunction with family support. For example, when in the care environment, children are provided with a wide range of healthy food and drink to meet their individual nutritional needs. Tey should also be encouraged, with the help of their parents, to choose and eat healthy meals and snacks outside the care environment.

Mealtimes can provide opportunities for children's cognitive development as carers can interact with the children, discuss types of food and encourage healthy eating habits.

All children are fascinated by new experiences with food and children love activities that result in a physical product, so cooking and eating provides an excellent opportunity to enhance cognitive, language and social skills. Food and eating is also a major part of many cultures, so having children help prepare and then eat a meal of a diferent culture is an excellent way to broaden their experiences and stimulate discussion.

Infants

As infants are fed, especially when introducing solids for the frst time, discuss the colour, texture and taste of food. Fussy eaters can be encouraged with fun eating games, such as 'Watch the aeroplane', as a carer pilots the food to the child, making the appropriate plane noises and verbalising positively as food is consumed. Carers should also ensure they tell the infant exactly what they are eating to assist their language and comprehension skills; for example, 'Here comes a piece of carrot', or 'Let's try some nice green peas'.

Toddlers

Toddlers' cognitive development can be supported by having them participate in activities as they eat, especially if they are fussy eaters. Creative activities and games can promote healthy eating behaviours and provide excellent opportunities to introduce children to diferent types of healthy foods. These activities can also be used to assist cognitive development by classifying foods into groups according to types, weights, colour, texture or cultures.

Preschoolers

Preschool children can be encouraged to learn the names of diferent foods in languages other than English and how diferent foods can be prepared. Meals from diferent cultures can be placed on the menu and discussed. For example, the children can discuss the relevant culture, festivals and celebrations and what foods are served.

Other cognitive development opportunities that can stem from this activity include discussing the diferent ingredients, tastes, smells, colours and textures, comparing cooking utensils and methods, discussing measuring and pouring, making a recipe book and comparing and enacting diferent ways of eating food.

Promoting Physical Activity

Regular physical activity is also important to support children's cognitive development and carers may need to support parents to understand the relationship between physical activity, good health and cognitive development.

Children's parents and family members should be encouraged to promote a physically active lifestyle away from the care environment as children who lead healthy and active lives early, are more likely to continue to do so in later years. When planning physical activities, ensure the environment is safe, as some physical activities may involve an element of risk.

Infants

Infants should be given ample opportunity for unrestricted movement and encouragement to physically explore their environment even though they may have limited self-mobility. Carers should promote activities that encourage exploring and the development of skills such as reaching, rolling, sitting up, crawling, pulling up and walking. These activities all aid in the development of motor skills and teach children to be active from a very young age. Opportunities should be provided such as:

- placing the infant on your lap and bouncing them while supporting them in the standing position
- using toys and brightly coloured objects to promote the infant's auto motor responses
- holding the infant's legs and gently making them 'run'
- placing objects in front of the infant on the foor mat to encourage the child to try to reach for them.

When arranging equipment the carer should ensure the area is clear of hazards; gives the infant adequate room to reach, stretch and crawl; and is comfortable.

An infant's physical activity should promote the development of gross motor skills, so equipment should be used that is safe, fun and promotes an infant's physical development, such as play mats, paddle pools and sandpits. This equipment should be arranged so infants can access it, with or without the assistance of a carer, but always under close supervision.

Younger infants are somewhat limited in their ability to play actively until they have developed coordination and motor skill ability; however, they should still be encouraged as much as possible. Terefore, limit the amount of time an infant spends in prams, rockers, baby walkers, cots and capsules.

Toddlers and Preschoolers

Toddlers and preschoolers must be given ample opportunity for daily, unstructured physical activity to beneft health and development. Equipment should be arranged to encourage toddlers to develop movement skills that are building blocks for more complex movement tasks; and for preschoolers to encourage them to develop competence in and hone their movement skills.

Toddlers and preschoolers should have access to indoor and outdoor areas where they can perform large muscle activities. When setting up equipment it is important children are able to select what they wish to play with. This helps foster independence and allows the child to use their decision-making and problem-solving skills. It is important to provide a wide selection of toys and equipment at the child's level (for example, on low shelves, or in boxes on the ground) so they can access them easily themselves. This physical activity and interaction with other children provides the child with opportunities to further develop their language, social and cognitive skills.

Providing for Interests

A child is more inclined to excel at something that he or she is interested in. As an educator, your role involves discovering that interest (with parental partnerships) and fostering growth in that area, while still providing a balance of other interests. Note that if a child is encouraged in a particular subject they will become more interested in that subject as they are naturally inclined to seek praise and attention.

The following example illustrates the provision of an appropriately challenging opportunity for a toddler to expand their interests.

Jake is 3 years old and is particularly interested in trucks. His mother says that she likes his interest, but wants to ensure he is developing a 'more rounded set of cognitive skills'. Rosey is the group leader and primary caregiver for Jake. She assures his mother that they can create many learning opportunities involving Jake's current interest. These opportunities include:

- using a book with a truck as the main character to read and learn about sharing, and counting such as counting the page numbers and objects on each page with Jake.
- Jake playing with wooden and metal trucks both inside the centre, in the sand box, and under the tree on the grass. Rosey provides small wooden logs for Jake to create lumber yards, roads and bridges, and to lift with the trucks.
- showing Jake that the metal trucks can get hot to touch when left outside, so Jake knows to bring them in or use the wooden trucks.

Rosey continues to describe the many ways that Jake's interests could be used to create interesting learning tools. Jake's mother is thrilled with Rosey's explanation. She asks if she can donate more books to the centre including some of Jake's favourite truck books to continue the great work she is doing.

Jenna is 18 months old and is developing her motor skills and has been walking now for three months. Her interests include 'anything pink or white', and reading time as she enjoys pointing and contributing to stories.

Develop at least three appropriately challenging opportunities for Jenna to further her thinking and problem-solving skills.

Ensure you can justify each activity against the appropriate stage of Jenna's cognitive development.

Teaching the Child About Consequences

Childhood is about trial and error and education is about limiting the amount of error required to learn something new. The carer's role is to facilitate a safe and nurturing environment that allows for trial of new experiences and learn what is and isn't acceptable or safe.

As adults, we ofen want to jump in and correct a child's grammar, spelling, mathematical solution, or even pencil grip. Learning requires a certain amount of trial and error. A carers role is to facilitate an experience where the child learns from their actions and choices in order to develop better skills and knowledge.

The experiences can range from open-ended questions, which allow children to hypothesise, reason and explain their ideas, to demonstrations and imitations of tasks (like cooking, cleaning, or pencil-holding techniques). The child can think about and process the information, carry out an action, and see what result they get.

Consequences relating to negative or poor behaviour can be demonstrated through a number of techniques such as the following:

- *Reference to posters, books, movies or stories* – for older children (toddlers and above), discuss the themes of posters, books, movies or charts which depict unacceptable behaviour. By agreeing that the behaviour illustrated in the media is unacceptable, the child recognises his or her own poor behaviour and is less likely to repeat it.
- *Mirroring* – a technique of mimicking unacceptable behaviour to refect the actions back to the child performing negatively. This method, originally attributed to psychologist, Milton Erikson, has the efect of transforming a situation immediately. The negative behaviour stops and the child (ofen shocked by the performance) must deal with the refection of their own behaviour.
- *Discussion* – for children who are able to talk and comprehend, discussing the consequences of bad behaviour can have a profound efect before and/or afer any such behaviour is conducted. Discussion should centre on the child's feelings (the cause) and the feelings of those facing the unacceptable behaviour (the efect).

Learning from Experiences

The theory of experiential learning involves creating meaning from your direct experiences. This theory supports the notion of providing opportunities for children to experience the consequences of their actions. The theory suggests that we learn from:

- a concrete experience
- observing and refecting upon the experience
- abstract concepts about what we've seen

- testing what we think in new situations.

For children, who are less able to ponder the application of their experiences, the process is still observed over time. In the example of learning language, they try to use the words they understand as being correct and learn each time they use them. Tink of any time a child has mixed up their words or pronounced something incorrectly. As an educator, you should allow children to come to the correct use of language through some tactful questions.

Opportunities for Infants

Infants interact with the world physically and through the use of emotion and sound. To provide opportunities for them to experience the consequences of their choices, carers should ofer two or more possibilities to the infant during activities. For example, holding up a rattle in one hand and a music shaker in the other and asking 'Which one should we play with?', then choosing one and removing the other from view. Repeating this process demonstrates the consequence of choice.

Where an infant has done something natural (such as wetting or soiling their pants) the carer should acknowledge the child and say something like 'Good job! That feels better, doesn't it?' This reinforces the action while maintaining a positive environment. Infants do not perform bad actions, as they are merely reacting to their environment. The carer's role is to adapt the environment, where applicable, to allow the infant to feel secure, safe and engaged. Consequences of crying, laughing, scratching, mouthing sounds and other developmental occurrences should be positive reinforcement only.

Opportunities for Toddlers

Toddlers are beginning to gain a sense of self and a strictly egocentric personality. Tey are walking and learning to balance, run, talk, build, reason and much more. Tey will make rapid advances in their development and they will make mistakes.

Carers should encourage toddlers to decide between tasks and activities and expand their knowledge of the world through exploration and inquiry. Consequences for exploration, enquiry, inquisitiveness and failure during attempts at new skills, should all involve support and reinforcement. Harsh or negative reactions to a failed attempt will discourage the toddler from trying again.

Of course, toddlers are also learning to push the boundaries of their environment. Tey will test and respond to the reactions of adults and peers. If they get what they want, they will continue that behaviour. It is important for carers to establish boundaries with toddlers so they become aware of social and personal consequences if the boundaries are broken.

Opportunities for Preschoolers

By this age, children are beginning to accept common social contracts such as behaviours that are and are not allowed in social situations. For example, they learn it is not acceptable to scream at others or cry to get their own way but accepting others input and sharing is rewarded and praised. Carers can provide social opportunities through group games, free play and story times. Additionally, they can provide posters, stories and facilitate discussion about inappropriate behaviour.

Encouraging Children to Explore, Understand and Solve Problems

Children can learn by constructing the elements of their environment so they make sense. Tey can also construct knowledge from social interaction by observing and reacting to various causes and efects within the group. In a childcare role, you should be aware that this work has led to our current understanding of the need for children to explore, understand and solve problems on their own, as well as interact in groups, with peers or with children of diferent ages.

Opportunities to Explore

A child must be encouraged to explore his or her surroundings. The extent to which you allow this is dependent on the child's age.

Age-specifc Opportunities

Consider the opportunities you might provide to a toddler to explore their surroundings. How might they difer from a preschooler or infant? You must ensure that the opportunities you provide are realistic and within the abilities of the child. For example, age-specifc opportunities to develop problem-solving skills might include the following.

Limitations to Providing Opportunities

In a childcare centre environment, the opportunities you may provide are limited by a range of factors as follows:

- *Distance and proximity of the new experience:* A child can only explore within the vicinity of the centre; however, service policy may outline certain areas where the children may be taken outside of the centre. Be sure you are aware of the requirements for taking any children outside of the centre grounds. Given this limitation, you should seek to provide a wide range of possible experiences in the centre itself.
- *Risks and hazards*: The child's safety is the highest priority of centre staf. You should only encourage activities for which you have considered the risk factors. There is no harm is sending children on an egg hunt during Easter, but if there is a lightning storm approaching, you'd probably re-think your strategy.
- *Time available:* Sometimes you're restricted by the time available, especially when the opportunity to explore or solve a problem occurs without prompting (as it usually does!).

Maintaining Children's Interest in Solving Problems

There are a variety of ways for a child to learn and an equal variety of methods and resources available to support that learning. When a child is not interested in an object or activity, learning is not likely to take place. So matching the right method and resources to the child's interest is paramount.

Consider how a child's interest and learning coincide when they are immersed in a new toy, subject, game or story. When a child is not otherwise distracted or anxious, they seek out novelty and curiosity; they enjoy, manipulate and explore new things. Equally, when the child has satisfed their curiosity, they will move quickly on to the next thing. Your role is to enable this curiosity to have an outlet and seek ways to move the child from one thing to another to maintain interest and learning.

Strategies for Maintaining Interest

There are three main reasons why a child may lose interest in an object, activity, situation or person:

1. The curiosity has been satisfed.
2. The task is difcult and frustrating.
3. The adult fails to guide the child, loses interest or does not pay attention.

Let's consider how you can manage each of these causes.

When the Child's Curiosity is Satisfed

A child's curiosity can stem from necessity or desire and the motivation should be intrinsic. It should be an internal motivation to learn something new. When a child feigns interest to impress a parent, the interest disappears as soon as the parent does. If a child has their own motivation for learning, the interest is maintained.

A curious child is one who 'reacts positively to new, strange, incongruous, or mysterious elements in the environment by focusing attention on them, moving toward them, manipulating them and/or seeking information about them'.

There are several theories which attempt to explain a child's curiosity. It might simply be:

- a trait that they possess
- a perception of a type of surprising, incongruous or complex stimuli
- a desire to master their surroundings
- their ethology (biologically driven behavioural desire)
- an innate desire to solve problems
- as a result of socialisation agents or how the child is infuenced by their group/ parents/educators.

Each of these factors has its role in helping you to understand the behaviours of children, but few empirical studies have shown how to maintain a curious nature.

If a child's curiosity is satisfed easily and they solve the problem quickly or master the subject easily, there is little you can do to force the child to maintain interest in that subject. The child's learning at that point is complete and they will need something new to investigate. As a childcare worker, your goal is to continue to challenge the child.

Dealing with Difcult or Frustrating Tasks

This is the most common difculty experienced by both the children and the educators (including parents and teachers). It is an inevitable part of childhood. Each new task or subject the child attempts to master will ofer difculties and hurdles. Consider when you frst learned to tie your shoes, ride a bike or whistle!

The challenge for the carer is to ensure a child's frustration does not lead to self-esteem issues. In a child's mind, seeing older children and adults coping easily with the tasks they have yet to master, creates a huge gap between 'I can' and 'I can't'. And this can easily lead to 'and I never will'. According to Sparrow (2009), the child must learn to do the following:

- *Control the feelings generated from frustration:* These might include anger, despair, sadness or rejection. Self-control can be encouraged by ofering calming strategies such as slow breathing, cuddling a favourite toy, remembering a happy occurrence or going for a walk.
- *Develop self-belief:* A child needs to maintain a sense of self-worth as a matter of healthy development. This can be damaged by frustration. To avoid the damage, you can remind the child of past successes, put the activity into perspective by recalling bigger triumphs and focus on their strengths like determination and endurance.
- *Keep trying:* An example that is cited regularly is the child's determination to walk. Tey don't quit until it's done; then balance and nimbleness develop as the skill is mastered. This example can apply to all tasks such as writing their name, throwing a ball or learning new words. Instil a determined nature by regularly referring to words like 'practice' and 'patience 'and describing the words through pictures, examples or stories.

When the Adult Loses Interest

Young children naturally want to impress their parents and other adults. In their frst year, children learn the value of rewards and the feeling of esteem and confdence that coincides with completing a new task. This feeling stays with most of us for life. Equally, a child who receives no praise will likely experience learning difculties and social issues.

Praise can be verbal or nonverbal. One of the easiest forms of praise is attention. Paying attention to your child is the frst step of good parenting, and an essential practice for childcare professionals.

Attention is not just being physically present; it includes asking the right questions and asking them in the right way. It is relatively instinctive, but involves listening to the child and observing them frst, then interacting in a way that shows you're interested in what they're doing.

In a busy childcare centre, undivided or complete attention to each child is virtually impossible. Maintaining a child's interest in a subject requires a skilful approach to asking the right questions. The *right* question is the one that allows the child to:

- think about the answer
- problem-solve
- explore further
- be creative.

The following example demonstrates this type of question.

Developing a Child's Attention Span

While it is important to continually challenge the child, you must be aware of the child's propensity for distraction and ensure that a loss of interest is not merely caused by a distraction rather than conquering a problem. To do this, there are several techniques designed to increase a child's attention span and ensure they complete one activity before moving onto another.

Strategies for Developing Attention Span

The approach to developing a child's attention span is usually determined by the child's age. Some suggested strategies for diferent age groups are listed below.

Infants

The best time to start developing a child's ability to focus their attention is while they are still an infant. Reading and talking to the infant are the best methods to develop attention spans. It doesn't matter what you say because although they may not understand the words you say, the sound of your voice and the expressions on your face will keep the infant intrigued for quite some time.

In a childcare facility, the sound of other children and adults in the room is comforting as is your continued talking and using the child's name. This is a good practice to develop with parents to encourage consistency between the service and home.

Reading aloud to children of any age stimulates their brain development and is encouraged as a starting point for attention development.

Toddlers

For this age group, a good method for building attention span is to use art and craf activities. As mentioned, children have an easier time giving their undivided attention to something they enjoy and are interested in. Adult participation is also benefcial, if not essential, at least to get them started. It creates a bond between child and carer in addition to encouraging the child to give the project the attention it deserves.

Identify the areas in which the child shows interest or talent and encourage those abilities, such as drawing, building or even colouring for young children.

Preschoolers

For older children, one of the best ways to challenge and improve their attention span is through the allocation of responsibility. Looking afer animals (some centres allow pets) encourages children to focus on something besides themselves. This supports Piaget's observations that children of this age become less egocentric. Tey also learn to display love, responsibility and earn self-respect.

If a pet is not an option for your centre, giving the child tasks with rewards or privileges can teach respect, appreciation and responsibility, and how to focus attention to achieve these things.

Knowing when the Child is Ready to Move on

A child should move on from an activity when:

- it is no longer challenging or interesting
- the task has been completed
- the problem has been solved
- time allocated has expired at which point a future time allocation should be made
- more urgent or important activities must be done
- the activity is no longer safe or a health concern exists such as prolonged exposure to the sun or a video screen, which could risk the child's health.

Disposition and Temperament

Early childhood educators place importance on the idea of individual diferences and the value in providing suitable care for individual children. Every child has a diferent personality and ways of responding to other people, diferent temperaments and dispositions that are displayed from birth.

Temperament is based on three key elements:

1. Emotionality, which is the tendency to be distressed or display fear, anger and dramatic episodes; emotionality can manifest in many ways and is most recognisable by the extremes of behaviour exhibited by the child.
2. Sociability, which refers to a child's social disposition and tendency to prefer the company of others.
3. Activity levels; for example, having high energy levels and always being on the move, or displaying low levels of activity and a calm nature.

It is important to develop the correct disposition or attitude within a young child so they may go on to learn efectively when they reach primary school. Developing a well rounded attention span, one that allows for the efective completion of a task in a given time, is a lifelong skill that will develop further during the child's school years. Without a frm foundation, their learning progress can be negatively afected.

A child's disposition may be afected by diet and other brain-afecting conditions such as attention defcit hyperactive disorder (ADHD), Asperger's syndrome, and pervasive development disorders. These efects can negatively impact on a child's cognitive development. Alternative strategies are needed to assist children with special needs. This information is covered more in the Aspire workbooks *CHCFC504A Support emotional and psychological development in early childhood* and *CHCIC512A Plan and implement inclusion of children with additional needs.*

Introducing New Ideas

A child learns by experiencing an event, observing and considering how it applies in diferent contexts, trialling the event in a new context, and fnally creating a concrete memory of the event. Once the event is complete, the child is ready for the next challenge.

This constructivist approach to learning can be thought of as a series of building blocks. Each new skill or piece of knowledge is used with others to form the next. Soon, direct experience will not be necessary to consider what might occur during a cause and efect event. The child can make educated guesses based on what they've already experienced.

Creating New Knowledge and Skills

Learning for a child can be an exciting and deeply satisfying adventure. As they learn new things, their understanding of the world around grows. This can happen incrementally, as with the wind in the sails example, and sometimes exponentially, as ofen happens when a child realises their own cognitive pattern for solving addition and subtraction problems.

The child's understanding, in this sense, can develop and extend over diferent situations and subjects. Here are some examples:

Knowledge	*For example*
Mathematical understanding	Understanding in this area might include how different figures fit together, counting and arithmetic, patterns and rhythms, tables and estimations, and even the linear understanding of time and motion.
Scientific principles	Learning how things work in the natural and built environment might include the laws of motion (including gravity), chemical and physical reactions, how sound waves bounce, and so on. While the intricacies and details aren't demanded during the early years, it's still highly beneficial for a child to observe natural causes and effects to gain perspective of their environment.
Social understandings	How people interact and the socially appropriate ways to act and talk around others is learned primarily by observation of adults and older children. Again, cause and effect demonstrations or discussions can illustrate how appropriate and inappropriate behaviours can affect the child. This includes lessons on tolerance, diversity, communication and respect.
Geographical awareness	This can start at a local level such as the streets, buildings and natural environment which make up the child's immediate world. Awareness then progresses to information about the state, cities, the country and other nations. Maps and other references are excellent tools to develop this understanding. Try looking for both illustrated and photographic maps to expand the child's perception of the world as they grow.
Historical understanding	As a child progresses from toddler to preschooler, you can begin to introduce relevant historical events as stories, videos, talks from experts, and excursions. Learning history has the effect of developing the child's understanding of self and position in the world. They

(Contd....)

(Contd...)

	begin to understand that much has happened before today and that more will happen in the future.
Mechanical understanding	Some children have a higher level of mechanical understanding than others. This is thought to be a predisposition and those who possess it should be encouraged to explore the workings of things. Children who do not possess this disposition may still work through the mechanics of a puzzle or complex object, but tend not to see the interrelationships between the components as readily.
Potential of computers	Computers are in more than 67 per cent of family homes in Australia. The percentage of people with access to computers has increased from 31 per cent to 75 per cent in the 10 years to 2008 *(www.abs.gov.au)*. The increasing awareness and inextricable use of computers in daily life drives the need to introduce computers to children in their early years. Carers should explore the various areas of potential with children. These areas include: • researching things of interest • playing educational games • creative work such as drawing, writing and music.

Extending Knowledge

Carers must look for opportunities to extend the knowledge of children by recognising interests and developing new challenges for learning. Children need to be exposed to elements of the world around them to help them develop knowledge or understanding. The following table outlines these diferent elements and provides examples.

Elements	*Examples*
The natural environment	The elements of their environment which make up the natural world such as flora and fauna, fire, wind, rain and sunlight.
The social world	The interaction of people in different contexts such as home, school, playgrounds, cities, country towns, dances, sport and so on.Observing and participating in social settings develops a child's understanding of the causes and effects of social interaction.

(Contd...)

(Contd...)

The cultural environment	Children also grow through exposure to cultures different from their own and the cultural heritage specific to them.Learning through observation of cultural behaviours, listening to a range of music and stories, smelling and tasting foods from that culture, and touching cultural artefacts, if appropriate, should be encouraged regularly.
The world of ideas	Understanding that ideas can develop into objects, actions and situations is an important lesson for children.Why ideas are important and how creativity can lead to discovery.Understanding how and why we think in certain ways helps us to recognise our own thoughts, ideas and originality.
Human-made environment	Also called the built environment, this simply means the surroundings that are artificially created and can include buildings, bridges, canals, roads, cars and all the elements in the centre made through some form of manufacturing process.Explaining how things are made is a key developmental step for children and something many children are very interested in.

Children's understanding of the world can be challenged and expanded through activities such as those outlined below.

- *Excursions/incursions*: This means planning trips away from the centre, or to particular parts of the centre, where elements of the world can be discussed and explained. It may also involve having people or things being brought into the centre such as choirs, animals or guest speakers.
- *Maps, posters, books*: These tools are relevant sources of information and knowledge throughout the child's life. Exposure to these sources of self-directed investigation helps the child develop the skill of research. He or she will learn to seek out the information from a sign, poster, book or map rather than rely solely on an adult's advice.
- *Music*: Playing and listening to music, rhythms, beats and songs develops a child's knowledge of the creation of sounds, their emotional and physiological relationship to music and dexterity to create the sounds on instruments by themselves.
- *Walks in the local area*: While excursions usually involve a bus or car ride to a facility or site, walks in the local area can also prove very

educational. Children are not only exposed to the natural and built environments but they also have the opportunity to learn the layout or geography of the area.

- *Community resources*: Local communities can include schools, parks, zoos, libraries, pools, fountains, shopping centres, restaurant districts, universities, council chambers and so on. Exposure to these and other local resources expands the child's knowledge of their local environment and his or her understanding of how communities are created and arranged.

The following example illustrates how staf can introduce new activities to build on existing knowledge and interests.

Developing Children's Abilities to Observe

Observation is essential to discovery and is the cornerstone of the scientifc methods that help us explain the natural world. While a child might not understand *how* observation contributes to learning, they will understand that seeing something makes it *real* to them. You can support and enhance the child's ability to observe their surroundings through a number of nonverbal and verbal techniques.

Questioning Techniques to Support Observation

There are dozens of questioning techniques designed to evoke specifc responses. If you are seeking to enhance a child's ability to observe his surroundings, there can be nothing more powerful than a cleverly placed question. Diferent types of questions include:

- closed questions
- open questions
- direct and indirect questions.

Closed Questions

A closed question is one that elicits a single correct/incorrect response. Tey are perfect for establishing existing knowledge. For example, 'What shoes are you wearing today?' or 'Why do you wear sunscreen?'

These questions are not asking the child to think beyond an initial reaction to, or observation of, a fact. Tey elicit a 'true or false' kind of answer, a 'yes or no', or a statement of fact. For this reason, they are not ideal for developing a child's cognitive skills, but serve as a review mechanism which helps the child recall facts and establish memories.

Open Questions

An open question is designed to elicit a thoughtful response. For children, the technique varies with age, as stages of development have an efect on the type of answer you're likely to receive. For example, a pre-teen is not likely to give you a long, thoughtful answer and a toddler may need to have the question reworded in several diferent ways to understand what is being asked.

Despite this, open questions are perfect for developing a child's observation skills. Using the right question can direct a child's interest and attention towards something in order to provide you with an answer. For example, 'How does that work, Anna?' or 'Why do you think the sky is blue, Prakesh?'

Each open question should lead to another in order to 'steer' the child in the direction of discovery.

Direct and Indirect Questions

A direct question is aimed at a single child, while an indirect question may be aimed at a group. These can be open *or* closed and are designed to establish learning or promote discussion. For example:

- Direct (closed) –'What type of dinosaur is that, Teagan?' Direct (open) – 'Why do you think dinosaurs walk like that?'
- Indirect (closed) – 'Who has fnished their drawing?'

  Indirect (open) – 'What do you think makes the trees grow?'

The correct use of indirect questions should involve follow up questions or statements supporting each child's response, and if necessary, direct further questions to individuals to involve them in the group.

Nonverbal Support

You can direct and encourage a child to observe their surroundings without words. The following table outlines types of nonverbal communication techniques and how these may be used with the child.

Nonverbal communication	*How you use type of communication*
Movement and body position	You can demonstrate actions such as running, jumping, angry expressions, smiling, posture, eye contact and gestures which allow the child to observe the effects on you and your surroundings.Through imitation, the child can observe how their own actions might lead to similar outcomes.
Demonstration	Consider a child's reaction to a demonstration of an activity they haven't seen before. The power of an effective demonstration cannot be underestimated. For example, a carefully constructed role-play with older children or staff can demonstrate concepts like stranger danger, environmental care or even hygiene.
Posters and other teaching aids	These can illustrate environmental awareness across various categories depending on the children's needs. They are a useful learning tool as well as a handy reference for carers who are teaching children about their surroundings (both close and distant environments).

Paralanguage

Paralanguage is the term given to how you make sounds, infections, emotions, grunts, melodies, and so on. You can use this technique to convey relevant messages to children without the use of complicated words. The way you say things is ofen more important than what you say. Indeed, when communicating with infants, the sound of your voice can be more powerful than any words.

Monitoring Children's Cognitive Development

The role of an educator is to provide opportunities for learning. The educator must also ensure that the learning continues through a monitoring process. This involves both formal and informal questioning and observations. Most childcare centres have established policies that require daily or weekly observations be recorded on a child's fle. This is also the avenue for recording all cognitive development observed and tested by the educator.

Reasoning and Problem-solving

A child's ability to reason comes from exposure to problems and the observation of causes and efects. You can observe and monitor the development of these skills through a process of informal testing. This is done by:

- providing problems to solve on a regular basis
- recording the child's approaches to solving the problem
- recording the outcome of the test such as whether the child did or did not solve the problem without assistance
- reviewing the results and progressing to the next problem.

While this sounds very clinical, the actual process can be very interactive and enjoyable for the child. Notably, most centres do not record 'negative' comments about cognitive development in children's folders, so ensure you word any observations in line with your centre's policies.

Developing Understanding and Explanations

Solving problems tests a child's ability to think in a logical or progressive manner. Efective cognitive development requires that a child also develops understanding. This allows the child to create abstract applications of his or her knowledge and skills which leads to further and ongoing development.

Monitoring a child's understanding is best done through formal and informal questioning. That is, asking the child why something occurs or how something works.

You'll notice that (in accordance with Piaget's stages of learning) children will respond in some fanciful and funny ways to these sorts of questions. You can reassure them and help them to understand through demonstration or explanation, but remember that very young children cannot distinguish between real and magical. You should ask age-appropriate questions to monitor this development.

A positive sign is that the child *attempts* to explain what they're seen, tasted, heard and so on. Explanations that involve fairies, robots or magicians are all acceptable; however, as educators, it is pertinent to explain real functions as *real* functions where appropriate.

For example: 'Where does water go when you pour it on hot cement?'

If the answer is that 'a dragon blows hot air on it and boils it away', then you should endeavour to develop the child's understanding of evaporation through experiments or diagrams. Of course, dispelling Santa and the tooth fairy is well outside your job description!

Critical Thinking

From a very early age, children can begin to think about their efect on others. Even though they are generally egocentric until they are in their 7th to 12th year, they are able to focus on concepts like purpose, questions, information, inferences and emotions.

According to Fran (2006), thinking is question-driven. When children are regularly encouraged to ask questions, they improve and develop their ability to think.

To identify and monitor a child's ability to critically think, you can record his or her involvement in asking questions and problem-solving. If the child asks questions and appears to learn from each answer (that is, they don't repeat the question afer it is understood), then development has been observed.

You can ask children to develop their own questions as a task. This might be for any subject that interests them or their peers. The reactions and questions may be recorded for development monitoring.

Use of Mathematical Concepts

Improvement in the use of mathematical concepts is relatively easy to monitor. The child can be tested by giving real world scenarios, playing counting games, relating sounds or movements to numbers and so on. Improvement can be recorded and reviewed periodically.

Inventing, Discovering and Planning

As a child's cognitive processes improve, so will their desire to invent, explore, discover and plan. Interest is maintained through challenging tasks and attention to the child's specifc needs. Monitoring this behaviour is through observation. You will have the opportunity to see the child discover new approaches to problems, try new tasks, explore the environment and talk with others.

Planning at this level refers to the child's ability to think ahead of the situation. To monitor this, you may wish to discuss options with the child about a project or task they are about to undertake. Record the child's perceptions and the way they approach the task to monitor their development in the skill of planning.

PROMOTING OPPORTUNITIES IN SCIENCE AND TECHNOLOGY

It is important to provide children with a wide variety of creative opportunities as they grow and develop. Creative play stimulates their senses, allows them to explore their emotions and helps them become socially active beings. It is equally important to encourage children to learn to think logically, to reason and to develop their curiosity about how things work.

Developing activities and promoting opportunities for children to explore the concepts of mathematics, science and technology can help to stimulate logical thinking and reasoning abilities. Developing activities that deal with our environment can teach children to become responsible citizens of the world.

Presenting Experiences in Science, Maths and Technology

Developing a child's capacity for logical thinking and reasoning does not need to be tedious or boring. There are many ways in which a child can learn to look at numbers, the natural world around them and be flled with the wonder of new discoveries. A carer's role is to ensure that this is the case.

The Concept of Numbers

Early development of the concept of numbers plays an important part in developing positive attitudes about mathematics at an early age. There is a range of special methods and activities that can help children to develop early numeracy skills. As young children need to experience new things by 'doing' and 'saying' before concepts make sense to them, these methods will need to include the use of motivating and engaging concrete materials that children can manipulate. As early as two years of age, many children can already parrot the words 'one', 'two', 'three', 'four', 'fve' and so on. However, they do not yet understand that the number refers to an item or a set of items.

Suggestions for incorporating numbers into activities can include:

- using numbers in daily vocabulary such as 'let's put the two books we've read back on the shelf'
- counting children in the room such as asking 'how many children are here today?' and then touching each child as you count 'one, two, three …'

- counting the number of blocks a child is playing with
- introducing concepts such as 'many' or 'lots' such as 'there are many children here today' or 'there are lots of apples in the bowl'.

Introducing numbers and concepts in this way will gradually build up the appropriate language and understanding of these concepts in children.

Measurement Concepts

Engaging children with a variety of measurement concepts is a great beginning. For example, a child will take joy in telling people that they are 'bigger' than their sister or brother or 'taller' than the lamp or that they are 'higher' than the dishwasher. Young children will also think that they have 'more' in their cup simply because their cup is taller. This type of language needs to be promoted and children need guidance to help with any confusion about these concepts through experimentation and play. Further, children can be encouraged to explore the concept of measurement by weighing and measuring objects; using scales and rulers to determine how one object is heavier than another and how one object may be longer or shorter than another.

Classifcation

Classifcation is a pre-number concept that children need lots of experimentation and communication with. We classify things on a regular basis without even considering that we're actually doing it. We look in indexes that are alphabetised or numerically arranged, we purchase groceries in areas of food groups, we classify to sort laundry, we sort our cutlery before putting it away. Children can beneft from a variety of classifcation activities which will also support early numeracy concepts.

Classifcation activities can include:

- using blocks to engage young children to repeat patterns such as blue, green, orange
- using shapes to encourage children to determine what comes next such as triangle, square, circle, triangle
- asking children how many items in the play room are square or round or heavy
- asking children to say how many things are made of wood, plastic or metal

- extending classifcation activities to include more than one attribute such as heavy and small, or square and smooth.

The Wonders of Science

Children are inherently curious about the natural world: everything is new and needs to be explained. The level of understanding children require is refected in their level of cognitive development. For example, there is no need to explain photosynthesis to 3-year-olds; it is probably enough for them to know that leaves are green and turn brown when they fall from a tree.

Activities that stimulate children to learn about science can be developed around themes including:

- water
- wind
- sight and sound
- colours
- machines
- insects
- plants and fowers
- food and drink.

Materials such as rocks, leaves, bark and so on can be arranged on tables with equipment such as magnifying glasses so that children can touch, feel and examine the objects.

It is also easy to extend activities and introduce ways of collecting and recording their fndings:

- Selecting and collecting natural objects. Sensory understanding of the texture and physical limitations of objects develops children's comprehension of how natural elements work together. Consider a collection of powder, sand, stones and rocks; each refecting stages of erosion that can be easily demonstrated to a child.
- Observation is the key to scientifc discovery. Children enjoy demonstrations and experiments as they learn frst-hand how diferent objects and elements interact with each other. You can encourage them to draw or write what they see to explain what they have witnessed. This also challenges their language and cognitive development.

Using Technology

Children today are much less cautious about the use of technology than their parents and grandparents. Computers, televisions and the Internet have formed part of their environment since birth (with variations due to socioeconomic circumstances or cultural beliefs). Using a keyboard and a mouse and understanding the concept of movement and text created on the computer screen is no more amazing to a child than driving in a car; they all form part of the 'built world' in which they exist.

It is important for a carer to understand how best to aid learning and what types of learning could be facilitated through the use of technology. Computers should be viewed as more than tools for bringing efciency to traditional approaches. Instead, they can be used to open new and unforeseen avenues for learning. Tey allow children to interact with vast amounts of information from within their care facilities and homes and connect children from across the world.

The physical environment can also afect children's social interactions. For example;

- placing two seats in front of the computer and one at the side for the carer can encourage positive social interaction
- placing computers close to each other can facilitate the sharing of ideas among children
- centrally located computers invite other children to pause and participate in the computer activity.

Technology can be used from a very early age to teach children concepts in mathematics and in science. Nothing, however, provides a better learning experience than personal experience.

Stimulating Learning about the Environment

Children need to be encouraged to take an interest in the environment around them and how we, as human beings, impact and afect that environment.

Stimulating General Curiosity

Children are naturally curious and with the right encouragement can be set on a path of lifelong learning. Methods of stimulating a child's desire to learn about the environment in which they live could include the following activities or strategies.

Strategies	***How to implement these strategies***
Provide genuine age-appropriate choices	This means ensuring that the activities that are planned are not too hard for the younger children to understand or too easy for the older ones to enjoy.Providing children with activities that are pitched specifically at their age group will help them learn at an appropriate pace.As each stage in their growth and development is reached, the activities can increase in complexity.
Observation	Encourage children to observe what is going on around them and ask questions about things that arouse their curiosity.
Provide a safe, stimulating environment	Provide a place where children can explore without fear or without exposing themselves to harm.A safe, secure environment in which to explore also encourages a safe level of risk-taking by the children.
Encourage children to work together	Cooperation helps stimulate discussion about discoveries made and ideas and problems can be solved collaboratively.Working in cooperation with other children will also help them learn from each other and discover that there are differing opinions, ideas and approaches.
Encourage problem-solving	This can be achieved by acting as a role model and by modelling cooperation, negotiations and communication skills to the children.Explaining the process of problem-solving and using appropriate intervention and support strategies can also help children learn problem-solving skills.
Asking questions that will stimulate investigation	Nothing can be more effective than asking the right types of questions in an easygoing manner.Questions that you ask should have simple and proper wordings. For example, questions you could ask to develop analytical skills could include:, Tell me one simple difference between a plant and a baby., Can you tell me more about this flower?, Compare this bird and that bird. Tell me what the difference is., What do you think would happen if ...?
Promote use of own judgment	Provide opportunities where children need to use their own judgment by encouraging them to consider the consequences of their choices.
Time	Provide plenty of time to work and talk through their discoveries and/or problems.

Environmental Activities

Carers can help children develop an understanding of the environment and improve their critical-thinking skills by incorporating nature into early learning experiences. An excellent example of how to incorporate this learning in a long-term project that will build knowledge and respect for nature could be to immerse them in environmental activities year-round.

To begin, identify a theme such as:

- Spring is in the air
- Explore your playground
- Where are the leaves?
- Wintertime for animals

Once a theme has been established, take the children on a walk around the outside play area and identify changes within the same setting over time. Such activities can be an excellent opportunity to develop young children's observation skills.

For example, have children compare the shapes, forms, and conditions of trees at diferent times of the year. Observing trees with or without bark, leaves, fowers, or fruit each month helps children develop an awareness of the cyclical processes of nature. Or mark tree shadows at diferent times during the year. Keep a record of the time, date, and length of the shadows and help the children compare the records.

Activities of this nature can be developed to suit a range of age groups and can be stimulating and fun for both the children and the adults supervising them.

Recognising Children's Abilities

All children have particular talents that need to be noticed and nurtured so they will do well in school and in their later lives. In the past, childcare facilities and schools ofen used a very narrow defnition of what constitutes intelligence. It did not account for the diferent ways that children show their abilities, or that some children have difculty in showing their talents at all. Today, childcare facilities and schools have adopted broader and fairer methods to recognise a child's potential and abilities.

Theory of Multiple Intelligences

Howard Gardner, Professor of Cognition and Education at the Harvard Graduate School of Education, developed the theory of multiple intelligences to more accurately defne the meaning of intelligence and to measure human cognition in its fullness. For example, he claimed that intelligence can be shown in the following areas.

Area of intelligence	*What this means*
The natural environment	The elements of their environment which make up the natural world such as flora and fauna, fire, wind, rain and sunlight.
Linguistic intelligence	Children who are 'word smart' are most likely to enjoy reading and writing for pleasure and talk about what they have read. They can use language effectively to express themselves and have a wide vocabulary. They are often fascinated by words and enjoy playing word games and puzzles.
Logical-mathematical intelligence	'Number smart' children can display the capacity to analyse problems and reason logically. They frequently score well in mathematical tests, like number games and counting and are also interested in science, love detecting patterns and figuring how things work.
Musical intelligence	'Music smart' children are fascinated by sounds. They love to sing or hum either to themselves or as a performance. They are appreciative of music, have the capacity to recognise songs and create their own rhythms and tunes and they may also play musical instruments.
Bodily-kinaesthetic intelligence	Children who particularly enjoy physical or hands-on activities are 'body smart'. They are skilful at using their bodies, may display good balance, coordination and agility and love sports, drama or dancing. When engaging others they use plenty of hand and facial gestures and are very tactile.

Family and Community Infuence on Cognitive Development

Cognitive development, the process by which reason, thought, ideas, and critical thinking emerge, is signifcantly impacted by interaction with family and community members. The term indoctrination, referring to the process of learning ideas, attitudes and even cognitive approaches without question or critical examination, is commonplace in almost every community on Earth. Children are indoctrinated into their specifc societies, families, and religions and the rules and laws which apply to them. Generally, this type of learning is accepted as the price paid for a secure and safe society and therefore holds a strong position within the cultural beliefs of any given society.

Carers must respect children's individuality as infuenced by exposure to family and community groups, while still encouraging them to explore, investigate and solve problems on their own. For example, a child born into a bohemian family that values music, art, self-sufciency and a non-materialistic lifestyle, must be accepted and respected by carers. Tey must be given the opportunity to develop cognitive processes as well as creative outlets that improve the child's ability to learn and develop.

Recognising Ability in a Child

Understanding the diferent ways in which a child can display abilities is the frst step in actually recognising and responding to them. In the course of a working day, a carer will be working with a variety of children both individually and in groups. The key to recognising particular abilities in a child is in observation and communication. This can include paying attention to the questions they ask and the games they play.

Watch out for the following:

- What type of questions is the child asking?
- Do they seem focused on specifc subjects or areas of interest?
- Do their questions display an understanding of the topic above their usual comprehension levels?
- Do they play specifc games with particular interest?
- Are they displaying a particular level of expertise or knowledge when playing games?
- Are they able to undertake tasks or activities that other children in the group are still having difcutly with?

Recognising these abilities in a child does not necessarily mean that this child will have above-average intelligence, or that they will become a child prodigy. It does mean that the child has a specifc interest feld that can be nurtured and developed, perhaps to levels of greatness, but at least to levels that can be useful and enjoyable throughout their lives.

Responding to Potential

Children's talents should be developed as early as possible so they can achieve their full potential. Having discovered a child's interest or abilities, a carer should develop activities designed to encourage and stimulate that interest. Programs should be developed in cooperation with other staf in the childcare facility with whom the child has contact and also with the child's family. This cooperation between the home and the care facility can reinforce the child's abilities and talents by ofering them consistency and the opportunities to display them in both environments.

Responding to a child's potential can include the following:

- Provide the child with 'project work'. This gives the child the opportunity to apply a range of diferent investigative and problem-solving skills as well as motivation to persevere until the project has been completed to their satisfaction.
- Interact with the child and encourage them to communicate their ideas and thoughts with the adults in their lives, and the children with whom they interact on a daily basis.
- Provide materials and resources appropriate to their interest area and encourage them to use them in new ways.
- Help them develop language and literacy skills by asking them questions designed to develop their thinking and reasoning ability.
- Provide a stimulating, safe environment where they can explore and experiment with new ideas and concepts.
- Encourage imaginative substitution by asking questions like 'What would happen if …?'
- Ensure that activities and plans are age-appropriate.

Encouraging participation

Engaging children in activities is not always easy. Teir attention spans are fairly short when they are still very young and they tend to be very easily distracted. In order to encourage a child to become and stay involved with a project it must hold their interest.

Science, mathematics and technology can be learning experiences a child will look forward to with anticipation if they are designed and presented in ways children will fnd enjoyable. Joanne Hendricks is Professor Emerita of Early Childhood Education at the University of Oklahoma and suggests that the following priorities should be observed when planning for cognitive development:

- Maintain the child's sense of wonder and curiosity.

- Let cognitive learning be a source of genuine pleasure for children and the carer.
- Bind cognitive learning to afective experiences whenever possible.
- Accompany cognitive learning with language wherever possible.

Age-appropriate Activities

All children develop as individuals and it is important to keep this in mind at all times when developing activities for children in a care facility. As a general guideline, children aged 2 can be introduced to the concept of maths and science and can complete very simple activities with adult assistance. Children aged 3 can complete tasks and activities with slightly less assistance afer directions are given and children aged between 4 and 5 can generally complete activities with minimal assistance. Remember that all tasks should be appropriate for the children's ages and levels of cognitive ability.

Engaging Children in Science and the Environment

As computer games and television increasingly occupy children's time in their everyday lives, it can be increasingly difcult to interest them in traditional activities such as playing outside or spending time in the garden. However, it is possible to engage children in the outside world by making activities as enjoyable and interesting as possible, to compete with the many diferent hobbies available in the digital age.

The following examples can be followed to encourage children to take an interest in spending time outdoors while at the same time introducing them to the concepts of science and the environment.

Science concept	*How you can encourage children*
Grow an edible garden	Encourage children to participate in gardening by setting up a garden bed or a few 'edible' baskets and pots, with tomatoes and herbs such as parsley, thyme and basil. All these things are easy to grow from seed. Children will enjoy seeing what they can grow and you can also experiment with carrot tops and cress, apple pips and seeds left over from lunch.
Take an interest in trees	Learn with children by getting to know all the names of trees in the surrounding area. To keep it fun and interesting the children can collect leaves, dry them out and press them, and then stick them in an album or make a montage.

	The leaves could even be laminated and then made into mobiles or pictures to hang in the children's play areas.
Encourage composting and recycling	You can make environmental awareness fun for children by promoting composting and recycling in the garden. Give children ownership of the compost bin by helping them to decorate it in any way they want, and paint recycling bins in different colours. Encourage children to take part in helping the environment by suggesting ways to recycle different materials in the childcare centre and in the home and by drawing charts and finding new uses for old things.

Engaging Children in Maths

Maths can be either a really fun subject or really boring for children. It doesn't have to be boring as you can easily relate it to children's lives. For example:

- Give the children real-life objects to count rather than the same old plastic counters they have been using. Children love counting objects that they are familiar with, like fruit or toys.
- Relate the maths to the child's real-life interests. Use characters from television shows in your maths problems.
- Create fun word problems for the children to solve. Place the children's names in the word problems and use real-life experiences in the maths problems, such as 'Brian had three lunches on the feld trip and lost two.'
- Instead of measuring everything in centimetres, use some edible tools to measure items, such as carrot or celery sticks.

There are also many commercial and educator-made maths games, including sets of animals, fruit, vehicles, shapes, board counting games, board classifcation games and various spinners and large dice, which are useful in reinforcing one-to-one correspondence and classifcation. Remember, when developing learning activities for children, maintain the child's sense of wonder and curiosity and let the cognitive learning be a source of genuine pleasure for children.

Stimulating Children's Curiosity and Learning

Children are generally curious by nature. Tey explore, question, and wonder, and by doing so, they learn. From the moment of birth we are drawn to new things. When children are curious about something new, they want to explore it and discover how things work. For example, by turning the light switch on and of over and over again, a child is learning about cause and efect. By pouring water into diferent-shaped containers a 4-year-old is learning basic concepts of mass and volume. By exploring new things, a child can discover the sweetness of chocolate, the sourness of lemon, the heat of the stove, and the cold of ice.

Keeping Curiosity Alive

A child's potential (emotional, social, and cognitive) is expressed through the quantity and quality of their experiences. Curiosity plays an enormous role in the depth and breadth of these experiences. Generally speaking, if a child's curiosity is nurtured and encouraged, they are more likely to make new friends, have more rewarding social lives and be interested and excited about new activities and experiences. Because of this enthusiasm, the curious child is usually easier to teach and motivate.

There are three common ways adults dim the enthusiastic exploration of a curious child.

1. *Fear:* When a child's world is in turmoil or when they are afraid, they will not like anything new. Tey will usually look for anything familiar, staying within their comfort zone, unwilling to leave and explore new things. For example, children impacted by war, natural disasters, family distress or violence have their curiosity crushed by day-to-day fears about survival.
2. *Disapproval:* Parents and carers sometimes tell children 'Don't touch. Don't climb. Keep it down. Don't take that apart. Stop getting dirty'. This can have a very negative impact on a child's sense of curiosity. Children can sense and respond to adults' fears, biases and attitudes.
3. *Absence:* Children respond to the care and interest of an adult. It provides them with a sense of safety and happiness. The ability to share their discoveries with adults and receive encouragement and positive reinforcement proves an impetus for continued learning.

Keeping children stimulated and flled with curiosity can be easily achieved. Strategies for stimulating children's curiosity and learning include the following:

- Recognising the child's style of curiosity. Some children may want to explore only with their minds, while others explore in more physical ways by touching, smelling, tasting and climbing. Some children are more shy than others while some are more comfortable with novelty and physical exploration.
- Redefning the concept of failure. Curiosity ofen leads to more mess than success. It is how we, as carers, handle the mess that helps encourage further exploration, and thereby, development. For example, if a 5-year-old is learning to jump rope and they trip a thousand times, this is not a thousand failures – it is determination. Always take a positive approach to a child's exploration and attempts.
- Using attention and approval to reinforce the eforts of the exploring child. Positive reinforcement and encouragement can have a signifcant efect on a child's determination and resilience when exploring and learning new tasks or dealing with new situations.

By allowing a child to explore in safe, supportive environments you could, potentially, be developing a lifelong love of learning in that child. According to Bruce Perry the following natural cycle results by inspiring and supporting a child's curiosity:

- Curiosity leads to exploration.
- Exploration leads to discovery.
- Discovery leads to satisfaction.
- Satisfaction leads to repetition.
- Repetition leads to mastery.
- Mastery leads to new skills.
- New skills leads to confdence.
- Confdence leads to improved self-esteem.
- Self-esteem leads to a sense of security.
- Security leads to further exploration.

Language and Creativity

A child's brain constantly forms new neural pathways by learning new things, storing memories and gaining new skills. The areas of the brain are not yet confgured as they are in an adult and therefore, new experiences are trapped in a number of diferent regions interconnected by experiential knowledge and basic sub-conscious motor skills.

Language is thought to be one of humankind's most distinctive skills. The cognitive development of language in a child is surprisingly fast, with new words, meanings and understandings being added to the child's memory on a daily basis. An educator's responsibility is to feed the growth of language and speech by providing new words to digest, and new contexts in which to use those words.

Similarly, the creative centres of the brain are growing quickly during this time. Creativity is displayed across many disciplines including art, mathematics, science, language, movement, music and social understanding. Cognitive development can be stimulated through exposure to a wide variety of disciplines that allow children to explore, test and discover their unique abilities and interests.

Stimulating Experiences

Presenting the kind of experiences that will stimulate a child's curiosity will depend on a child's age and stage of development. In keeping with Gardner's theory of multiple intelligences, curiosity will also depend on their particular talents and abilities. For example, children who lean towards verbal or linguistic talents are normally avid talkers, like to play word games and enjoy listening to and telling stories. Children who are more mathematically talented are able to handle long chains of reasoning and like to know the reason for doing things. Tey can solve problems rapidly and ask lots of how and why questions. Some children might have musical talents and have a great sense of pitch, tone and rhythm. Tey can remember songs easily and can pick up melodies quickly. Children with visual or spatial talents have very active imaginations and can create complex mental images. Tey are able to place things in relationship to others and enjoy designing and decorating. These are only some examples of how children can difer greatly from one another. It is the role of the educator to develop and present activities that will keep them engaged and willing to explore new concepts and themes. This should, ideally, be done with the child's particular interests and talents in mind.

There are many and varied ways of stimulating a child's curiosity, some of which have been presented throughout this chapter. One of the most efective ways of engaging a child, however, is the creative use of questions.

Using Questions to Stimulate Curiosity and Learning

Questions can be used to make a child think about what they are doing and to assist them in reasoning through and solving problems. Diferent kinds of questions can be used for diferent results as outlined in the following table.

Type of question	*Examples*
Valuing questions	These questions can be used when a child is asked to express an opinion. For example: 'What do you think of …?' or 'How do you feel about …?' or 'Which of the two pictures do you like best?'
Information questions	These questions can be asked to encourage a child to research and find answers. For example: 'How does x work?' or 'What makes x go?' or 'How can flies walk on the ceiling?'
Creative questions	These questions will help a child to think 'outside the box' – to extend their normal way of thinking about things. For example: 'What would you do if x happened?' or 'How would you solve this problem?'
Reasoning questions	Ask these questions if you want a child to draw relationships of cause and effect or to compare or classify items. For example: 'Which of these things match?' or 'What is the difference between a paint brush and a pencil?'

Providing Opportunities to Concept Development

As children explore, their experiences gain in complexity. This fuels their development on a social, physical, emotional, and intellectual level. The more a child explores, the more they discover and learn.

As a child develops, you will need to challenge them intellectually and this ofen means introducing more complex puzzles and concepts for them to work with and explore. This can be achieved by making their tasks and activities more in-depth and by introducing projects for them to focus on.

Using Projects as a Tool

A project is a set of activities that aim to create an outcome over a specifed time. In early childhood education, a project can be started in consultation with the child concerning his or her interests or developmental needs (as defned by the carer or parents). The project takes shape over time as resources are made available and progress is made in the creation of the 'thing of interest'. You are able to interact throughout the project to monitor various areas of development and provide support and encouragement to the child to reinforce his or her commitment to the task.

A project allows the child to incrementally develop skills and knowledge as they draw from previous experiences and apply their new learning and understanding.

Depending on their stage of development, a child may be encouraged to demonstrate their progress by:

- talking with peers or adults
- drawing or writing about what they have discovered
- creating a sculpture or model
- acting out what they've learned in dramatic play or a role-play.

You must take care to facilitate, acknowledge, and comment on the child's self-review to foster ongoing exploration and evaluation.

References

Frensch, P. A., & Funke, J. (Eds.). (1995). *Complex problem solving: The European Perspective*. Hillsdale, NJ: Lawrence Erlbaum Associates.

Hayes, J. (1980). *The complete problem solver*. Philadelphia: The Franklin Institute Press.

Mayer, R. E. (1992). *Thinking, problem solving, cognition*. Second edition. New York: W. H. Freeman and Company.

Newell, A., & Simon, H. A. (1972). *Human problem solving*. Englewood Cliffs, NJ: Prentice-Hall.

Sternberg, R. J., & Frensch, P. A. (Eds.). (1991). *Complex problem solving: Principles and mechanisms*. Hillsdale, NJ: Lawrence Erlbaum Associates.

Wagner, R. K. (1991). Managerial problem solving. In R. J. Sternberg & P. A. Frensch (Eds.), *Complex problem solving: Principles and mechanisms* (pp. 159-183). Hillsdale, NJ: Lawrence Erlbaum Associates.

8

Psychological Type and Learning

This chapter focuses on the natural differences among students that need to be considered in the planning of instruction and for handling interpersonal relationships. By accounting for such differences we can not only retain the students we have, but also attract the nontraditional groups that are underrepresented in engineering.The personality instrument discussed in this chapter, the Myers-Briggs Type Indicator (MBTI), has proven to be a successful tool in engineering education for recognizing and accommodating these differences.

The essence of the theory behind the MBTI is that "much seemingly random variation in behavior is actually quite orderly and consistent, being due to basic differences in the way individuals prefer to use their perception and judgment". "Perception" refers to the ways that we process information or become aware of the world around us. "Judgment" has to do with the ways we make decisions on the basis of what has been perceived. These ideas are based on the theories of the Swiss psychologist Carl Jung and their application and extension by Katherine Briggs and Isabel Briggs Myers. The MBTI has been used in education and industry as well as career and marriage counseling to help identify personality types in order to improve communication and open the possibilities for learning. Such knowledge is very important for professors and beneficial for students.

An indicator, not a test, the MBTI is a self-reporting instrument which offers a forced-choice format between equally valuable alternatives. In answering the questions or responding to certain word-pairs, we can discover our preferred way of dealing with, and living in, the world. Intrinsic preferences, though possibly inborn, aren't always available to our conscious minds. The way we are raised and the situations we confront may force us to react in ways opposed to our inherent preferences. The MBTI allows us to arrive at a "reported" type and then examine the conclusion in light of our experiences, beliefs and feelings, all the time being free to accept or reject the result. Over the years, the MBTI has become the most widely used personality measure for non-psychiatric populations. What the MBTI does not do, however, is merely classify people. Type does not refer to something that is fixed, permanent. Each type has its own ways of reacting to situations, but no one is true to type all the time. As McCaulley et al. point out, good type development often involves responding in ways that one does not spontaneously prefer. "The word *type* as used here refers to a dynamic system with interacting parts and forces. The characteristics and attitudes that result from the interactions of these forces do differ, but the basic components are the same in every human being".

From Jung to The MBTI

The seminal work on type theory was done by Carl Gustav Jung, the Swiss psychologist and contemporary of Sigmund Freud. His study *Psychological Types* was published in 1921 after almost twenty years' work in treating individuals and discussing problems and solutions with colleagues, as well as "from a critique of [his] own psychological peculiarity". In his difficult yet eminently readable book, Jung looks at the problem of type in the history of classical and medieval thought as well as in biography, poetry, philosophy, and psychopathology.

An excellent biography of Katherine Cook Briggs and her daughter, Isabel Briggs Myers, is Frances Saunders' book; and *Gifts Differing* gives an excellent discussion of their theory. Katherine Cook Briggs was a lifelong student of the differences among individuals and how they relate to the way in which one functions in the world. In part her interest in personal differences grew out of her desire to be a writer and create fictional characters, and for this reason she was particularly interested in Jung's treatment of biography in his book.

Discovering Jung's work in the English translation in 1923, Briggs is alleged to have said, "This is it". Unfortunately, she was so impressed with Jung's work and terminology that she burned her own notes and adopted the latter's terminology. She shared this interest in personality with her daughter Isabel (later Isabel Briggs Myers) who continued studying type. With the onset of World War II, Myers desired "to do something that might help people understand each other and avoid destructive conflicts". She decided to find a way to put the theory to practical use and from this came the idea for a "type indicator." Her first task was to develop an item pool that would reflect the feelings and attitudes of the differing personality types as she and her mother had come to understand them. The first period of development involved item validation with friends and family and then collecting data on 5000 high school students and 5000 medical students. The second period began in 1956 when the Educational Testing Service (ETS) became the publisher. After the 1962 publication of the MBTI manual and form F, the popularity and use of the MBTI began to grow slowly. In 1975, Consulting Psychologists Press took over publication, and since then the use of the instrument has expanded greatly. It has now been translated into Japanese and Spanish, and is also being used in England and Australia. According to McCaulley, the fact "that similar career choices by the same types occur in disparate cultures suggests that Jung's theory taps some fundamentally important human functions that cut across cultural teaching."

Psychological Type: Attitudes and Functions

In *Psychological Types,* Jung postulated that everyone has a basic orientation to the world which indicates the directions in which energies or interests flow: to the outer world of people and events (extroversion, E) or to the inner world of ideas (introversion, I). He referred to this as an attitude toward the world. Either type, in the conscious aspects of life, processes information either through the senses (S) or by intuition (N) and makes decisions on the basis of this information either by logical, impersonal analysis (thinking,T), or on the basis of personal, subjective values (feeling, F). Jung regarded both thinking and feeling to be rational processes and so the term "feeling" here does not carry the common connotations associated with emotions. As to why there are four functions (S, N, T, F), not more or less, Jung (1971, pp. 540–41) says he arrived at that number on purely empirical grounds. Through sensation we establish what is present, with its meaning determined through thinking. Feeling tells us its value, with possibilities delineated by intuition. The jungian dichotomies are as follows:

Direction of energy/interest:	E or I
Perceiving functions:	S or N
Judging (decision-making) functions:	T or F

To these three Jungian pairs, Katherine Briggs added a fourth: a judging (J) or perceptive (P) orientation to the world. In her research she discovered that individuals tend to function primarily in either the perceiving or the judging mode. That is, some people (P) like to gather more and more information and adapt to situations as they arise; others (J) prefer to lead a more structured, ordered existence, making lists, and trying to control events.

A person's preferences are indicated by these dichotomies, but each person is free to use sensing or intuition, and, similarly, thinking or feeling. As with handwriting, anyone can write a signature using either the left or the right hand; however, most have a preference for one over the other and tend to develop the skill in one more than in the other. The four dichotomies (EI, SN, TF, JP) can be arranged in a four by four table or matrix, giving sixteen personality types from interactions.

Orientation to Life: Extroversion (E) And Introversion (I).

The first pair, extroversion and introversion, focuses on how one approaches the world. Ever since Jung first posited these descriptors of behavior, the terms have become part of the language and as used here they carry the standard psychological connotations. The outer-directed extrovert enjoys social contact and depends on interaction with others for personal satisfaction. The inward-looking introvert, on the other hand, tends to withdraw from such interactions, preferring quiet for concentration rather than the quick action of the extrovert. The easy communication of the extrovert is a problem for the introvert, who, preferring ideas, may have trouble communicating. In problem-solving, the extrovert tends to place greater weight on the situation and other people's views, whereas the introvert tends to focus more on the conceptual framework of the problem. No one is purely extroverted or introverted, though some individuals clearly may represent extremes of each type. Instead, the terms refer to preferred orientations. Anyone can exhibit both introverted and extroverted behavior. For example, an introverted teacher may approach a class with some fretfulness, mustering up all of his or her energy to begin the class, but once settled into the course, may feel comfortable and act the complete extrovert—within the confines of the class. Yet, the preferred orientation is that of a cautious introvert. Each person carries the capability of developing both orientations but by preference tends to develop one of them. The same is true of the other three function pairs. This is an important point to remember while reading about the MBTI. Myers and McCaulley caution that the Indicator is no substitute for good judgment and that the proper way to use it is as a stimulus to the user's insight.

Extrovert (E). (roughly 70 percent of the general population; about 33 percent of the engineering student population)

- Likes people.
- Likes action.
- Acts quickly.
- Communicates easily.
- Is applications-oriented.
- Feels energized by interaction with others.

Introvert (I). (30 percent of the general population; about 67 percent of the engineering student population)

- Prefers quiet for concentration.
- Likes ideas and concepts.
- Has trouble communicating.
- Relies on inner illumination.
- Prefers to work alone and is energized by doing so.

Perception or Becoming Aware: Sensing (S) And Intuition (N)

The second pair, sensing (S) and intuition (N), characterizes the perceptive function, or how one becomes aware of, or perceives, the world. The sensing person leans toward working with known facts rather than looking for possibilities and relationships as the intuitive person often prefers to do. He or she also tends toward step-by-step analysis and prefers to work by established methods. Intuitives favor inspiration and may work in bursts, quickly jumping to conclusions or solutions. Unlike sensing individuals, they are impatient with routine and may appear to be more imprecise. Using their imaginations, they see possibilities, whereas sensing individuals use their senses and work through the powers of observation. To a sensing type, soundness, common sense, and accuracy characterize real intelligence, which for an intuitive is shown by flashes of imagination and insight in grasping complexities. Attitudes characteristically developed from the preference for intuition include a reliance on sudden insight, an interest in the new, and a preference for learning through an intuitive grasp of meanings. A synopsis of the two types shows the following.

*Sensing (S). (*70 percent of the general population; 53 percent of engineering student population)

- Uses senses and powers of observation.
- Works through step-by-step analysis.
- Likes precision.
- Prefers established methods.
- Is patient with routine.
- Works steadily.

Intuition (N). (30 percent of the general population; 47 percent of the engineering student population)

- Is imaginative, sees possibilities.
- Relies on inspiration.
- May be imprecise.
- Jumps to solutions (is quick).
- Works in bursts.
- Dislikes routine.

Decision Making: Thinking (T) And Feeling (F)

Once all the data are in, whether by sensing or by intuition, one must then decide how to process the information and come to a decision. A person who prefers to be logical and analytical, weighing facts impersonally and objectively, shows a preference for thinking (T) as the mode of decision making; someone who bases decisions on subjective, personal values and standards uses feeling (F).

Both poles are accessible to everyone, and often most individuals move freely between them; however, each person has a preferred mode.

Thinking (T). (60 percent male/40 female in general population; 74 percent of engineering students: 77 percent male/61percent female)

- Is objectively analytical.
- Works through cause and effect.
- Tends to be logical.
- Tends to be tough-minded.
- Tends to be impartial.

Feeling (F). (40 percent male/60 percent female in general population; 26 percent of engineering students: 23 percent male and 39 percent female)

- Understands people.
- Desires harmony.
- Stresses interpersonal skills.

Living In The World: Judgment (J) And Perception (P)

The fourth preference pair is used to identify the way an individual functions in the world. The previous sections considered the attitudes (E and I) and the functions (S, N, T, and F) which Jung used to categorize conscious mental processes. In an elaboration of Jung's ideas, Briggs and Myers added a further dimension: the attitude a person takes toward the world. This attitude is based on the person's relationship to or preference for the functions of perceiving and judging. An individual who prefers to use a perceiving function (S or N) to run his or her life tends toward being open to new perceptions, adapting to situations, and in general taking in information. This flexibility often leads to minimal planning and organization. For someone who uses a judging function (T or F) to conduct his or her outer life, the impetus is toward planning, organization, and closure. Thus, the JP preference indicates how an individual prefers to live in the outer world. If you are curious as to which of these applies to you, just think about the way you plan a vacation. Are you content to fly somewhere and then to take it from there, making plans as you go (P)? Or are you appalled by the thought of such a trip, preferring to schedule hotels, routes, stopovers, and so forth, well beforehand (J)? Do you find yourself taking in more and more information before finally writing that report—often at the eleventh hour (P)? Or do you plan it and work on it section by section, day by day (J)? As with all the pairs, both ways of living in the world are of course accessible to the individual. And even someone given to doing jobs at the last minute may find him- or herself having to be very much the schedule maker and planner in structuring family plans. So both choices are available. The dynamic interplay of all of the preferences (EI, SN, TF, JP) leads to sixteen combinations or types.

Judging (J). (50 percent of the general population; 61 percent of engineering students)

- Prefers to live in a planned, orderly way.
- Likes to regulate and control events.

Perceptive (P). (50 percent of the general population; 39 percent of engineering students)

- Prefers to be flexible, spontaneous.
- Likes to understand and adapt to events.

Dominant and Auxiliary Processes

According to type theory, children are born with a predisposed preference for some functions over others. Lynch maintains that the dominant function is usually reflected by kindergarten age. In engineering terms, they are hardwired for a given type. This preference leads to fuller development of the preferred function and greater competence in it. A preference for sensing, for example, leads to the development of characteristics commonly seen in a practical-minded sensing individual. At the same time, the opposite pole of the preference tends to be ignored; in the above example a sensing child gives less priority to intuition and thus develops along quite different lines from another child who prefers intuition. It is apparent then that environment ("software programming") plays a key role in one's development, either reinforcing or demotivating development along certain lines. This "falsification" of type can lead one to develop a less preferred function but overall still not feel in control or confident in his or her abilities. In good type development each person uses all four processes, but one process becomes the leading or dominant.

In the literature about type, the roles of the dominant and the auxiliary are often compared to those of a general and an aide. In an extrovert, the general (dominant function) is at the forefront making decisions and taking the lead, for all the world to see. As a result, we say that for an extrovert,

"What you see is what you get." For an introvert, however, the aide (auxiliary function) stands as an intermediary with the outside world while the general makes plans inside a tent. The introvert, who focuses on the inner world, is difficult to know until one gets close enough to the individual. The dominant function remains hidden, which is why introverts are often misunderstood.

To see how the dominant and auxiliary functions are determined, consider an INFP and an ENFP. For the ENFP, the fourth pair (that is, the choice between judment and perception which indicates how the person lives in the world), here the P, indicates that this person prefers to conduct his or her outer life in the perceptive mode. So we only have to look back to the perceiving slot (the second letter, here N, intuition) to find the function used by this person in the outer world. If asked to characterize this individual's type, another person would see the intuitive aspects. Now, by definition, extroverts show the world their strongest function; therefore, the N in this case is the dominant function. For the ENFP the dominant is extroverted intuition; the auxiliary is a balancing introverted feeling (F) (introverted because the auxiliary always balances the dominant, which here is extroverted), with thinking as the third and sensing as the fourth or least developed. So for an ENFP:

Dominant:	N
Auxiliary:	F
Third:	T
Fourth:	S

For an INFP the P indicates the person extroverts his or her perceptive function. Thus a judging function is dominant since an introvert's strength is within. The other perceptive function is third, and the fourth, or least developed, function, is judging (T). Thus,

Dominant:	F	(introverted feeling)
Auxiliary:	N	(extroverted intuition—what world sees)
Third:	S	(sensing)
Fourth:	T	(thinking—least developed function)

These individuals trust introverted feeling the most and use it the most in directing their lives, with intuition in support of the thinking. To the world, they appear intuitive. Like most introverts they are easily misunderstood because their strength is inside, not as open to the world as the strength of an extrovert.

Good Type Development

Type development is seen as a lifelong process of increasing mastery or command over the functions of perception and judgment that one prefers, and corresponding but lesser development of the less interesting but essential processes. Myers and McCaulley summarize the process :

- Development of excellence in the favorite, dominant process.
- Adequate but not equal development of the auxiliary for balance.
- Eventual admission of the least developed processes to conscious, purposeful use in the service of the dominant process, even though this use may require the dominant and auxiliary to temporarily relinquish control in consciousness so that the third or fourth function can become more conscious.
- Use of each of the functions for the tasks for which they are best fitted.

Applications of the MBTI in Engineering Education

The differences described by type theory are familiar parts of everyday life, and so the theory can be used for a wide range of applications: education, counseling, career guidance, situations involving teamwork issues, and communication. Any university counseling or psychological center can provide the necessary testing services, or individuals can be certified through the training sessions such as those offered by the Association for Psychological Type (APT), the Center for Applications of Psychological Type (CAPT), or the Consulting Psychologists Press. Thomas offers some preliminary results on "rapid MBTI self-classification."

Jensen and DiTiberio extensively examine its relevance in the teaching of writing. Provost and Anchors discuss the uses of the MBTI in higher education. McCaulley *et al.* consider the results of the ASEE-MBTI Engineering Consortium of eight universities. In the MBTI manual Myers and McCaulley give numerous rankings of students and colleges by means of various preferences. Schurr, Ruble, and Henriksen look at the effects of different admissions practices on the MBTI and gender types. Several authors discuss the MBTI and problem solving, with McCaulley offering a jungian model. Yokomoto et al. discuss improvement of problem-solving performance and also consider student attitudes toward ethical dilemmas.

Three ethical dilemmas were presented to students, who were required to make a decision on what further action, if any, might be taken to resolve them. Analysis of the results showed several biases arising from personality differences, with feeling types recommending action more strongly than thinking types in one situation. Campbell and Kain investigated whether some types prefer certain forms of information presentation in problem solving. They found that the most time-efficient types (N and J) were also the least accurate, similarly for NT's and NF's. S, P, SF, and ST types tended to be more accurate but took longer to achieve their accuracy. Campbell and Kain conclude that type plays a small role in a person's preference for presentation form, but a larger role in the accuracy and time efficiency of problem solving.

Teaching Methods

Lawrence synthesizes learning style research involving the MBTI. The MBTI can be used to develop teaching methods to meet the needs of different types, especially on the sensing-intuition dichotomy. As McCaulley points out, S and N types approach problems from opposite directions: S moves from the specific to the general; N from the "grand design to the details." She then makes a telling point: "In fields with relatively equal numbers of S and N students, such as engineering, the faculty have more of a challenge maintaining student interest than in fields, such as counseling, where students and faculty are more similar".

Smith, Irey, and McCaulley found that personality traits influence student attitude and performance in self-paced instruction. They further note that a major weakness in college teaching appears to arise from a teacher's and student's lack of recognition of each other's differences, which gives rise to the need for different learning activities. Self-paced instruction, according to the authors, can be made more effective if instructional modules or packages are designed which fit different styles of student perception and judgment. Provost, Carson, and Beidler studied a sample of professor of the year finalists to see how outstanding teachers use their type preferences. This limited study doesn't conclude that most outstanding teachers will have a certain preference or be a certain type; however, it does show that type affects teaching style, assumptions one might make about teaching, and attitudes about what aspects of teaching are seen as rewarding. These teachers have been able to relate to other types and to appreciate the inherent diversity. From the students' standpoint, Rodman et al. looked at the self-perception of engineering students' preferred learning style and related it to the MBTI. Among other conclusions, their work shows that in engineering education major differences among types occur in the sensing and intuition classifications.

The sensing-intuition (SN) dichotomy is perhaps the most important one for an engineering educator, both from the standpoint of the instructor and from that of the students (especially as sensing relates to mastering a body of knowledge and the corresponding skills central to a field of practice). Intuition has to do with the ability to think complexly and contextually. The percentages of type in the general and university populations alone tell a significant tale. Sensing types predominate in the general population; intuitives, in a university environment. More college professors are intuitive types than sensing types, and they tend to write exams that more frequently fit their own type. If memorization and recall are important, sensing and judging types will perform better; if hypothesizing and essay tests are required, intuitive students will have an advantage. Aptitude tests are also designed to measure knowledge in the domain of introverted intuitives (IN). The data show that introverts consistently score higher than extroverts on the SAT-Verbal. Intuitives also consistently score higher than sensing types. The sensing-intuition differences, according to Myers and McCaulley, are greater than the extroversion-introversion differences.

In the classroom, the thinking-feeling (TF) preference appears to have less importance than the others, but it can be argued that a predominance of thinking types in a class could "freeze out" the few feeling types. Is it possible that feeling types self-select out of engineering because of the more impersonal emphasis of the predominant thinking types in engineering? One colleague has suggested that it might be easier to teach ethics if students were more interested in human motivations (feeling types), rather than being concerned with building the best device (ST) or developing the most elegant theory (NT). Finally, it is important to remember that type theory does not make judgments on intelligence: All types can succeed in any area, and all types are represented in every area. What is important is that every type can learn to survive in the academic world. Paying attention to type differences and taking them into account in teaching goes a long way toward promoting such success. The fact that certain types predominate in certain careers says more about a type's attraction to the field than whether he or she will succeed in it. Once an individual has gotten past the educational barriers to a given field, being different from the prevailing type can be an advantage since he or she will see things that others miss.

Motivation

The MBTI can also be used to help students if the instructor understands the ways that different types are motivated. An instructor can help students gain control over their own learning and thereby reach more students. Even something as simple as a phrasing can be important. For example, feeling types respond better to a question that is phrased "How do you feel about... ?" whereas the thinking type prefers "What do you think... ?" Also, the quickness of the N types may discourage an S type, and in a classroom the quicker student is often more praised and honored; the "slower" student quickly forms an impression that he or she is lacking what the "best" students have. We use quotation marks to indicate that intelligence is not the consideration here. In the long run, the "slower" but more thorough and accurate S may be more correct and/or successful. And if not demotivated by the instructor, such a student may be a valuable addition to the class.

Curriculum and Materials

The MBTI can be used to analyze curricula, methods, media, and materials in light of the needs of different types. This should be done in conjunction with the other aspects of learning theories, such as that of Kolb. And it can be used to provide extracurricular activities that will meet the needs of all types

Interpersonal Relationships

The MBTI can also be used to help teachers and administrators work together more constructively. Type data from one sample show that administrators tend to be heavily J types [86 percent in Lawrence's sample]. As in other areas, such as personnel cases in industry, awareness of type differences can lead to a more harmonious working environment. On a personal level, knowledge of type can be very helpful in counseling. Carey, Hamilton, and Shanklin use type theory to look at the relationship between communication style and roommate satisfaction. The differences between judging types and perceptive types can often lead to conflicts. What a perceptive sees as a strength in the desire to have complete information or knowledge before proceeding, a judging person often sees as procrastination. And what a judging type sees as decisive action, a perceptive may see as close-minded and precipative behavior. Differences on the extroversion-introversion and thinking-feeling dichotomies can also lead to problems. From type theory, interpersonal competence is related to extroversion and feeling. The focus of extroverts is on people and the external world; that of feeling types is on the effects of their actions and decisions on themselves and others.

In engineering, a great deal of work is done in teams. Clearly, it's important that the members work together harmoniously. A good preparation for this takes place in undergraduate laboratories. Accounting for type differences and making students aware of each other's different strengths can go a long way toward easing the tension that arises when, say, a perceptive can't put an end to a literature search which his or her judging partner needs for the next day's oral report. Giving and receiving criticism in these situations can also depend on the individual's preferred way of functioning.

Student Retention

Retention and attrition are complex issues which every college or university must face. Godleski considers use of the MBTI to increase retention of underachieving college students. His preliminary results showed that there was no difference in extroversion or introversion, but a significantly larger number of sensing over intuitive types and perceptive over judging types who were in academic difficulty. Provost found type patterns among freshmen experiencing first-year difficulties, with analyses showing overrepresentation of TP combinations. Schurr and Ruble found that high school performance and the judging preference (J) were the best predictors of college performance. This report was a follow-up to their 1986 study which followed an entire entering college class. McCaulley describes a study at the Fenn College of Engineering at Cleveland State University comparing freshman who wanted to become engineers and seniors who successfully completed the program. McCaulley offers some reasons for this pattern :

1 People learn in different ways. If the faculty teaches one way, they will favor some types over others.

2 Faculty members serve as role models for students, but there appear to be no data to indicate that engineering faculty are appropriate models for engineers in industry. Students may not realize this.

3 Choice of textbooks (and programmed learning courses) can favor the learning pattern of some types and cause difficulties for others.

Staiger also uses type to identify subsets of electrical engineering students who need special attention from the point of view of retention and maintains that curriculum redesign should include teaching styles that will accommodate diverse learning styles, including guided design, cooperative learning, and developmental instruction. Kalsbeek offers a conceptual model for understanding student attrition. His comment offers an appropriate close to this section: By relating type data to student attrition, educators can consider how different types of students interact with types of academic environments and thereby respond appropriately to the challenges posed.

Distributions of Types in Engineering

All sixteen types are represented in all areas of engineering; however, even the quickest glance reveals that certain types self-select into and are retained very markedly in engineering. For example, the corners of the table are strongly over-represented—what has come to be called the "tough-minded" TJ types; what is missing, relatively, is participation by the feeling types. McCaulley raises the question "Are engineering schools preparing their students adequately for the 'people complexities' of the profession?" That feeling types are in such a minority may indicate that the answer is no. It is these groups which tend to drop or transfer out of engineering. One speculation worth exploring is whether underrepresented groups in engineering, such as minorities and women. If it is true, as the data to date indicate, that women classify more as being F than T, it could be that they view the heavy T orientation of engineering as cold and unfriendly. If the ranks of engineering are to be filled in the future, and clearly the standard pool of potential engineering candidates of the past is dwindling, it is these groups that educators will have to look to and encourage.

The report of McCaulley *et al.* with the ASEE-MBTI Engineering Consortium provides data showing the breakdown of engineering students by type preference. Among their results were the following.

1 Engineering students markedly prefer thinking (74 percent) and judging (61 percent), with the stereotypical engineer falling into the TJ group.

In the consortium data, this group accounted for almost half of the sample (males, 49 percent; females, 44 percent; with the males more often introverted, 56 percent). One would expect all majors to have the same proportion of each type (with 25 percent in each group if the distribution was equal); the fact that the opposite is true gives evidence to the usefulness of the theory.

2 Male engineering students differ in type from female engineering students. In engineering, 77 percent of the males were T, whereas 61 percent of thepercent), geological (69 percent), computer (69 percent) and general (70 percent) engineering. Engineering students differ from other college students. Compared with a sample group of college freshmen, engineering students are more often introvert, thin females were T. The proportions of S and N were about the same.

3 Engineering disciplines attract different types of students. The fields with the highest proportion of extroverts were industrial (56 percent), computer (55 percent), petroleum (51 percent) and mineral (51 percent). Introverts were more frequent in aerospace (61 percent), geological (60 percent) and electrical (59 percent) engineering. The fields with the highest proportion of the practical sensing types were civil (69 percent), industrial (61 percent), mechanical (61 percent), and mining (60 percent). Intuitives were frequent in geological (62 percent), aerospace (60 percent) and metallurgical (54 percent). As noted above, all fields had a majority of T types, with the highest proportions in aerospace (82 percent), electrical (80 percent), mechanical (80 percent) and physics (76 percent). The fields with the lowest proportion of T types were undecided students (68

5 All types survived to year two, but atypical types had lower retention rates. Judging types were slightly, but significantly, more likely to be retained (entering students were 63 percent J, retained were 65 percent J, $p < 0.01$). The practical SJ types were 34 percent of entering students but were 40 percent of those remaining. Note that there were no differences in retention between male and female, and feeling types were as likely to persist as their more analytical T counterparts.

Implications of Consortium Study

The implications drawn from the consortium study merit serious consideration.

1. Clearly, and one might say expectedly, many logical, analytical, and decisive types of students are drawn to engineering; however, overemphasis on these characteristics tends to result in an underemphasis on skills related to listening, understanding, and getting things done through people. Since a great part of engineering work depends on communication and teamwork, it is important that faculty stress the importance of these skills and even teach them specifically (which of course will be appreciated by the extroverted, feeling, and intuitive types).
2. Less typical engineering students, extroverts and feeling types, learn better if given frequent feedback and appreciation; unfortunately, the types which are attracted to the field are the least likely to give such feedback. So it is up to the faculty to teach and model such behavior, which in turn will encourage students to do the same in their own work. Type knowledge can also help in identifying behavioral patterns and needs that may be beneficial in advising students.
3. Since the numbers of sensing (S) and intuitive (N) types are roughly equal, the implication, though debatable, is that half of the students learn best deductively, and about half, inductively. The sensing types benefit from clear instructions, starting with their practical experiences, and with new material presented with a step-by-step approach. Intuitives, on the other hand, prefer theoretical principles first, followed by mastery of details through problem solving. In order to reach the greatest number of students effectively, instructors must keep these differences in mind. Tests and other measures of evaluation should also be varied so that different types are given a fair chance.

Difficulties with Psychological Testing

The MBTI is prone to the same kinds of problems that plague any psychological test:

1. A student may not understand a question because of phrasing or vocabulary. Though not likely applicable for an engineering student population, the MBTI requires at least eighth grade language skills (for children, the Murphy-Meisgeier Type Indicator is used for grades two through eight).
2. The wrong box may accidentally be marked.

3 Students may mark what they feel they "ought" to think or may try to "psych-out" the tester. Unconscious biases may also affect the results.

4 Current environmental stress may change one's answers temporarily.

5 Results may be misinterpreted. With the MBTI a little learning can be a dangerous thing, for it's easy to turn the occasion into a parlor game and make it little more than a horoscope reading. Accurate interpretation is assured if a qualified tester is present such as a psychologist, a counselor, or someone certified to administer the MBTI.

6 Reliability. The MBTI is reliable, but people can change. Times of stress may lead to differing results, and over a period of years growth may be reflected in a change of type. However, such changes are expected and predicted within type theory. For example, as one enters middle age, it's common for compensatory development to occur in the less preferred functions. Although one's type doesn't change, the way it is experienced and reported may change and give different MBTI results. Seventy-five percent of people who have retaken the MBTI after one to six years have not changed or have done so in only one category. More information can be found in the reliability studies reported in of the manual by Myers and McCaulley. Hammer and Yeakley conducted a study to investigate the relationship between "true" type and reported type.

7 Validity. The MBTI has good face validity. The results seem true to the test taker. Does the MBTI measure what it is trying to measure? This is a problem with all psychological tests: What they try to measure is usually based on a psychological theory. Thus, is the underlying theory valid? If it is, does the test accurately measure this?

The Myers-Briggs Type Indicator offers engineering educators a workable instrument with which to meet the changing needs of engineering education. Measuring preferences as indicated by the students themselves, it is not meant to measure the strength of a trait, as other psychological instruments do. Consequently, it is fairly simple to implement and interpret without requiring a staff psychologist within an engineering department. Attention to differences also makes tremendous common sense as the diverse needs of a new population of students must be met before they can succeed in engineering. We can increase participation in the field as well as increase productivity. Quite possibly, as McCaulley points out, use of the indicator may help move students toward greater maturity of cognitive development in Perry's model. Finally, to stress that engineering educators must acknowledge that students learn differently, Staiger concludes: "It would help to have the phrase 'equal opportunity for learning' included in all university admission statements as a constant reminder".

References

Jung, C. G., (1971). *Psychological Types,* Princeton University Press, Princeton, NJ.

Kalsbeek, D., (1987). "Campus retention: The MBTI in institutional self-studies," in Provost, J., and S. Anchors (Eds.), *Applications of the Myers-Briggs Type Indicator in Higher Education*, Consulting Psychologists Press, Palo Alto, CA,, pp. 31-63.

Lawrence, G., (1982). *People Types and Tiger Stripes: A Practical Guide to Learning Styles*, 2nd ed., Center for Applications of Psychological Type, Gainesville, FL.

Lawrence, G., (1984)."A synthesis of learning style research involving MBTI," *J. Psychol. Type*, 8, 2

Lynch, A. Q., (1987)."Type development and student development," in Provost, J., and S. Anchors (Eds.), *Applications of the Myers-Briggs Type Indicator in Higher Education*, Consulting Psychologists Press, Palo Alto, CA, pp. 5–29.

McCaulley, M., (April 1976). "Psychological types in engineering: Implications for teaching," *Eng. Educ.*, 66, 729

9

Learning Theories

Learning theories are conceptual frameworks that describe how information is absorbed, processed, and retained during learning. Learning brings together cognitive, emotional, and environmental influences and experiences for acquiring, enhancing, or making changes in one's knowledge, skills, values, and world views.

There are three main categories of learning theory: behaviorism, cognitivism, and constructivism. Behaviorism focuses only on the objectively observable aspects of learning. Cognitive theories look beyond behavior to explain brain-based learning. And constructivism views learning as a process in which the learner actively constructs or builds new ideas or concepts.

Merriam and Caffarella highlight four approaches or orientations to learning: Behaviourist, Cognitivist, Humanist, and Social/Situational. These approaches involve contrasting ideas as to the purpose and process of learning and education - and the role that educators may take

Informal theories of education breaks down the learning process, learning authentically and with practicality. One theory deals with whether learning should take place as a building of concepts toward an overall idea, or the understanding of the overall idea with the details filled in later. In Marzano's restructuring knowledge, the informal curriculum promotes the use of prior knowledge to help students gain big ideas and concept understanding. This theory states that new knowledge cannot be told to students, but rather the students' current knowledge must be challenged. By challenging students' current ideas, students can adjust their ideas to more closely resemble actual theories or concepts. By using this method students gain the big idea they're taught and later are more willing to learn and keep the specifics of the concept or theory taught. This theory further aligns with the studies of Brown and Ryoo, who support that teaching concepts and the language of a subject should be split into multiple steps.

Other informal learning concerns regard sources of motivation for learning. Deci argues that intrinsic motivation creates a more self-regulated learner yet schools undermine intrinsic motivation. This is not ideal for learning. Critics argue that average students learning in isolation perform significantly lower than those learning with collaboration and mediation. Students learn through talk, discussion, and argumentation.

Transformative learning theory explains the process of constructing and appropriating new and revised interpretations of the meaning of an experience in the world. Transformative learning is the cognitive process of effecting change in a frame of reference although it is recognized that important emotional changes are often involved. These frames of reference define our view of the world and we have a tendency as adults to reject or deem unworthy any ideas that do not ascribe to our particular values, associations, concepts,etc. Our frames of reference are composed of two dimensions: habits of mind and points of view. Habits of mind, such as ethnocentrism, are more fixed and influence our point of view and the resulting thoughts or feelings associated with them, whereas points of view may change over time as a result of influences such as reflection, appropriation and feedback. Transformative learners utilize discourse as a means of critically examination and reflection "devoted to assessing reasons presented in support of competing interpretations, by critically examining evidence, arguments, and alternative points of view." When circumstances permit, transformative learners move toward a frame of reference that is more inclusive, discriminating, self-reflective, and integrative of experience. Transformative learning leads to autonomous and responsible thinking which is essential for full citizenship in democracy and for moral decision making in situations of rapid change.

Constructivism and The Scientific Learning Cycle

What makes students go through the agony of such reconstructing? The answer appears to be the disequilibrium caused by new data which cannot be explained by the old model, and the inability to solve required problems.

Bodner notes that many students find mathematical arguments and lectures with little discussion insufficient reason to discard the pre-newtonian model. Experiments with an almost frictionless system (such as a dry ice puck) are required to make students revise their model of the world. The inconsistencies between a student's model of the world and these new data should be forcefully pointed out. The second step is the availability of a plausible and understandable new concept or model which can eliminate the disequilibrium by explaining the new data. The student will restructure or assimilate new data only if accommodation fails and he or she is motivated to reconcile anomalies and reduce inconsistencies.

This example illustrates several important points about the constructivistic theory. Since the pre-newtonian model has been reinforced by years of practice where it worked, this knowledge structure is securely lodged in the brain. Removing any entrenched knowledge structure will be difficult. Thus, an extended period of time focused on Newton's laws is required both in and out of class, which helps to explain why learning new material is often slow. Frequent and timely feedback on mistakes helps to strengthen the necessary but not sufficient disequilibrium. Since forming new knowledge structures is difficult, students must be motivated. Direct contact with faculty can have a very positive effect on reorganization of the knowledge structure, particularly for students who identify with authority figures. The reorganization is aided by presenting information in hierarchical form with explicitly stated rules for generating hierarchies. Learning new material in a form which is easy to recall from memory is aided if students are given objectives which help them key on important material and if the material is presented in a well-organized fashion.

The usual lecture-homework sequence requires formal operations. Students still in the concrete operational stage in physics have difficulty revising their knowledge structures. For those in this stage, the concrete operations of the laboratory can be instrumental in helping them accept the new organization of knowledge. The laboratory exercise has other advantages as well. In the laboratory the student must be active, unlike in a lecture where a passive approach is allowed and often encouraged. Reconstruction requires active mental effort by the student. The laboratory is also often a group activity which encourages students to discuss their understanding of physics actively, and the experience provides support from the group. Finally, this example helps to explain why beginning physics is widely considered to be the most difficult first-year course. Many students are overwhelmed by the need to use formal reasoning to revise well-entrenched commonsense knowledge structures quickly and totally in a large class which often appears unfriendly.

It is interesting to compare the constructivist view of learning with the traditional view of knowledge which is implicitly assumed by many professors. In the traditional view knowledge exists independent of the individual. The mind is a *tabula rasa,* a blank tablet, upon which a picture of reality can be painted. If the student is attentive, learning occurs when the teacher unloads his or her almost perfect picture of reality through well-designed and well-presented lectures. Most experienced professors can attest that this model does not work for most students. Unfortunately, the traditional model focuses on the delivery system and not on the learner. Or, in computer language, the focus is on output devices and not input devices. The minds of the learners are not blank tablets upon which the teacher can write at will. The constructivist theory says the tablets are not initially blank and only the individual can do the writing. The traditional delivery system, the noninteractive lecture, satisfies the conditions of the traditional theory, but not the conditions of the constructivist theory. Fortunately, lectures can be modified so that the conditions necessary for learning are satisfied.

There are exercises and homework assignments professors can use to help students develop a knowledge structure. One useful assignment for every book chapter or section of the course is the development of a *key relations chart.* A key relations chart lists and diagrams the key ideas, equations, relations, definitions, and so forth, on a single page. The instructor can first illustrate this procedure by handing out his or her own chart for a chapter; then students can be required to do the same for homework. The chart can be evaluated for accuracy, completeness, and conciseness. Finally, the assignment is no longer made, but students are urged to continue developing the charts. Some professors allow students to consult key relation charts during tests. Since the preparation of such a chart is a useful exercise, this is an interesting alternative to open book tests.

A related exercise is to have small groups of students develop a *memory board,* which is similar to a key relations chart but is significantly more complete and is prepared as a group exercise. It can include more equations, rules, interrelationships, and problem-solving hints. Construction of a memory board is a group activity, which makes it useful for support and motivation, particularly for the extroverts in the class. Working in groups also provides social pressure for students to change constructs which appear to be incorrect.

A third related exercise is to have individual students or groups of students develop *concept maps* or *networks*. A concept map or network visually represents the relationship between concepts, usually two-dimensionally. Both the hierarchical relationships and the key cross-links between concepts are shown. Concept maps are complementary to key relations charts and memory boards since the concept map does not give equations, definitions, or ideas. It shows the relations between concepts without full explanation of the concept. Since it is a visual representation, a concept map is often fairly easy to remember. Students need to be taught how to construct concept maps and then encouraged to develop them on their own. Smith et al. illustrate a scoring model for evaluating concept maps.

Constructivism can help to explain how individuals solve problems. Problem solving appears to require both a general problem-solving strategy and specific knowledge. For routine problems, the specific knowledge structure is probably sufficient since it includes a pattern for solving routine problems. When confronted with unusual problems, the solver finds that no pattern exists for solving them. General problem-solving heuristics help one to start reconstructing the knowledge structure to solve the problem. Without specific content knowledge the general procedures are insufficient. Thus, engineering professors need to teach content and procedures.

Piaget's ideas and constructivism have led to a theory of how to teach science which is known as the *scientific learning cycle*. (In the literature this is simply called the *learning cycle*. We have added the word "scientific" to differentiate it from Kolb's learning cycle.) This method was independently developed by Robert Karplus in physics and Chester Lawson in biology. It has been extensively used and tested in science education at a variety of school levels. There is considerable experimental evidence that the scientific learning cycle is more effective in teaching science than are the more traditional methods.

In the exploration phase, students explore new phenomena with minimal guidance; for example, given a new mechanical linkage or a new circuit, their assignment can be to determine how it works. In this phase they discover for themselves some of the patterns and concepts involved. The exploration can be done individually or in groups.

In the second phase, called term introduction, invention, conceptual invention, or concept introduction, the professor introduces terms and definitions. Students are encouraged to use these new terms to describe the patterns as completely as possible. The professor then fills in the missing parts of the pattern to give a complete scientific picture. This phase can be accomplished through lecture, readings, video, guided discussion, and so forth.

In the third phase, concept application, concept expansion, or idea expansion, students apply the new ideas, terms, and patterns to new examples. For instance, if the exploration phase involves development of a new physical law, then the law can be applied in new ways. This phase can involve homework, group discussions, or laboratory.

Although developed originally for use with laboratory manipulations in the exploration phase, the scientific learning cycle can be modified for other types of experiences. For example, the exploration phase can involve a computer simulation game which allows students to explore the simulated properties of some process or device. Alternatively, students can explore through video, slides, or even a lecture-question format. The key is to have students discover concepts on their own instead of being "spoon-fed."

The scientific learning cycle follows the ideas of constructivism. The exploration phase uses experiences (often concrete) to present data which cannot be explained by the students' existing knowledge structures. Students are encouraged to develop new knowledge structures by assimilation or accommodation, and the teacher ensures that this information is encoded with the correct terms. The concept application phase helps to organize the new knowledge structures.

The scientific learning cycle can easily be adapted to engineering education if appropriate laboratory equipment or computer simulation games are available. Adoption of the learning cycle to lecture-style classes is more problematic but is certainly possible. Demonstrations in front of an entire class can represent a concrete chance to explore, although with less freedom than with individual laboratory equipment. Exploration can also take place in lectures if the instructor describes phenomena and then has the students "experiment" by asking questions. The instructor has to be careful to allow them to discover concepts on their own. This approach may seem less efficient than the traditional lecture, but if efficiency is defined as student learning per amount of time, then the scientific learning cycle is more efficient.

Learning and Teaching Styles

Individual preferences for learning and teaching are varied. Since mismatches can cause problems, professors should understand these styles.

Dichotomous Styles

Many investigators have described dichotomies in learning styles. The Meyers-Briggs scheme includes the sensing-intuition dichotomy, while Belenky et al. introduce the dichotomy between separate and connected knowing into Perry's scheme. In addition, both Piaget and Perry note the dichotomy between rote memorization and true learning. Other ways of looking at dichotomous learning styles are briefly discussed below.

Reflection versus impulsivity measures the tendency either to reflect over possible answers or to impulsively select a solution. This appears to be a relatively stable trait, but individuals can be taught either to slow down or to speed up. Students who lean toward impulsivity need to be taught to slow down so that they at least read all the possible answers. Students who reflect for such a length of time that they either become immobilized or take an excessively long time on tests can become a bit more impulsive. When people live or work together for a long period, they tend to approach each other on this dichotomy (that is, some learning occurs).

Information processing can be either deep or shallow. Deep processors learn the meaning and connections of ideas, whereas shallow processors tend to learn in terms of symbols and by memorization. For example, a deep processor learns the meaning of an equation and is able to use the equation if the symbols are changed.

A shallow processor learns the equation in terms of symbols. If the meaning of symbols is changed, the shallow processor may have considerable difficulty in using the equation. Most students are capable of both types of processing. The professor, through homework and tests, exerts considerable control over which type they use. If the homework and tests emphasize rote learning, then shallow processing is reinforced. This is probably a good reason for not requiring the memorization of a large number of equations.

Students in the concrete operational stage of development or on the dualistic levels of Perry's model may not be able to do deep processing, since deep processing skills appear fairly late in the developmental process.

Another learning style dichotomy involves deductive versus inductive learners. Deductive reasoning starts with general principles and then deduces consequences from these general principles. For example, a variety of specific equations can be deduced from very general equations such as Maxwell's equations or the Navier-Stokes equations. Inductive reasoning starts with specifics and then proceeds to induce generalities. Inductive reasoning may appear to be a slower way to present new material, but it is the natural learning style. The inductive reasoning process is the natural way to construct a knowledge structure in a new area and is the style used in the scientific learning cycle. Inductive reasoning can be used by individuals at any level of development, whereas deductive reasoning requires that the individual be in the formal operational stage. When students are seeing the material for the second time, deductive reasoning is a very effective presentation style. Since a preliminary knowledge structure exists in this case, they have something on which to build their deductions. The apparent success of deductive reasoning in these cases has seduced many professors into employing deductive reasoning at all times. Introductory textbooks are much easier for students to understand if they are written in an inductive style, starting with fairly specific simple cases and building to generalities. A deductive style may be advantageous for advanced textbooks where students are seeing the material for the second or third time. At Arizona State University Anderson found that engineering students preferred an inductive style, while professors preferred to teach deductively. Clearly, there is a mismatch.

Field-independent versus field-sensitive learning represents another useful dichotomy for understanding the dynamics of teaching and learning. Field-independent individuals are less cognizant of the surroundings or field when they are working on a given task. For instance, these individuals can study effectively in a crowded, noisy college union. Field-independent individuals are more likely to be autonomous, and they often self-select into analytical fields such as engineering, mathematics, and science. Field-sensitive individuals are strongly influenced by authority figures and peer groups. They tend to be more people-oriented and are often good at working with others because they are aware of subtle messages. Achievement in a course does not appear to correlate with this dichotomy, but attitude and survival in a curriculum probably do. Groups which are underrepresented in engineering, women and some minorities, have a large percentage of field-sensitive individuals. Teaching methods such as collaborative learning which are attractive to field-sensitive individuals will probably help retain individuals in engineering.

People appear to process information either serially (sequentially) or globally (holistically). Serialists take information in logical sequence and build their knowledge structures step by step. They can function quite well without seeing the big picture and they learn best in well-defined, logical classrooms. Since most elementary and high school classrooms follow a sequential procedure, serialists often do quite well in school. Holistic learners are driven early in the process to create a knowledge structure which shows the big picture even though most of the details are missing. As they learn, holistic learners fill in the details. Serialists tend to be better at details, and holists are better at overviews or seeing how everything fits together. Obviously, skill at both tasks is useful. Advance organizers are extremely useful for holists and are probably ignored by most serialists. Since globalists often struggle, particularly in introductory courses, it is important for professors to provide some aid and encouragement. In advanced classes globalists may have an advantage since they can see connections and do syntheses which are difficult for serialists. At Arizona State University sequential learning was the preferred learning mode for engineering students and the preferred teaching style of professors.

The final dichotomy to be discussed involves active and reflective processing of information. Active experimenters want to do something with the information in the external world. For example, they want to discuss, teach, solve, or make something. They want to try the activity and learn by doing. This dimension is closely related to extroversion. Reflective individuals want to process the information internally (introversion). They want to ponder it. However, a noninteractive lecture is optimum for neither style of learner. As in the case of all the dichotomies discussed, individuals can learn to learn better if they can use both techniques when appropriate. Anderson found that engineering students prefer active processing, while the preferred teaching style is reflective.

Whether these dichotomies are independent constructs appears to be doubtful. Claxton and Murrell report that Kirby hypothesized that there may be only two fundamental groups which he calls "splitter" and "lumper" types and which overlap with left-brain and right-brain analyses. The splitters include field-independents, serialists, abstract, separate-knowledge individuals, whereas the lumpers include field-sensitive, holistic, concrete, connected-knowledge individuals. If this is true, then the dichotomies are not independent, but each dichotomy adds to the picture of how people learn. However, individuals are complex and have the disturbing habit of not fitting into any theory.

Auditory, Kinesthetic, and Visual Modes

People use three different modes for perceiving the world: auditory, kinesthetic, and visual. Everyone without a major physical handicap has the ability to use all three modes. For example, at a feast you can first enjoy the sight of the food and the table. Then you can enjoy the smell, taste, and feel (all kinesthetic) of the food and drink. Finally, after the meal you can sit back and enjoy the feast again by talking about how wonderful it was. As in other aspects of learning, most of us have developed a favorite mode of perception for learning about the world. This favorite mode affects how we learn in different situations.

Kinesthetic learning includes taste, touch, smell, and feelings. Kinesthetic learning is important for chefs, athletes, therapists, artists, skilled craftspersons, and others. Kinesthetic learning occurs in engineering education when students work in laboratories and handle real components such as circuit boards, valves, and machine tools. Passing objects around during a lecture not only spices up the class but also incorporates kinesthetic learning. Touch can be useful to understand the smoothness of objects or the heat generated when a bearing is binding. The sense of smell can be used as part of the learning process for food process engineers, chemical engineers, and environmental engineers. Smell can help tell if a process is operating correctly or incorrectly. Feelings or affective aspects of learning are always present. Success and praise can help engender a positive attitude (feelings) toward the course, while failure and criticism do the reverse. Although criticism is often necessary, professors should never try to humiliate or belittle students. Writing about something is a good way to learn, partly because it involves both kinesthetic and auditory learning.

Visual learners prefer to process information in pictures, and they prefer to learn from pictures, charts, diagrams, figures, actual equipment, photographs, graphic images, and so forth. This appears to be the preferred mode of learning for most people and was the preferred mode for engineering students. The phrase, "A picture is worth a thousand words," is a common-sense way of saying that most people prefer visual learning. Visual information appears to be easier to understand and place into memory than words. Visual learning can be incorporated into engineering education in a variety of ways. Plotting equations to show their shape makes them much more real for many students. This can be done conveniently with calculators with plotting screens. Graphical solution methods are easier for many students to understand than solving equations analytically. Showing that the intersection of two curves is the simultaneous solution of two equations helps students understand what this means. Graphical solutions to more complex problems such as a McCabe-Thiele diagram in distillation or a Bode plot in control, help many students understand the solution procedure. Showing graphical integration procedures and comparing these to Simpson's rule or other integration procedures helps clarify for the student the meaning of the integration procedure. Correlations of data should be shown both in a figure with the scatter of data and as an equation with the correlation coefficient. Equipment sketches and diagrams should be insisted on for the solution of all problems. Computer-aided three-dimensional diagrams can help to clarify complex concepts in mechanics and other areas. Field trips or at least professionally produced videos of plant sites help students see the "real thing." For many students this one-time exposure to real equipment makes an entire semester of equations and problem solving much more understandable. Students in co-op programs also benefit from this aspect of visual education.

Auditory teaching methods are most commonly used in Western education systems. This includes lectures and print material. Reading in Western cultures is a visual representation of auditory processing techniques. In contrast, Chinese ideograms are closer to visual processing, and Eastern education has a more visual character. Writing words or equations on the blackboard is also a visual representation of an auditory method. Few people prefer to use auditory learning if given a choice; however, the Western educational system does not usually provide for a choice. Successful students have adjusted to auditory teaching styles before they reach college. One of the basic tenets of learning theory is that learning is more thorough and is retained better if multiple modes are used to input and process the information. Stice reports on some early data from the Socony-Vacuum Oil Company which supports this contention. For reading alone, the learner's retention was 10 percent; for hearing alone, 26 percent; and for seeing, 30 percent. If the learner both saw and heard, retention was 50 percent; if the learner said something, retention was 70 percent; and if the learner said and did something, the retention was 90 percent. Thus, auditory styles of teaching should be heavily supplemented with visual and, to a lesser extent, kinesthetic learning opportunities. Opportunities for the student to speak, write, and solve problems should be incorporated in the course. With a little creativity this can often be done without major changes in the course format or coverage. Since visual learning is the preferred style for most students, it is also useful to consider if the entire course can be presented in a mainly visual style. This revision would probably require major changes in the course.

Kolb's Learning Cycle

Kolb developed a two-dimensional circular or three-dimensional spiral model of how people learn. Kolb's model starts with two dichotomies which are considered to be orthogonal to each other. The first is active experimentation (AE) versus reflective observation (RO). This dichotomy refers to how individuals prefer to transform experience into knowledge. Individuals who favor active experimentation like to get things done and see results. Reflective observers prefer to examine ideas from several angles and to delay action.

The second dimension in Kolb's theory is the dichotomy between abstract conceptualization (AC) and concrete experience (CE). This dimension distinguishes between how an individual grasps or takes in information. Abstract conceptualizers prefer logical analysis, abstract thinking, and systematic planning. Individuals who favor concrete experience want specific experiences and personal involvement, particularly with people, and tend to be nonsystematic.

Kolb considers each of these four areas to be steps in learning. McCarthy modified and extended Kolb's model to apply it to teaching. The complete learning cycle shown in Figure 1 requires all four steps; thus, a proficient learner is able to complete all steps in the cycle although he or she prefers certain modes of operation. The cycle can be entered at any of the four steps, but usually starts with the concrete experience method of grasping information. This information is then transformed or internalized by reflective observation (RO). For complete learning the individual should continue around the circle and use abstract conceptualization to perceive the information that has now been changed by reflection. Next the learner processes the information actively and does something with it. For complex information the circle is traversed several times in a spiral cycle. The spiral may extend through several courses and on into professional practice as the individual learns the material in more and more depth.

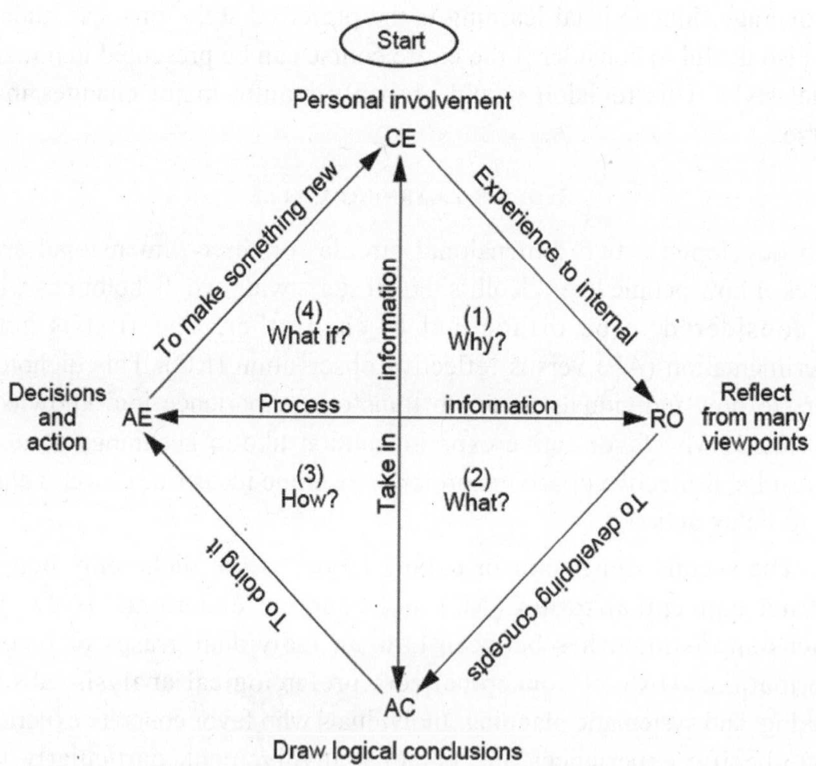

Figure 1. Kolb's learning cycle (Modified)

Kolb's learning cycle is a theory describing the steps required for complete learning. Unfortunately, students often take short-cuts and employ only one or two stages in the cycle, which results in significantly less learning. A study of the retention of knowledge showed 20 percent retention when only

AC was used, 50 percent with RO and AC, 70 percent with CE, RO, and AC, and 90 percent when all four stages were employed. Most college education is geared to abstract conceptualization, but retention (hence long-term learning) is involvement by students increases learning because additional stages in the learning cycle are used. Cooperative education and summer jobs aid learning because they involve the student in doing and in concrete experience.

Kolb's learning cycle is useful for conceptualizing how people learn and for developing courses and training programs. Stice first discussed applications in engineering education. A lecture (RO) can be followed by requiring students to think about the ideas (AC), do homework (AE), and observe demonstrations or do laboratory experiments (CE). Retention should be significantly better than in a course requiring only regurgitation of lecture (RO) and homework (AE). McCarthy showed that Kolb's theory is similar to many other theories of learning. She extensively modified Kolb's theory and applied it to teaching a variety of topics at all levels. McCarthy's 4MAT system has been applied to engineering classes by Harb et al., Terry et al., and Todd. We will discuss the modified and extended Kolb learning cycle or 4MAT system in more detail.

This teaching and learning system starts each instructional unit with concrete experience (CE) and leads to reflective observation (RO). The student learns why the material is important in the first quadrant of Figure 15-2. This is the motivation step which professors often skip. McCarthy suggests performing first a right-brain-mode activity and second a left-brain-mode activity to create reasons for learning material.

The right-brain-mode activity can be experimental such as going out "on the street" and seeing and feeling the need for a bridge at a specific location. The left-brain-mode activity can then reflect on the need for the bridge. McCarthy suggests breaking down the learning activities in all four quadrants into both right and left activities. Possible teaching and learning activities are listed in Table 1.

In the second quadrant students move from reflective observation (RO) to abstract conceptualization (AC). They think and learn concepts. The key question is what? What are the facts? What body of knowledge are the students supposed to learn? For students studying bridge building various aspects of bridge design are covered in class. The teacher's role is to teach.

Table 1. Teaching And Learning Activities

Diverger (1)	*Assimilator (2)*	*Converger (3)*	*Accommodator (4)*
Motivation	Information and facts	Try it	Do it themselves
"War" stories	Lecture	Homework problems	Self-select projects
Brainstorming	Reading	Laboratory	Design
Observations:	Instructor or	Simulations	Open-ended problems
Field trips	TV demonstration	CAI	Write problems
"On street"	Patterns	Problem solving	Field trips
Logs	Organizing	Short answer	Work experience
Journals	Analyzing	Reports	Simulations
Role playing	Objective tests	Demonstrations	Teach yourself
Discussion	Library Work	Experiment	Teach someone else
Questioning	Problem-solving examples	Tinker	Think tank
Visualization	Seminars	Record	Make things work

In the third quadrant students move from thinking to doing. They want to answer the question How does it work? This is where homework assignments, laboratory sessions, and fieldwork fit into engineering education. In the example on bridge building, students can do homework on bridges and test model bridges in the lab. The professor coaches them and facilitates their efforts but lets them do it themselves. Engineering and technology programs include at least some courses where the third quadrant is heavily used.

In the fourth quadrant students remain active and move from active experimentation to concrete experience. This completes the cycle, but the students return to concrete experience with a very different understanding of the knowledge. In this fourth quadrant they can teach themselves and others, ask what-if questions, and do something with the knowledge. They can create their own experiment or construct a model of their design. For example, for the class on bridges students can choose from a variety of projects such as designing a new bridge, building a model, producing a portfolio of bridge photographs, and so forth.

The usual college education uses what McCarthy calls a "pendulum style" of teaching. That is, it oscillates between quadrants 2 and 3. This style never goes around the entire cycle. Thus students are seldom motivated and seldom have the opportunity to do it themselves unless they have co-op or summer jobs. The pendulum style reduces retention and, as we shall see shortly, does not satisfy the favorite learning style of many students.

Kolb also developed a theory of learning styles. A short psychological test which provides numerical scores for the grid is available. The four styles are illustrated in Figure 1. Convergers prefer abstract conceptualization (AC) and active experimentation (AE) (quadrant 3). They enjoy logic, practical application of ideas and theories to solve problems and are often quite focused. They tend to use deductive reasoning and are good at solving problems with a single answer. Many engineers, technologists, computer scientists, and physical scientists are convergers. The favorite learning style of convergers is in quadrant 3 where they can do experiments and design equipment. If too convergent, these individuals may tend to act without reflection and to think without feeling. As a result, they may be perceived as being arbitrary and cold. Since convergers need to relate theory to practical applications, case studies, laboratory, field trips, and work experience are a very helpful part of their education.

Assimilators prefer abstract conceptualization and reflective observation (Quadrant 2). They are excellent at understanding information and developing logical forms, prefer inductive reasoning, and are good at creating theoretical models. They can be contrasted with convergers since they do not worry about practical aspects. They do share the AC aspect with convergers and are often more interested in ideas than in people. Many teachers, writers, lawyers, mathematicians, scientists, and engineers with a scientific bent are assimilators. Assimilators often do well in lecture classes, and their favorite learning style is in quadrant 2. Assimilators are systematic planners, but they may ignore the human aspect.

Accommodators prefer active experimentation and concrete experience (Quadrant 4). They are similar to convergers in that they like to act and to get things done. They differ from convergers in that they are less logical and are more people-oriented. If the theory does not fit the experiments, they will often discard the theory and go with what works. They enjoy new experiences and are often willing to take risks. Accommodators are often found in business or large organizations where they enjoy marketing, sales, managing, politics and public relations. They do well in hands-on group activities in class or group laboratory assignments. They prefer quadrant-4 activities. Accommodators may be seen as pushy and nontheoretical (a no-no in engineering education), and they rely heavily on trial and error.

Divergers are the opposite of convergers, preferring concrete experience and reflective observation (Quadrant 1). Often imaginative, emotional, and good at seeing the global picture, they tend to do well in working with people, recognizing problems, and generating many alternatives. Unfortunately, if too divergent, they may not make decisions and will not get things done. Divergers often become artists, actors, personnel managers, counselors, and social workers. In a classroom, divergers do well in quadrant-1 activities such as group exercises, particularly brainstorming-type activities.

Table 2. Distribution Of Preferred Learning Styles

Diverger (1)	*Female (%)*	*Male (%)*	*Total (%)*
Learning styles:			
Diverger (1)	25.0	19.4	23.0
Assimilator (2)	27.5	37.5	31.1
Converger (3)	14.8	23.5	17.5
Accommodator (4)	32.7	19.6	28.5
Dimensions:			
Concrete (1 plus 4)	57.7	39.0	51.5
Abstract (2 plus 3)	42.2	61.0	48.5
Reflective (1 plus 2)	52.5	56.9	54.1
Active (3 plus 4)	47.5	43.1	45.9

It is important to note that these are *preferred* styles, but that everyone has the capability to use and the need to develop all four styles. Working through Kolb's entire cycle automatically has students use all styles. In addition, every student has an opportunity to shine when the learning activity is in her or his favorite quadrant. The distribution of preferred learning styles for teachers and administrators was determined by McCarthy and is given in Table 12. It is interesting to note that higher percentages of men than of women are assimilators and convergers, which are the typical engineers, scientists, and technologists. Men tend to prefer abstract methods for taking in information, while women prefer more concrete approaches. These style preferences are not cast in stone. Students who are in a program which heavily emphasizes a given learning style tend to shift their preferences toward that style (if they survive). Also, as people get older they tend to process information more reflectively and less actively.

Individuals who prefer any of the four learning styles can find a niche where they will be successful engineers. After school, accommodators tend to move toward management, sales, and marketing; divergers move toward personnel and creative positions. Convergers tend toward hard-core engineering jobs such as plant operations, design, and construction. Assimilators gravitate toward research, development, and planning. Since technically trained people are needed in all these jobs, it is important to design educational programs to retain students with each of these styles. In school, convergers and assimilators are likely to find more kindred spirits among both teachers and their peers. Thus, it is the accommodators and the divergers who are most at risk in engineering education.

Teachers also have styles. If these styles differ from those of their students, the mismatch can cause problems. For example, assimilators emphasize logic, abstract theories, and ideas without applying them to practical problems. Convergers in the class do not consider the class to be practical and may not see the practical applications of the material. All students may have problems applying the material if later classes are taught in a convergent fashion. This mismatch often explains why engineering students are unable to use the mathematics they studied earlier. The teacher can help all students by including all aspects of Kolb's learning cycle. This provides some activities that are appropriate for each student, and helps each student broaden his or her repertoire of skills.

Motivation

Regardless of the student's learning style and basic intelligence, he or she will not learn if not motivated. Unfortunately, "nobody can't teach nobody nothing". Thus, student motivation is crucial to learning. Although much of this motivation is beyond the teacher's control, he or she can do a great deal either to motivate or demotivate students.

Motivation is usually considered either intrinsic or extrinsic. Intrinsic motivation is internal. It often satisfies basic human needs which include physiological needs, as well as the need for safety, belongingness, love, esteem, and, finally, self-actualization. Extrinsic motivation is externally controlled and includes many things that the instructor can do, including grading, providing encouragement and friendship, and so forth. The differences between intrinsic and extrinsic motivation are not always sharp. For example, a high salary might be considered to be an extrinsic motivator, but it can also enhance an individual's self-esteem. Both intrinsic and extrinsic motivation will be discussed in terms of Maslow's theory of human needs and motivation.

Student Motivational Problems

Students can have a variety of motivational problems. Since the "cure" often depends upon the problem, it will be helpful to list some of the problems briefly.

1. The student does not want to study engineering or even to be in college. A surprising number of students are in engineering because of parental pressure. Failure is one way the student can prove that the parents are wrong. Research clearly shows that students who do not believe in the importance of education have lower success in school.
2. The student is not under pressure to be in engineering but is uncertain if engineering is the best choice. Since many outstanding engineers were once in this category, a major motivational effort may be appropriate. Since students need to see meaning in their studies, the motivation effort can focus on this. Once purpose is instilled, these students can become outstanding engineers.
3. The work ethic is absent. Many students coast through high school and find engineering painfully hard work. Installing a work ethic at this late date may be difficult, but it is important for success in engineering.
4. The background in prerequisites is inadequate. Success is very motivating, but with an inadequate background students may be unable to be successful in a specific course or in the entire curriculum.
5. The student feels isolated and perhaps discriminated against. This can particularly be a problem for women and minorities who are traditionally underrepresented in engineering. It can also be a problem for international students.
6. The student finds engineering classes or classes in general distasteful. If the student's learning styles are very different from the professors' teaching styles, the student may find classes unrewarding even if they are not difficult. Some students find engineering classes too competitive or feel they never get rewarded for their efforts.
7. External problems are overwhelming. A death in the family, health problems, financial difficulties, relationship problems, and so forth, can prevent students from being motivated in their studies.

8. The student becomes overly anxious during tests or while doing homework. The discomfort caused by excessive anxiety can reduce motivation. High stress on tests is detrimental to all students but hits women harder than it does men. Anxiety and stress can be controlled by desensitization procedures (such as giving more tests), by relaxation methods, and by giving the student more control of the grade he or she will earn.
9. The student wants only a grade or a degree and does not care about learning the material. Although the professor may think that the student is motivated for the wrong reason, these motivations can be used to get the student to learn.
10. The student is not intelligent enough. We placed this reason last since, contrary to the opinion of many professors, the lack of intellectual ability is seldom the major reason for a lack of motivation, although it may contribute, particularly for concrete operational students. A significant body of research shows that "accomplishment in a particular activity is often more dependent upon hard work and self-discipline than on innate ability".

Maslow's Hierarchy of Needs

According to Maslow's theory of motivation, which has become widely accepted, individuals have a hierarchy of needs. When a need is unfulfilled, the individual is very motivated to fulfill that need. Once needs at the lower levels are satisfied, higher-level needs become important and the individual becomes motivated to satisfy these needs. If one of the lower-level needs is suddenly not satisfied, then this need becomes the most important need until it is again satisfied. For example, a Ph.D. in engineering who is lost in the woods and starving thinks only about food and rescue, not about abstract theory. Maslow noted that the hierarchy is not invariably followed by all individuals.

Western society tries to satisfy the physiological and safety needs for everyone, although not always successfully. Since professors and most students have these needs satisfied, we tend to ignore their importance. Professors need to remember that for some of their poorer students these needs may be very important. It is difficult to focus on studying if one is wondering where money for food or rent will come from. This type of external problem needs to be solved with financial aid, not by exhortations to study. A student who is terrified to walk back to a dorm after dark will not benefit from help sessions or the availability of a computer laboratory. These safety needs must be met by proper campus lighting, police patrols, and an escort service before the student can focus on studying.

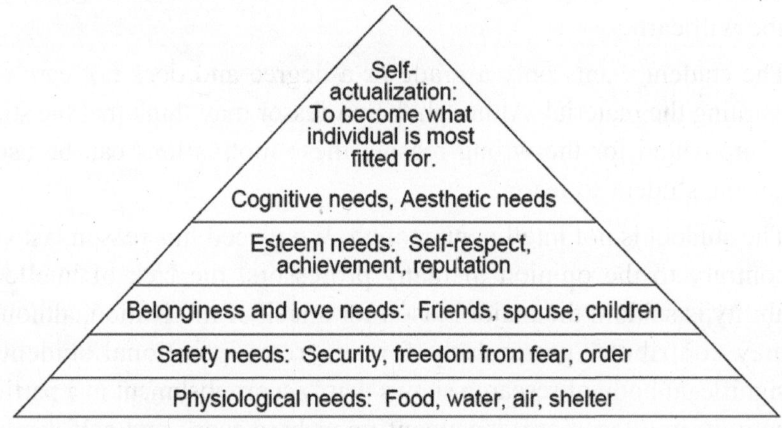

Figure 2. Maslow's Hierarchy of Needs

When students leave home to go to college, they often find that the needs for belonging and love are no longer satisfied. Parents and friends several hundred miles away may be insufficient to satisfy these needs. Part of the adjustment process for freshmen, transfer students, and graduate students involves satisfying the belongingness needs in a strange location. The adjustment process tends to be worse for freshmen because they have less experience in satisfying these needs on their own. The school can help by encouraging students (and for freshmen, their parents also) to visit before registration. Mixers and other get-togethers are useful in helping new students meet others. Living in a residence hall is particularly helpful to freshmen and also helps their development on Perry's scale.

Professors have an important role to play in helping to satisfy belongingness needs. Retention of students is significantly enhanced when students are integrated into the university both socially and academically. Academic integration includes contact with faculty and staff, involvement in the curriculum, and academic performance. Students who have made significant contact with a faculty member during the first six weeks of the semester are more likely to become academically integrated and remain at the university. To make contact with students the professor must at a minimum learn everyone's name. A more active approach such as inviting small groups of students to his or her house or for coffee at the student lounge can have a positive impact. It is interesting that significant contact almost always occurs for new engineering graduate students, but at large universities is often absent for freshmen. Students who do not want to be in engineering or who are unsure about engineering have more difficulty achieving academic integration.

Counseling, support, and encouragement can help these students. The ability of engineering to satisfy other needs may help them become academically integrated. Thus, spending some time in introductory classes talking about the many joys and advantages of being an engineer helps some students get past a difficult period. Strong negative feedback attacks both the need for belonging and esteem. Unfortunately, the sting of negative feedback lasts much longer than the glow from positive feedback. Professors need to be creative in finding ways to use positive instead of negative feedback.

Students with very different learning styles often do not feel that they belong in engineering. A relatively small amount of course modification to include other learning styles can help these students feel they belong. A particularly important change for many students is to make learning more cooperative and less competitive. Cooperative group exercises and grading which does not pit students against each other can help convince them that the true adversary is ignorance, not the professor or each other. The need to belong can have a negative impact on the student's desire to study since some groups may exclude students who do too well in class. This can be combated by developing groups such as honor societies, study groups, or professional organizations where academic excellence is appreciated.

A major need that can be fulfilled in class is that for esteem. Grades are often the most important motivating device because they directly relate to the esteem needs, and grades are under the professor's control. Achievement, reputation, and self-respect can all be enhanced by good grades. The perception that one is doing well is very motivating. Excusing students from the final because of good grades during the semester can be an excellent motivator for the better students. Yet grades won't motivate if students believe that high grades will interfere with their belonging, and the belongingness needs are unfulfilled. When unfulfilled, the lower-level needs are more important. Good grades must also be seen to be achievable. Students with poor academic backgrounds and poor study habits quickly learn that they cannot achieve good grades. For them, grades are a demotivator. Remedial help and tutoring can help these students succeed. Another modification which involves considerable effort, but is extremely valuable for some students, is to use a flexible time frame and allow the students to spend more time learning. This can be done in mastery or self-paced classes. Since every student can achieve if given sufficient time and encouragement, these classes can be very motivating.

Needs for esteem and belongingness are also met by respect from faculty and by positive feedback. Eble states that respecting students as human beings without requiring them to prove themselves is one of the most important things a teacher can do to help them grow. Feedback should be immediate, and if at all possible should contain some positive aspects. Effort should be praised even if it is somewhat misplaced. Professors can learn from successful coaches in this respect. For example, in basketball when a player fouls, the coach may praise the player for a good hustle and then correct him or her for the foul. Negative feedback should be avoided if at all possible, but if necessary it should be focused entirely on the performance and not on the person. Unfortunately, negative reinforcement may result in unexpected and undesired behavior changes such as avoiding class entirely to avoid being yelled at. Criticizing a student as lazy is an attack on the person. In the long run, it is usually more productive to point out that the performance is not up to the student's ability and is not satisfactory. Smiles, nods, and encouragement for responses are all positive reinforcement. Greeting a student by name with a smile in the hall or in your office is also positive reinforcement which can help to meet the student's esteem needs. This reinforcement is unexpected and intermittent and thus is very powerful. Many students who leave engineering cite discouragement and the lack of support as major reasons.

Assignments and tests motivate students to keep up with the class since they tap into the need to be successful and avoid failure. Motivation for doing tests and assignments appears to be highest when there is a fair but not certain chance for success. The professor should introduce assignments and tests with positive expectations for student performance. These positive expectations are in themselves motivating.. Success is motivating. It is worthwhile to ensure that there is some aspect of an assignment or course at which each student can be successful. The workload should be reasonable since excessive work is demotivating and reduces the chance of success.

The prospect of a good salary upon graduation is often considered to be a crass extrinsic motivator. Based on Maslow's theory, there are often good reasons why the promise of salary is a strong motivator. If the student experiences periods when physiological or safety needs are not met, then the salary can be a way of ensuring this does not happen again. Engineering should promote itself as a way up and out of poverty. Parental pressure to go into engineering may arise from the parents' desire to have a son or daughter earn a good salary. If satisfying parents helps meet belongingness and love needs, then the student may be positively motivated. For many students the salary helps to satisfy the need for esteem. Since salary after graduation is a long way off for a freshman or sophomore, the more immediate reinforcement of a summer or a co-op job may be a better motivator.

The chance to present a paper at a meeting and to be a coauthor on a published paper can help meet a student's need for esteem and reputation. This can be a tremendous motivator for graduate and undergraduate students. Students work harder on research when they have a self-imposed deadline (paper presentation or the desire to graduate) than when pushed by the professor.

The highest level in Maslow's hierarchy, self-actualization, is the need for individuals to reach their potential. The need to self-actualize is what causes individuals to write poetry at 2 A.M. when they have to report to a respectable, well-paying job at 8 A.M. Cooking gourmet meals when something simpler would suffice may represent the need to self-actualize. Creativity and the need to create can be considered part of the need to self-actualize. Maslow notes that for extremely creative individuals the need to create may be more important than the lower needs. People require time to learn how to satisfy their needs. Thus self-actualization occurs in mature individuals and based on Maslow's studies is uncommon. Self-actualized students are more likely to be encountered in graduate or continuing education classes.

Self-actualized individuals have a need to guide their own destiny. In class they appreciate the chance to do individual projects and delve into a topic of their choice at considerable depth. Bonus problems and other methods which give them some control over what they do are appreciated. In research they want to guide their own projects. The professor's job is to step back and serve as a resource person when asked.

Maslow notes that cognitive needs are present throughout the five stages. There is joy in learning and creating which can be used to motivate. However, professors must make an effort to remove barriers that prevent students from achieving the joy of learning. The professor's enthusiasm and joy in learning the subject can be contagious. Sleeping students are not learning. Lecturing with energy, excitement, and some humor at least keeps students awake. And students enjoy classes more and learn more when the professor performs.

The force of curiosity is most evident in young children and in self-actualized individuals. Professors can use curiosity as a positive motivator in the classroom. For example, in a lecture questions can be asked and not be answered. We have found that questions which ask the students to use their engineering knowledge to explain nature often pique their interest. Why does a car window frost over at night when the window on an adjacent building does not? What is wind chill? Or, have the student estimate how long it will take for a person to respond on a very long-distance telephone call. Other variations of the socratic approach can be used. The important point is to ask questions which are thought-provoking for a group of students. This use of curiosity, like all motivating techniques, will work for only a portion of the class.

At all levels of Maslow's hierarchy the locus of control is important. People who believe they have some control over their work life are more strongly motivated. Students can be provided with a modicum of control with grade contracts, a choice of projects, a choice of problems on a test, or a vote on the test date. Graduate students, in particular, can be given significant control over their projects and often respond with extraordinary energy.

All writers on motivation in college teaching note that teachers need to be creative in developing motivational techniques. With a creative effort the professor can often find just the right thing to do to motivate a particular student. For example, we have seen graduate students become very motivated when given the opportunity to present a paper at a meeting or to tutor students. The chance to coauthor a research paper has sparked some undergraduates. Having a piece of equipment actually constructed and used while on a co-op assignment has turned students on to engineering. Taking a mastery class and being able to succeed academically for the first time in college has been a tremendous motivator for some students. One student obtained the help he needed once a professor took the time to sit and talk with him about the potential career consequences of his inability to communicate. Informal parties at a professor's house have helped many students feel at home at the university and thus have satisfied their belongingness needs. Often it is the attention and not the actual action which increases the students' motivation. This is the famous "Hawthorne effect". A professor can motivate classes by continually creating the Hawthorne effect by always experimenting. Professors control motivation in a class by their actions. If they give lip service to creative problem solving but always emphasize drill on homework and tests, the students will do drills. To obtain creative solutions there must be a focus on the activity. Many other examples could be cited.

References

Kolb, D. A., (1985).*Learning Style Inventory*, McBer & Co., Boston.

Kolstoe, O. P., (1975).*College Professoring: Or, Through Academia with Gun and Camera*, Southern Illinois University Press, Carbondale, IL.

Kurfiss, J. G., (1988).*Critical Thinking: Theory, Research, Practice, and Possibilities*, ASHE-ERIC Higher Education Report No. 2, Association for the Study of Higher Education, Washington, DC.

Lawson, A. E., Abraham, M. R., and Renner, J. W., (1989). *A Theory of Instruction: Using the Learning Cycle to Teach Science Concepts and Thinking Skills*, Monograph *1*, National Association for Research in Science Teaching, Cincinnati, OH, 1989.

Lowman, J., (1985).*Mastering the Techniques of Teaching,* Jossey-Bass, San Francisco.

Maslow, A., (1970). *Motivation and Personality*, 2nd ed., Harper and Row, New York.

10

Models of Cognitive Development

Cognitive development is the construction of thought processes, including remembering, problem solving, and decision-making, from childhood through adolescence to adulthood.It was once believed that infants lacked the ability to think or form complex ideas and remained without cognition until they learned language. It is now known that babies are aware of their surroundings and interested in exploration from the time they are born. From birth, babies begin to actively learn. They gather, sort, and process information from around them, using the data to develop perception and thinking skills.

Cognitive development refers to how a person perceives, thinks, and gains understanding of his or her world through the interaction of genetic and learned factors. Among the areas of cognitive development are information processing, intelligence, reasoning, language development , and memory.

Historically, the cognitive development of children has been studied in a variety of ways. The oldest is through intelligence tests, such as the widely used Stanford Binet Intelligence Quotient (IQ) test first adopted for use in the United States by psychologist Lewis Terman (1877–1956) in 1916 from a French model pioneered in 1905. IQ scoring is based on the concept of mental age, according to which the scores of a child of average intelligence match his or her age, while a gifted child's performance is comparable to that of an older child, and a slow learner's scores are similar to those of a younger child. IQ tests are widely used in the United States, but they have come under increasing criticism for defining intelligence too narrowly and for being biased with regard to race and gender.

In contrast to the emphasis placed on a child's native abilities by intelligence testing, learning theory grew out of work by behaviorist researchers such as John Watson (1878–1958) and B. F. Skinner (1904–1990), who argued that children are completely malleable. Learning theory focuses on the role of environmental factors in shaping the intelligence of children, especially on a child's ability to learn by having certain behaviors rewarded and others discouraged.

Piaget's Theory of Cognitive Development

Jean Piaget was a Swiss psychologist whose research on the development of children has profoundly affected psychological theories of development and of the teaching of children. His theory has also been widely studied for its application to the teaching of science in grade school, high school, and college. Unfortunately, Piaget's writings tend to be somewhat obscure. We will present a significantly edited version focusing on those aspects of his theory which affect engineering education. Further information is available in Flavell, Gage and Berliner, Goodson, Inhelder and Piaget, Phillips, Piaget, and Pavelich.

Intellectual Development

Piaget's theory conceives of intellectual development as occurring in four distinct periods or stages. Intellectual development is continuous, but the intellectual operations in the different periods are distinctly different. Children progress through the four periods in the same order, but at very different rates. The stages do not end abruptly but tend to trail off. A child may be in two different stages in different areas.

The sensorimotor period, which is only of indirect interest to our concerns, extends from birth to about two years of age. In this period a child learns about his or her relationship to various objects. This period includes learning a variety of fundamental movements and perceptual activities. Knowledge involves the ability to manipulate objects such as holding a bottle. In the later part of this period the child starts to think about events which are not immediately present. In Piaget's terms the child is developing meaning for symbols.

The preoperational period lasts from roughly two to seven years of age. Piaget has divided this stage into the preoperational phase and the intuitive phase. In the preoperational phase children use language and try to make sense of the world but have a much less sophisticated mode of thought than adults. They need to test thoughts with reality on a daily basis and do not appear to be able to learn from generalizations made by adults. For example, to a child riding a tricycle the admonition "Slow down, you are going too fast" probably has no effect until the child falls over. This continual testing with reality helps the child to understand the meaning of "too fast." Compared to adults, the thinking of a child in the preoperational phase is very concrete and self-centered. The child's reasoning is often very crude, and he or she is unable to make very simple logical extensions. For example, the son of one of the authors was astounded when he heard that his baby sister would be a girl when she got older!

In the intuitive phase the child slowly moves away from drawing conclusions based solely on concrete experiences with objects. However, the conclusions drawn are based on rather vague impressions and perceptual judgments. At first, the conclusions are not put into words and are often erroneous (and amusing to adults). Children are perception-bound and often very rigid in their conclusions. Rational explanations have no effect on them because they are unable to think in a cause-and-effect manner. During this phase children start to respond to verbal commands and to override what they see. It becomes possible to carry on a conversation with a child. Children develop the ability to classify objects on the basis of different criteria, learn to count and use the concept of numbers (and may be fascinated by counting), and start to see relationships if they have extensive experience with the world. Unaware of the processes and categories that they are using, children are still preoperational. Introspection and metathought are still impossible.

At around age seven (or later if the environment has been limited) the child starts to enter the concrete operational stage. In this stage a person can do mental operations but only with real (concrete) objects, events, or situations. He or she can do mental experiments and can correctly classify different objects (apples and sticks, for example) by some category such as size. The child understands conservation of amounts. This can be illustrated with the results of one of Piaget's experiments. Two identical balls of clay are shown to a child who agrees they have the same amount of clay. While the child watches, one ball is flattened. When asked which ball has less clay, the preoperational child answers that the flattened ball has less clay. The concrete operational child is able to correctly answer this question. He or she becomes adept at addition and subtraction but can do other mathematics only by rote. In the concrete operational stage children also become less self-centered in their perceptions of the universe. Logical reasons are understood. For example, a concrete operational person can understand the need to go to bed early when it is necessary to rise early the next morning. A preoperational child, on the other hand, does not understand this logic and substitutes the psychological reason, "I want to stay up."

Piaget thought that the concrete operational stage ended at age eleven or twelve. There is now considerable evidence that these ages are the earliest that this stage ends and that many adults remain in this stage throughout their lives. Most current estimates are that from 30 to 60 percent of adults are in the concrete operational stage. Thus, many college freshmen are concrete operational thinkers; however, the number in engineering is small and is probably less than 10 percent. For reasons which will become clear shortly, concrete operational thinkers will have difficulty in an engineering curriculum. However, these people can be fully functioning adults. Piaget's theories at the concrete and formal operational stages measure abilities only in a very limited scientific, logical, algebraic sense. His theories do not address ethical or moral development. Thus a person may be a successful hard worker, a good, loving parent and spouse, and a good citizen, but be limited to concrete operational thought.

The final stage in Piaget's theory is the formal operational stage, which may start as early as age eleven or twelve, but often later. A formal operational thinker can do abstract thinking and starts to enjoy abstract thought. This person becomes inventive with ideas and starts to delight in such thinking. He or she can formulate hypotheses without actually manipulating concrete objects, and when more adept can test the hypotheses mentally. This testing of logical alternatives does not require recourse to real objects. The formal operational thinker can generalize from one kind of real object to another and to an abstract notion. In the experiment with the balls of clay, for example, the formal thinker can generalize this to sand or water and then to a general statement of conservation of matter. This person is capable of learning higher mathematics and then applying this mathematics to solve new problems. When faced with college algebra or calculus the concrete operational thinker is forced to learn the material by memorization but then is unable to use this material to solve unusual problems. The formal operational thinker is able to think ahead to plan the solution path and do combinatorial thinking and generate many possibilities. Finally, the formal operational person is capable of metacognition, that is, thinking about thinking.

Application of Piaget's Model

The importance of the formal operational stage to engineering education is that engineering education requires formal operational thought. Many of the 30 to 60 percent of the adult population who have some trouble with formal operational thought appear to be in a *transitional* phase where they can correctly use formal operational thought some of the time but not all of the time. Engineering students in transition appear to be able to master engineering material. This probably occurs because they have learned that formal operational thought processes must be used in their engineering courses, but they have not generalized these processes to all areas of their life. This domain specificity of many students is one of the major criticisms of Piaget's theory.

The relatively small number of engineering students who are in the concrete operational stage will have difficulties in engineering. These students may make it through the curriculum by rote learning, partial credit, doing well in lab, repeating courses, and so forth. Concrete operational students can be identified by repeated administration of tests with novel problems on the same material. On the first few tests students may be unable to work the problem either because of lack of knowledge or because of an inability to solve abstract problems. On the basis of a single test it is difficult to tell if lack of knowledge or poor problem-solving ability has caused the difficulties. Students who can use formal operational thinking learn from their mistakes, learn the missing knowledge, and fairly rapidly become able to solve difficult new problems. Students who are in the concrete operational stage do not appear to be able to learn from their mistakes on problems requiring formal operations. Thus, they make the same mistakes over and over. The solutions of these students do not appear to follow any logical pattern since they often just try something (anything) to see if it works and to see if they get any partial credit. These students have great difficulty in evaluating their solutions. In engineering, concrete operational students are likely to be quite frustrated and frustrating to work with.

The suggestion has been made repeatedly that freshmen-sophomore courses in engineering should be made available for nonengineering students. If this were done, the much higher percentage of concrete operational students in the general student population would likely cause problems in the course unless some type of screening or self-selection takes place.

Piaget's Theory of Learning

The presence of some concrete operational students in engineering leads us naturally to the question of how a student moves from one stage to another. This is another aspect of Piaget's theories. Piaget postulates that there are *mental structures* that determine how data and new information are perceived. If the new data make sense to the existing mental structure, then the new information is incorporated into the structure (*accommodation* in Piaget's terms). Note that the new data do not have to exactly match the existing structure to be incorporated into the structure. The process of accommodation allows for minor changes (figuratively, stretching, bending and twisting, but not breaking) in the structure to incorporate the new data. If the data are very different from the existing mental structure, it does not make any sense to incorporate them into the structure. The new information is either rejected or the information is *assimilated* or *transformed* so that it will fit into the structure. A concrete person will probably reject a concept requiring formal thought. If forced to do something with the data he or she will memorize even though the meaning is not understood. This is similar to memorizing a passage in a foreign language that one cannot speak. An example of transformation is a person's response to seeing a pink stoplight. Everyone "knows" that stoplights are red, and thus the pink stoplight will probably be registered as being red since red stoplights fit one's mental structure.

How does one develop mentally? How does one make the quantum leap from concrete to formal thinking? Mental development occurs because the organism has a natural desire to operate in a state of equilibrium. When information is received from the outside world which is too far away from the mental structure to be accommodated but makes enough sense that rejecting it is difficult, then the person is in a state of *disequilibrium*. The desire for equilibration is a very strong motivator to either change the structure or reject the data. If the new information requires formal thinking and the person is otherwise ready, then a first formal operational structure may be formed. This formal operational structure is at first specific for learning in one area and is slowly generalized (the person is in a transitional phase). The more often the person receives input which requires some formal logic, the more likely he or she is to make the jump to formal operational thought. Since this input takes place in a specific area, the transition to formal operations often occurs first in this one area. Also, a person with a less rigid personality structure and tolerance for ambiguity is probably more likely to make the transition. We emphasize that the transition to formal operations may not be easy.

Piaget developed a variety of experiments to test what stage children were in and to help them learn to make the transition to the next stage. Unfortunately, the experiments work well for testing the stage but not for moving people to the next stage. A method called the scientific *learning cycle* has been developed to help students in their mental development. In the scientific learning cycle the students are given firsthand experience, such as in a laboratory with an attempt to cause some disequilibration. The instructor then leads discussions either with individuals or in groups to introduce terms and to help accommodate the data and thus aid equilibration. Finally, students make further investigations or calculations to help the changed mental structure fit in with the other mental structures (organization). The scientific learning cycle is successful at helping people move to higher stages, but progress is very slow. Since concrete operational students may try hard but still have great difficulty in understanding abstract logic, the use of words like "obviously," "clearly," or "it is easy to show" by the professor is frustrating and demotivating to them. The scientific learning cycle is also useful for working with students who are already in the formal operational stage since these students also learn by being in a state of disequilibrium and using accommodation.

Perry's Theory of Development

William G. Perry, Jr., studied the development of students at Harvard University through their four years at the university. His team used open-ended interviews as the technique of measurement. Over a period of years a pattern of development could be distinguished among all the varied responses of the students. Perry then used this pattern of development to rate another group of students. This replication showed that the scheme was reproducible at least for the men at Harvard University. Since publication of the results in 1970, interest in Perry's theory of development during the college years has grown until now his book is being called "the most influential book of the past twenty years" on how college students respond to their college education. Perry's study has been criticized since the group studied was quite homogeneous and consisted mainly of young men from privileged backgrounds. Additional studies since 1970 have essentially duplicated Perry's results and shown that his scheme has fairly general validity except that extensive modifications need to be made for the development of women.

Although Perry's model has become quite influential in higher education in general, engineering education has lagged behind. The model appears to have been introduced in engineering education by Culver and his coworkers. Culver and Hackos presented an overview of Perry's scheme and discussed implications for engineering education. Fitch and Culver and Culver and Fitch presented data on the positions in Perry's model of engineering students, and discussed educational activities to encourage student development. Culver described a workshop on Perry's model and discussed a developmental instructional model based on Perry's work. Culver considered values in engineering education and specifically related them to Perry's model. Hackos discussed using writing to improve problem-solving skills and to enhance intellectual development. The next year Culver continued his series by discussing how Perry's model was useful in explaining the effects of motivation exercises. Culver described applications of Perry's model in encouraging students to learn on their own and presented a workshop which was an overview of Perry's model and of applications to engineering education. Pavelich and Fitch measured engineering students' progress through Perry's positions and concluded that it is slow. Culver et al. discussed the redesign of design courses and curricula to aid the progress of students on Perry's model.

It would be convenient if Perry's scheme started where Piaget's theory stops. Chronologically, the two theories do fit this way, but in other more important ways the theories are *not* a match. Perry does use Piaget's ideas of how students learn. That is, a certain amount of disequilibration is necessary for accommodation to occur. However, Perry's theory is not concerned with problem solving and the applications of logic as are the concrete and formal operational stages of Piaget's theory. Briefly stated, Perry's model is concerned first with how students move from a *dualistic* (right versus wrong) view of the universe to a more *relativistic* view, and second, how students develop commitments within this relativistic world. There is a strong learning connotation in Perry's model since students cannot understand or answer questions which are in a developmental sense too far above them.

Positions in Perry's Model

From his interviews and by extrapolation Perry postulated nine *positions* as shown in Figure 1. These positions and the movement from position to position represent the major contribution of Perry's model.

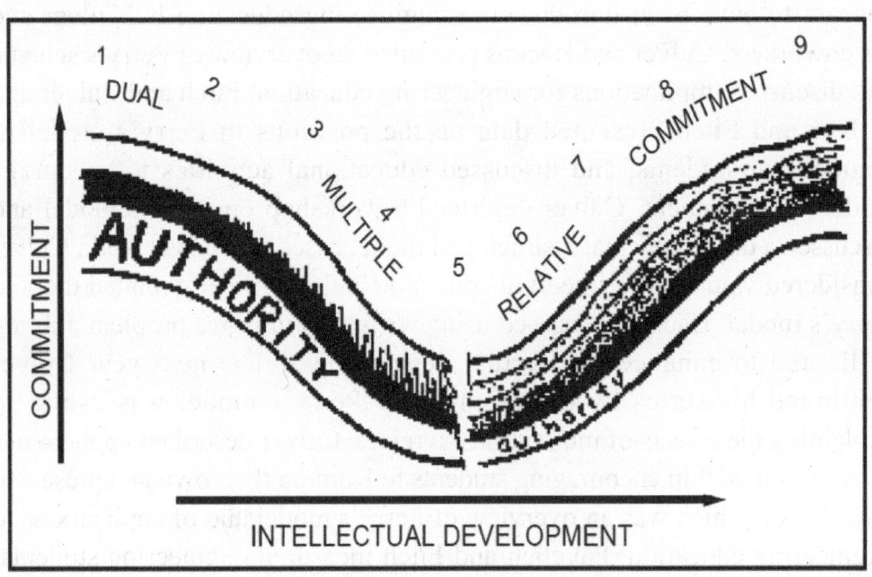

Figure 1. Positions in Perry's Model

Position 1: Basic Duality

The person sees the world dualistically, right versus wrong. There are no alternatives. Authorities know all the answers. Men appear to identify with the authority figure while women do not. The teacher as an authority is supposed to teach the correct answers to the students. Failure to do so means that the teacher is a bad teacher. Hard work and obedience will be rewarded. Authority is so all-knowing that all deviations from authority are lumped together with error and evil. Perry notes that this position is basically naive since there is no alternative or vantage point which allows the person to observe her- or himself.

Perry talked to freshmen after one year at Harvard. He did not talk to anyone in position 1 but inferred this position from student reports about what they had been like when they entered Harvard. Perry notes that this position's assumptions are incompatible with the culture of pluralistic universities and thus students will be unable to maintain this position if they stay at the university. Much of the confrontation with pluralism occurs in residence halls, which may be a good reason to strongly encourage freshmen to live in residence halls. Many other studies have reaffirmed the importance of residence halls in the development of students. Students may start in this position because of a culturally homogeneous or narrow environment, but they will quickly lose their innocence at a university.

Confrontations with their basic dualistic position both in class and in residence halls cause disequilibration. The student tries to accommodate the new ideas of multiplicity. This can be done by moving to position 2 or, at least temporarily, by modifying position 1. The modified position 1 assumes that absolute truths exist, but that authorities may not know what these truths are. Thus conflicts are explained since authority doesn't know the truth, but if one searches hard enough there is an absolute truth. This modified position itself leads to position 2 since the modified position admits that authorities can make errors. Unfortunately, there is another possible outcome to the stress induced by confronting multiplicity at the university. The student may leave.

In their study of the development of women, Belenky et al. included individuals from many social classes. By talking to women in social service agencies, they detected the presence of a position before (or below) position 1 which they called "silence." These women were from very deprived or abusive backgrounds. "Silent" women were unable to understand the words of others and were unable to articulate their own thoughts and feelings. With the steady increase in older students returning to college, some women who have once been in this position will become engineering students.

Position 1 is also the home of intolerance and bigotry. It appears to us that this is the basic position taken by some cults. Although engineering educators tend to shy away from moral arguments, there seem to be clear moral reasons to help students move out of position 1 into position 2.

Position 2: Dualism: Multiplicity Prelegitimate

In position 2 the student can perceive that multiplicity exists but still has a basic dualistic view of the world. There is a right and a wrong. Multiple views or indications that there are "gray" areas are either wrong or interpreted as authority playing games. Since it is possible for authority to be wrong, the absolutes are separate from authority. Thus, some authorities are smarter than others. This position may lead to the feeling that "I am right and authority is needlessly confused." The person may hold the view that there is one answer, but authority shows multiple answers as a game to make students learn how to find the one right answer.

An engineering student in position 2 can successfully solve problems, particularly closed-end problems, with a single right answer. These are the types of problems students in position 2 expect, and these students prefer engineering classes to humanities classes because the problems fit their dualistic mode of thought. In design classes, where problems have multiple answers, these students have difficulties, and they protest against open-ended problems. A student in position 2 wants the teacher to be the source of correct knowledge and to deliver that knowledge without confusing the issues. In this student's view a good teacher presents a logical, structured lecture and gives students chances to practice their skills. The student can then demonstrate that he or she has the right knowledge. From the student's viewpoint a fair test should be very similar to the homework.

Perry notes that students are bewildered and protest as they move from position 1 to position 2. The move from position 1 to position 2 may appear to be small; however, the student has made a major concession by allowing for some complexity and some groping into uncertainty.

In the two dualistic positions men and women use language differently. In general, men tend to talk and women listen. Since listening to authorities is the primary focus of women in the dualistic positions, Belenky et al. call these positions "received knowledge."

Position 3: Multiplicity Subordinate or Early Multiplicity

In position 3 multiplicity has become unavoidable even in hard sciences and engineering. There is still one right answer, but it may be unknown by authority. Thus the gap between authority and the one truth has been widened. The student realizes that in some areas the knowledge is "fuzzy."

This position has some built-in procedural conflicts. If authority does not yet know the answer, how can the professor evaluate the student's work? This is a considerable change from position 2 where honest hard work would presumably lead to the correct answers. Now, in position 3 honest hard work is no longer guaranteed to produce correct answers, and thus good grades seem to be based more on "good expression." The big question students ask is "What do *they* want?" The methods for evaluation become a very important issue and students want the amount of effort put into something to count. From the students' perspective a good professor clearly explains the methods used for determining the right answer even if he or she does not (temporarily) know the right answer, and the good professor presents very clearly defined criteria for evaluation.

For men education appears to play a significant role in the shift to multiplicity. From a developmental sense, one problem with engineering education is that there are few challenges at the lower levels to move the student into position 3 or 4. In class the challenges of multiplicity usually come in senior design classes and in graduate school. The lower-level classes are usually taught as if everything is known. This can lead to severe stress for students in a design course where multiple answers are expected and they are suddenly expected to function in a world with multiple answers. Students survive design courses but often do so without changing a great deal. This survival may occur because design is an isolated class which lasts only for one semester, and the legitimacy of multiplicity may not be reinforced in other classes or in the rest of the student's life. In addition, students who are academically very good can often hide from the challenges of multiplicity through competence (their design is likely to have fewer technical errors and they receive good grades). Beginning graduate students often become very frustrated as they try to determine what they are supposed to do. With less structure, fewer supports, a longer-term reward compared to seniors, and more pressure to adjust to a world of multiplicity, the graduate student's frustration is understandable. Graduate work in engineering and the physical sciences is similar to undergraduate work in the humanities in the respect that both confront the student with multiplicity and uncertainty.

For women formal education is relatively unimportant for the shift into "subjectivism" [the term used by Belenky et al. for multiplicity]. Women appeared to shift into subjectivism "after some crisis of trust in male authority in their daily lives, coupled with some confirmatory experience that they, too, could know something for sure".

Position 4: Complex Dualism and Advanced Multiplicity

The student tries to retain a dualistic right-versus-wrong position but realizes that there are areas of legitimate uncertainty and diversity of opinion. Students react to position 4 in one of two ways. They may conform to what authority seems to want and learn the forms of independent intellectual thought. These students learn that *independent-like* thought will earn them good grades. Genuinely independent thought has not yet been achieved or even considered as an issue. Most of the students Perry studied took this route. However, learning the forms is not enough, and these students may be tempted to *escape*.

The second reaction is that the student may oppose what authority wants in areas where multiplicity is important. The student may raise this multiplicity of opinions to a pervasive viewpoint that "anyone has a right to their own opinion." This raises areas of multiplicity and uncertainty to equal status with areas of dualism. "Everyone has a right to their own opinion" is obviously a wonderful position from which to fight authority. The danger of this position is that a bland "anything goes" attitude may prevail. The student may refuse to think since he or she believes everything can be solved by intuition. Men in this position fight authority openly, while women fight authority internally as "hidden multiplists". These women may be silently alienated from college. Since engineering does not affect their interior life, engineering may appear irrelevant and they may quit engineering even though they can do the work. This position was taken by fewer students and is probably rare for engineering students.

An engineer in position 4 can solve problems cleverly and creatively. The task of solving the problems becomes a game. Unfortunately, he or she cannot see that some problems are much more important than others. This person lacks vision and may solve problems considered unimportant or even immoral by others. Many engineering graduates with both baccalaureate and advanced degrees seem to be in positions 3 and 4.

Position 5: Relativism

In position 5 a person sees everything as relative, not because authority wants it that way but because that is the way he or she sees the world. There is a revolutionary switch from position 4 to position 5. In position 5 relativism becomes the common characteristic of everything and absolutes are a special case. One must then determine if complexity is *not* necessary. In position 4 the situation was the reverse: Dualism was the general principle, and relativism was a special case useful for certain classes of problems. Perry noted that this is often an extremely quiet revolution and that students hardly notice that it has occurred. The relativistic thought process becomes habitual without being noticed. For very focused students in engineering or science, position 5 may come as a shock when they realize that everything is relative in advanced classes.

Perry saw this position as occurring in three subpositions. First, the person divides the world into a relativistic area and into a dualistic area where authority still has answers. Then, the whole world is seen as relativistic, but this position alternates with a dualistic position. Finally, the whole world is seen as relativistic.

The relativistic position can be a very powerful one. There is room for detachment and objectivity. One can think previously forbidden thoughts. This ability to stand outside the situation and think objectively may, in Perry's words, "rank with language as the distinctive triumph of the human mind." The person in the relativistic position can get beyond the statement "all opinions are equal" by using the laws of evidence to develop positions which are more likely.

Belenky et al. noted that men and women may use different logical procedures in position 5, which they called "procedural knowledge." Most men and some women use the traditional logical approach with objective analysis and argument to form opinions. This *separate knowledge* or *objective knowledge* purposefully removes the person's personal experiences and feelings from the logical analysis. Separate knowledge emphasizes doubting and argument. It is the method one would expect from thinking types on the MBTI. This corresponds to the usual engineering approach. Arguments are supposed to be between positions, but many women have difficulty separating positions from people. Some women and men use an approach called *connected knowledge* which is an empathic treatment of divergent views. Connected knowledge personalizes knowledge and attempts to understand the reasons for another's way of thinking. Belief, not doubt, that the other is right from his or her viewpoint is the key stance of connected knowledge. Both feelings and thought are important. Connected knowledge would be expected of Myers-Briggs feeling types who are in position 5. In the same way that everyone has both feeling and thinking capabilities, everyone has the potential to learn both separate and connected knowledge. Individuals who strongly prefer to use connected knowledge as a way of understanding may find the environment at an engineering college somewhat hostile—since only separate knowledge is taught. Because these individuals can make major contributions as engineers (e.g., in life cycle design or conflict resolution), it is important to accommodate them in the educational system. For women the presence of a benign and encouraging authority appears to facilitate movement into position 5.

From the student's viewpoint in position 5 a good instructor acts as a source of expertise, but does not know all the answers since many answers are unknowable. This professor helps students become adept at forming rules to develop reasonable and likely solutions or solution paths. It is important for the professor to show that good opinions are supported by reasons. The student has become much more comfortable with being evaluated in a relativistic world and realizes that the evaluation is of her or his work and not of her or him.

There are problems in position 5. The world is full of possibilities, and there does not appear to be a clear way to choose. Decisions which were made earlier are now called into doubt. The student wonders whether engineering really is the right choice. Did he or she really marry the right person? And so on. Position 5 then represents both a period of strength and possibilities and a period of doubt and loneliness. Assuming that a person is eventually going to move into position 5, it is probably better to do so early while many important career and life decisions have yet to be made. Position 5 can also appear "cold" and even sinister to others because of the focus on method and the dissociation between means and values.

Position 6: Relativism. Commitment Foreseen

The way out of the uncertainty of relativism is *commitment*. In position 6 the student can see the need for commitment but has not yet made the commitment. This need for commitment may be seen as a logical necessity (this is likely for people who are a *T* on the MBTI or may be felt (people who are an *F*). Commitment may be looked forward to with eagerness, or the person may fight commitment. People who fight commitment may stay uncomfortably in position 5, or they may escape or retreat (these are discussed later).

Many students think they have already made firm commitments. Perry uses Commitment (with a capital C) to have a special meaning. Commitment is a mature decision made after one has accepted that the world can be viewed as relativistic and has seen all the possibilities. Previous decisions have been called into doubt and looked at objectively from a detached viewpoint. The new Commitment may be the same decision made previously, but the Commitment is deeper. Commitments can be made in a variety of areas such as career, religion, marriage, politics, values, and so forth. The Commitments one makes help set the person's identity and style. At this point one makes an objective decision on how much of the past to reject and how much to retain. This shedding of parts of the past is clearly different from adolescent rebellion which tends to be mindless.

For an engineering student who has invested a great deal of time in studying engineering, going through position 5 can be very unsettling. Position 6 can be something of a relief since the student sees that it is all right to commit to engineering if objectively that is a good decision. However, a major Commitment is not to be rushed, and the person may stay in position 6 for a while.

Positions 7 through 9: Levels of Commitment

Positions 7 through 9 are all levels of Commitment starting with initial Commitment in position 7. These positions represent degrees of development and depth of Commitment and are not as clearly defined as are the other positions. The person moves from position 6 into position 7 in one area by making a Commitment of his or her own free will. For some this is risky and may be done tentatively in relatively safe areas. As the person becomes more comfortable with making Commitments, he or she makes them in areas that are not as safe, eventually finding not only that a series of finite, discrete decisions have been made, but that a way of life has been developed.

Perry sees the student in position 7 first taking responsibility for who he is or will be in some major area of his life ("I'll stay in engineering"). In position 8, stylistic issues of Commitment become important. "If I am going to be an electrical engineer, how will I do it?" "What will my specialties be?" "What degrees should I get?" And so forth. Position 9 is a postulated position of maturity where the person has developed a sense of self in both Commitments and style. Perry postulated that this is a position reached some time after graduation. Women also make a commitment but it is to a life rather than the single Commitments men often make.

Belenky et al. added insight into the thought processes of the Commitment positions. The thought process uses *constructed knowledge* where procedural knowledge gained from others is integrated with personal or "inner" subjective knowledge based on personal experience and introspection. This constructed knowledge allows the individual to integrate thought and feeling and avoid the compartmentalization which Belenky et al. perceive as a shortcoming of objective knowledge. At the levels of Commitment a good instructor needs to provide freedom so that students can learn what they need to learn. The instructor also needs to forge linkages within the class.

Perry's model is a staged model which tends to ignore the situational specificity of behavior and knowledge. Real people in real situations have the annoying tendency to be complex. They don't fit into one stage, but depending upon the situation may be in several different stages. Despite this difficulty, Perry's model is a very useful model for conceptualizing the development of college students. A more recent model which builds on Perry's model is the reflective judgment model.

Alternatives to Growth

Perry hypothesizes that natural growth is from position 1 toward position 9. At Harvard he saw many students graduate in positions 7 and 8. However, he notes that growth is not inevitable. In engineering it is likely that many students leave in positions 3 and 4. The three alternatives to growth are *temporizing, retreat,* and *escape*. Note that these names incorporate Perry's hypothesis that movement from position 1 toward position 9 is growth and thus is desirable.

Temporizing

Growth does not occur linearly. Instead, periods of intense growth are commonly followed by pauses or plateaus. Perry defined *temporizing* as a pause in growth over a full academic year. All students go through plateau periods. Temporizing is just a rather long plateau and by itself is not bad. It may be a period in which the student gathers strength for the growth which lies ahead. In this case the student often seems aware that he or she is waiting for the correct combination of energy and will to move on. In an alternate mood of temporizing the student waits for fate to decide what will happen and may drift into escape.

Retreat

Retreat is regression to earlier positions. The most dramatic such retreat is movement back to position 3 or 2 when the complexities of relativism and multiplicity become overwhelming. (Retreat into position 1 is also possible, but in Perry's study these students presumably dropped out of Harvard.) Retreat into dualism requires an enemy. The student must be on her or his guard against the pluralistic university. Students seem to be most susceptible to retreating to dualism when they rely on authoritarian structures for emotional control. Retreat also occurs from higher levels but is not as dramatic. For example, a student may retreat from position 6 or 5 to position 4 where he or she can hide in the concept that "everyone has the right to his or her own opinion."

Escape

In escape the student avoids Commitment by exploiting the detachment afforded by positions 4 and 5. Perry's team noted two paths of escape both of which started from temporizing. In *dissociation* the student drifts into a passive delegation of responsibility to fate. She or he ends up in position 4. The alternate path is *encapsulation* which may be a favorite of engineering students. In encapsulation one avoids relativism by sheer competence in one's field. The student becomes very good at engineering but avoids any questions of deeper meaning or value. Engineers can use encapsulation to stay in position 4 or 5 for years. Escape need not be permanent, and people find different ways to resume growth.

Implications for Engineering Education

Perry's model has both value-free and value-laden implications for engineering education. Since the subject is less controversial, we will start with the implications which are relatively value-free. The major inescapable conclusion from Perry's model is that different students require different learning environments. This is no surprise since all models of learning come to the same conclusion. Students are not capable of understanding knowledge or questions which are too far above them as far as Perry's positions are concerned. If pushed to try to understand this material, they will become frustrated. How far above is too far? Perry does not address this issue. From our experience, questions which are one position above the student's position can, perhaps with considerable difficulty, be answered. Questions or knowledge two positions above the student's current position cause frustration. Students are capable of answering questions in positions below them although they may find these questions easy or may read too much into them. Appropriate teacher responses at each position were discussed with the descriptions of each position. How does the teacher provide an optimum learning environment for a heterogeneous class with students at a variety of levels? This is the key challenge of individualizing instruction, and there is no clear-cut answer.

Most of the applications of Perry's model to engineering education involve the value judgment that growth on Perry's scale is desirable (at least up to some level) and should be fostered. Perry considered this question and decided that growth was both natural and desirable. However, his sample contained no engineering students and in many ways was quite narrow. The faculty at each school need to face the question of whether or not to encourage growth on Perry's scale. Failure to encourage growth is equivalent to a negative answer. Currently, engineering students show little progress toward higher Perry levels and may actually regress slightly during their engineering studies. Thus, if the faculty decide that growth is desirable, engineering education must be changed.

As noted previously, we feel that there are clear moral grounds for strongly encouraging students in position 1 to grow into position 2. Students and practicing engineers in positions 1 and 2 will have significant difficulty practicing engineering in our multiplistic society. Fortunately, the samples reported by Fitch and Culver and Pavelich and Fitch showed very few students who were clearly in position 2 (and none in position 1). A large number of students were in transition between positions 2 and 3, and the mean position for all engineering students was about 2.8. Students in transition between positions 2 and 3 can see and accept multiplicity in some areas, and they accept that authority does not have all the answers. This transition region appears to be the minimum region in which a student can successfully study and practice engineering. These engineers cannot see the big picture, and without further growth they are unlikely to advance significantly in their careers. Fitch and Culver also reported many students in position 3 and a few in the transition between position 3 and 4. No undergraduate engineering students in positions 4 or higher were observed.

Pavelich and Fitch found that the written test used to measure students' developmental levels (Measure of Intellectual Development, the MID) was quite conservative. Interviews showed students who were at levels 4 and 5. This should be contrasted to Perry's sample of liberal arts students at Harvard where the average entering level was approximately position 4 and 75 percent were judged to be in position 7 or 8 at graduation.

The reasons for moving students to at least the transition between positions 2 and 3 are clear. Below this level they will have difficulty functioning as engineering students. Graduate students in thesis masters and Ph.D. programs will have trouble functioning below level 3 since they will not be able to answer the question "What do they want?" Research in graduate school seems to be structured to encourage the transition to position 3 if the student is not already there. Continued graduate study often moves the graduate student into position 4. Thus, engineering schools have implicitly made the decisions that undergraduates should reach at least the 2-to-3 transition and that graduate students should reach level 3 or 4 before graduation.

Is this sufficient? Probably most faculty will answer no. They want graduate students to operate at least at the level of the better students (position 4), and they want undergraduates to approach this level (say the 3-to-4 transition). In this regard Perry offers an interesting quote: "Fifty years ago, our researches suggest, a college senior might achieve a world view such as that of Position 3 or Position 4 on our scheme and count himself a mature man."

Superficially, it is easy to conclude that engineering education must change and take students past position 4. However, there are many dangers to this.

1 Taking the student to position 5 will fill the student with doubts about engineering as a profession. If a school purposely takes a student to position 5, the school must ethically help her or him to at least position 6. Some of these students will decide to make a Commitment to another profession.

2 It is difficult to take engineering students to position 5 even if we decide we want to. Engineering education at the undergraduate level reinforces positions 2 and 3, and at the graduate level does little to push students to position 5. Engineering students are very adept at escaping into competence once they reach position 3 or 4.

3 Many employers are happy with the current graduates at both undergraduate and graduate levels. This includes engineering schools as employers of Ph.D.s.

4 A consensus of engineering professors does not exist.

5 Absolute standards in physical laws are a useful mental construct despite the Heisenberg uncertainty principle. Perry's relativism can undermine this absolute standard

6 Some professors feel that there *should* be absolute standards in engineering ethics. This is a different value judgment than Perry's.

There are reasons for encouraging students to move beyond their current positions.

1 Growth appears to be natural and in this sense is "good."

2 Growth into positions 7 through 9 appears to be necessary to function well in important positions such as vice-president, dean, president, and CEO. In a technological society we need more engineers in these positions.

3 "The main trouble with engineers has not been their lack of morality. It has been their failure to recognize that life is complex"

4 For women, movement to higher-level positions is empowering and helps them act as equals with men.

What types of activities and teaching encourage growth? Fitch and Culver, Culver, and Culver and Fitch make the following suggestions based on the work of Lee Knefelkamp. First, since highly structured courses reinforce the lower levels, the curriculum should be restructured so that courses become progressively less structured. Second, a diversity of learning tasks is required, which means that the use of a single textbook in a course probably is not enough. Third, students need concrete learning experiences such as case studies, team projects, industrial experience, and so forth. These experiences should be designed to reinforce diversity. Fourth, a learning environment which supports risk taking needs to be developed in engineering classes and in the university as a whole. Additional suggestions can be added from the research of Belenky et al.. First, the student needs assurance that she is capable, and this support is needed from the beginning. Successful programs for women in engineering always include a significant component of support. Unfortunately, many women distrust praise from male professors.

"The women worried that professors who praised their minds really desired their bodies". Second, separating evaluation from instruction is valuable for many students. It is difficult for many professors to be supportive when they know they will have to evaluate later. Evaluation and instruction can be separated by using separate competency examinations scored by outsiders or by having separate help classes taught by instructors not involved in the graded class. Third, professors need to think out loud instead of presenting prepackaged thoughts as finished solutions. Finally, it is particularly important for professors of engineering and science "to avoid the appearance of omniscience".

One learning environment designed to encourage intellectual growth is the *practice-theory-practice* model developed by Lee Knefelkamp which has been applied in engineering education by Culver. In this model a concrete experience (practice) is used to introduce the concept. Then theory is developed to explain the experience. Finally, further practice is used to reinforce the theory and to provide an extension to other material. This type of cycle appears to be particularly important for women who found concepts useful in understanding their experience but balked at an abstract approach devoid of experience. To be effective for producing intellectual development, the experiences and theory must be understandable at the stage of development of the student, but the experience must also challenge the student.

Perry found that dormitory living was very important for moving students out of the lower levels. He also found that liberal arts courses were very valuable in helping students grow. Can liberal arts courses help engineering students grow on Perry's scale? The answer appears to be of the "yes, but" variety. Florman is strongly in favor of liberal arts for engineers, yet he notes, "One need not be a broadly educated scholar in order to be a topnotch engineer." Liberal arts courses can be useful, but some restructuring is probably needed. Certain courses such as beginning language courses and beginning economics courses have little effect. In other liberal arts courses engineers need to be mixed in with students from other areas. Putting all engineers into the same class defeats much of the purpose of achieving diversity. Since engineering students often see liberal arts courses as unimportant, the engineering *faculty* has to work hard to change this opinion. And since the students do not take a critical mass of liberal arts courses, ideas of multiplicity and relativism need to be reinforced in engineering classes. The liberal arts courses should be selected to challenge the student successfully no matter what his or her level. Dissonance, which is necessary for change, can be generated by writing or discussion but not by multiple-choice tests. Thus, courses must have significant writing or discussion.

One additional implication of Perry's model is somewhat disturbing. Mature students may find beginning engineering and science courses intellectually unchallenging and perhaps even stultifying. These students may find liberal arts or the social sciences more intellectually fulfilling and drop engineering. Evidence for this is contained in the study of Tobias exploring why some students drop science and engineering. A paradoxical result of this is that with current course levels it may be advantageous to delay intellectual growth until students have completed the lower-level courses. Obviously, there are many views on how much engineering education should do to move students on Perry's scale, but there is absolutely no correct view.

Piaget's theories have had a major impact on the teaching of science, but little impact in engineering. One possible reason for this difference is that engineers generally teach only engineers, whereas scientists teach everyone in the university. Thus, engineering classes have a small percentage of students who are in the concrete operational stage. Since there are few of them and most of them do not survive in engineering, it has been easy for engineering professors to ignore them.

Teaching Perry's model to graduate students can be an interesting experience for an engineering professor. We have encountered strong resistance to Perry's value judgment that growth on his model is positive. This resistance came from strongly religious graduate students. The most palatable presentation of Perry's model for these students clearly separated the observed behavior (the positions) from the value judgment. In addition, these students preferred to consider relativism as a way in which people *can* look at the world instead of Perry's formulation that this *is* the way the world is.

There is a strong tendency to demand equal rights and opportunities for women without looking at the real differences between men and women which were discovered in the research by Belenky et al.. In our opinion equal opportunity does not imply an education that is exactly the same for men and women. Since many current educational practices are more tuned to the ways men learn and develop, women have less opportunity to benefit.

Ideally, an equal opportunity education would involve many educational opportunities which are helpful for students with very different developmental needs and methods of knowing. Belenky et al. noted that there are different methods of knowing than those identified by Perry. The different paths appear to be the result of socialization, not hardwired gender differences. Once we admit to more than one approach to knowledge, it is logical while studying multiplicity to expect multiple paths caused by different socialization procedures in different societies. What other paths might there be? Palmer discusses a spiritual path. Another path is through dreams. The Senoi tribe in Malaysia clearly uses dreams as a path to knowledge. Although it is difficult to conceive of teaching engineering in Western society through dreams, they have often played a role in the solution of technical problems. Other paths to knowing exist and have been explored by anthropologists.

PLAY: AN IMPORTANT TOOL FOR COGNITIVE DEVELOPMENT

Early childhood educators often make the point that "children learn through play." But what does this statement really mean? In the scenario described above, what exactly is Gabriella learning as she plays? She is planning what she is going to do, carrying out her plan, and then recalling what she did (in the HighScope Curriculum, this is known as the plan-do-review process). But did we realize that she is developing key cognitive functions such as working memory, self-regulation (e.g., being aware of and controlling her feelings and actions), internal language or "self-talk," and the ability to organize, focus, plan, strategize, prioritize, initiate, and perform other skills that determine later success in school? Indeed she is, and these cognitive skills are all part of what we call executive function — the cognitive abilities that control and regulate other behavior. Play helps young children develop these abilities. Unfortunately, due to the demands for accountability in public schools and pressure to accelerate young children's academic learning, time for play is either being eliminated or limited, and play is much less often child-initiated or free from constraints.

The Importance of Play

Stuart Brown, Founder of the National Institute for Play, has said that "play is anything that spontaneously is done for its own sake...*appears* purposeless, produces pleasure and joy, leads one to the next stage of mastery". Edward Miller and Joan Almon describe play as "activities that are freely chosen and directed by children and arise from intrinsic motivation". Jeannine Ouellette refers to play as "activity that is unencumbered by adult direction, and does not depend on manufactured items or rules imposed by someone other than the kids themselves". When children play, they are actively engaged in activities they have freely chosen; that is, they are self-directed and motivated from within.

Kenneth Ginsburg, stating the position of the American Academy of Pediatrics, says that "play is essential to development because it contributes to the cognitive, physical, social, and emotional well-being of children and youth" Play is so important to children's development that the United Nations High Commission for Human Rights recognizes it as a basic right of every child.

The many books and articles written on the subject list a wide range of cognitive, emotional, interpersonal, and creative benefts (refer to the sidebar on p. 4 for some highlights).

Many experts agree that play provides the foundation for learning and later academic success. For example, research demonstrates the importance of child-initiated play (as opposed to play defned and directed by adults) in the development of language and literacy skills. When children determine the direction and content of their own play, they have many opportunities to hear and practice language. This type of language-rich play directly infuences future development of higher mental functions. When children are allowed to initiate their own play, they are then able to express those choices in words and to interact and converse freely with other children and adults. The International Association for the Evaluation of Educational Achievement (IEA) Preprimary Project, a cross-national longitudinal study, found that children's language performance at age seven was signif-cantly higher when teachers had allowed children to choose their own activities at age four.

Developmental psychologists identify four types of child-initiated play: *exploratory play* (discovering the properties of materials and tools, not to make something, but for the pleasure of doing it); *constructive play* (making things); *dramatic play* (acting out "make believe" or pretend situations and assuming various roles); and for older children, *games with rules*.

Gabrielle was engaging in the frst three types of play, but especially in dramatic (make-believe) play. When children spend time in make-believe play, they use self-directed talk and develop other features of the critical cognitive skills of executive function. We will look at how child-initiated play in general, and make-believe play in particular, help to develop executive function.

Components of Executive Function

Although researchers have not completely agreed on the elements of executive function, Chris Dendy outlines fve general components based on Russell Barkley and Tom Brown's work on attention defcit disorders.

Working Memory and Recall

The frst component of executive function is working memory and recall, which is the ability to hold facts in one's mind as well as being able to access them from one's long-term memory at any point in time. In the HighScope preschool daily routine, planning and recall times are opportunities for children to tap into their working memory and articulate their ideas, choices, and decisions about what they want to do (planning time), and remember and refect on their work-time actions and experiences (recall time). Planning builds children's self-confdence and self-control while leading to more concentrated, complex play. Recall time exercises children's capacities to form and talk about mental images, helps them build their memory skills, and expands their awareness of time outside the present. As presented in the diagram below, Gabrielle is exhibiting these functions during her planning and recall.

Activation, Arousal, and Effort

The second component includes *activation* (getting started), *arousal* (paying attention), and *effort* (fnishing work). On a larger scale, this would apply to the whole plan-do-review process. However, work time is the part of the day when children use these functions the most because children are following through with their plans by getting the appropriate materials, carrying through with their intentions while adapting to and solving any problems that arise, and then completing the task. During work time, these functions are used over and over again as children make new plans and follow through with them. As presented in the diagram on p. 4, Gabrielle sticks with her plan throughout work time, is highly engaged with pretend play, and solves problems and carries through with her intentions until cleanup time. It is important to recognize that it takes purposeful play for these cognitive functions to fully develop. Because their play is self-directed — and therefore meaningful and purposeful to them — children are highly motivated to maintain their engagement. Children who aimlessly wander around during free play are not exhibiting the highest levels of complex play and strategizing needed to use and develop these higher-level thinking skills. Likewise, when children's play activities are directed by adults, initiation (activation) is taken out of their hands, interest (arousal) is diminished, and actions (effort) may be aimed at pleasing others rather than thinking about and learning from their own experiences.

Child-Driven Play

When children pursue play under their own impulse and initiative, they

- Practice decision-making skills
- Discover their own interests
- Engage fully in what they want to pursue
- Develop creative problem-solving skills
- Practice skills in resolving conficts
- Develop self-regulation
- Develop trust, empathy, and social skills
- Develop language and communication skills
- Use their creativity and imagination
- Develop skills for critical thinking and leadership
- Analyze and refect on their experiences
- Reduce stress in their everyday lives

Controlling Emotions

The third component of executive function is *controlling emotions*, that is, the ability to tolerate frustration and to think before acting or speaking. This is part of self-regulation. Children with developed self-regulation are more able to control their emotions and behaviors, resist impulses, and exert self-discipline. Children who participate in a consistent, reliable problem-solving approach learn to express strong emotions in nonhurtful ways; appreciate their own views as well as the views of others; listen and discuss the details of problems; recognize that when there is a problem, there are lots of possibilities for solutions; and deliberate, negotiate, and collaborate with others while staying calm when confronted with a confict or a problem. When the magnetic tiles continued to fall down, Gabrielle could have had an emotional "melt down" or shown strong frustration by kicking at the tiles and walking away. However, due to her self-regulation skills, she stuck with the task and solved the problem by building with the tiles another way. There is evidence that some children who spend a signifcant amount of time using video games and watching violent media programming imitate what they see, thinking these are acceptable behaviors, and do not know how to self-regulate when frustrated. These children may get angry, even at the game itself.

Internalizing Language

The fourth component is *internalizing language* — using "self talk" — to control one's behavior and direct future actions. As adults, we internally talk to ourselves throughout the day (e.g., to master problems, control emotions, and plan) — we just remind ourselves not to talk back! With young children, private speech is key to these functions because it helps the children direct their own actions; for example, what to do with their hands, bodies, and voices, which in turn is part of developing self-regulation. Make-believe play in particular is most helpful for the development of private speech. Alix Spiegel quotes Laura Berk: "This type of self-regulating language...has been shown in many studies to be predictive of executive function" Returning to the opening scenario, as Gabrielle plays with the dogs, she uses private speech (internal dialogue) as she directs the pretend play. Children who spend the majority of their time in teacher-directed activities or watching television or computer screens — that is, listening to others talk — miss out on opportunities to develop self-regulation through internal dialogue and thought.

Complex Problem Solving

The ffth component of executive function is *complex problem solving* — taking an issue apart, analyzing the pieces, and reconstituting and reorganizing it into new ideas. During work time and small-group time, children are faced with many challenging problems as part of carrying out their plans and completing tasks. Part of problem solving with young children is helping them recognize that there is a problem and then involving them in the process of fnding a solution. When children are engaged and adults avoid jumping in and solving problems for them, the children learn to rely on their own ideas and decision-making skills and to see themselves as confdent problem solvers. For Gabrielle, through many experiences with magnetic tiles and solving problems, she needed no assistance in solving the problem and coming up with a new idea to continue her plans. Children who lack the experiences in play, and who spend most of their time in adult-organized activities, lack the creativity that it takes to solve problems mentally.

In summary, we as educators are entrusted with the responsibility of fully engaging children's minds and bodies in the way they learn best. By understanding the importance of play, how it helps to develop key cognitive functions, and what these functions are, we can become more effective in protecting purposeful play and more intentional in our interactions with children during their play. In this issue's "Classroom Hints" article, we will discuss strategies that assist in the development of execution function in young children. However, most important, we must remember that play is simply about having fun!

References

Kurfiss, J. G., (1988). *Critical Thinking: Theory, Research, Practice, and Possibilities*, ASHE-ERIC Higher Education Report No. 2, Association for the Study of Higher Education, Washington, DC.

Lawson, A. E., Abraham, M. R., and Renner, J. W., (1989). *A Theory of Instruction: Using the Learning Cycle to Teach Science Concepts and Thinking Skills,* Monograph 1, National Association for Research in Science Teaching, Cincinnati, OH.

Perry, W. G., Jr., (1970). *Forms of Intellectual and Ethical Development in the College Years: A Scheme,* Holt, Rinehart and Winston, New York.

Phillips, J. L., Jr., (1981). *Piaget's Theory: A Primer*, W.H. Freeman, San Francisco.

Piaget, J., (1950). *The Psychology of Intelligence*, Harcourt and Brace, New York.

11

Fostering Creativity through Education

Although the argument exits for long that whether creativity can be increased, there seems to be a consensus view within the realm of education that creativity is amenable to teaching. The attempt of fostering creativity through train-ing was given more attention in the mid twentieth century, when psychometric researchers, such as Guilford, Torrance, put efforts in extending and measuring individual's creativity. Guilford claimed that:

"Like most behaviour, creative activity probably represents to some extent many learned skills. There may be limitations set on these skills by heredity; but I am convinced that through learning one can extend the skills within those limitations".

Certain training programmes designed to help stimulate indi-vidual's creativity were then proposed, for instance, thinking tools and brainstorming technique were suggested to help people generate diverse thoughts and solutions. CPS (the Osborn Parnes Creative Problem Solving process) is another model that has been widely applied and researched. In addi-tion to pragmatic techniques of creativity training programmes, cognitive, social psychologists, and educational researchers have also generated implications for fostering creativity in school.

The insights and implications in developing creativity through education can be scrutinized into three aspects. First aspect is concerning about teaching, including how to provide creative and innovative practices which stimulates the development of multiple intelligence, possibility thinking, and higher-level thinking, or how to involve the opportunity of exploring and solving problem. The second aspect of the implications suggests creating an environment, both external and social, that is stimulating and supportive to learners' motivation/enthusiasm and creative behaviour. The third concern of nurturing creativity is about teacher ethos, which includes maintaining an open attitude towards creative ideas or behaviours, showing a humanistic pupil control ideology (as opposed to being authoritarian), being flexible, and valuing independence thinking.

Albeit these insights focus on different dimensions of developing creativity and the assumptions behind each view are not opposing and are even consistent, distinctions between pedagogical views were formed and varied terms used referring to a similar conception, due to different research approach. In light of this situation, a framework of creative pedagogy consisting of three interrelated elements is theorized with a confluence approach, in attempt to offer a more holistic view of fostering

The term for "environment" varies in the literature; other terms include climate atmosphere, conditions, classroom/school environment, and school culture creativity in education.

A Confluence Approach

Wehner, Csikszentmihalyi, and Magyari-Berck described the situation within creativity research with the fable of the blind men and the elephant, that people touch different parts of the huge animal but claim what they touch and know is the whole picture. As a result of the fractional findings of different approaches of creativity research, a confluence approach which integrated multiple dimensions and factors of creativity, has been developed since the last two decades of 20th century. Complex models, for instance, Amabile's three-factor componential model, Gruber and his colleagues' developmental evolving-systems model, and Csikszentmihalyi's systems model, were proposed to illustrate the multilevel interactions of different factors for creativity.

Likewise, confluence approach and complex model can also be found in researching pedagogical practices. In a review of modern conceptions of pedagogy since the 1930s, Watkins & Mortimore (suggested four phases of pedagogy research, including:

- a focus on different types of teachers. a focus on the contexts of teaching. a focus on teaching and learner

- complex models that offer an integrated conceptualization of pedagogy

Watkins & Mortimore explained that the last phase represents a more current view of pedagogy, and complex models are employed to describe relations between the teacher, classroom context/content, and the view of learning. The model differentiates itself from the previous phase of pedagogy research which focused on linear cause-effect chains and simplified prescriptions for action.

Keen Efforts Without Clear Guideline

Since the late 90's enhancing creativity has become a global-wide interest reflecting social and economic changes and the need to raise competitiveness in globalization activities. The function of education is re-conceptualized as building human capital by equipping youngsters with innovation and creative capacities in addition to knowledge delivering. Curriculum reform has been carried out and creativity has been included in education policy in western countries such as the US, UK, France, Germany, Sweden and Australia.

Many Asian countries have also responded to this trend. For instance, educational reform is urged to release children's creative potential in China, since the phenomenon of students' high achievement in math in international tests yet low ranking in imagination and creativity was noticed. In Hong Kong, creativity is recognized as one of the three generic skills to be developed in education, and several general principles for developing creativity are suggested in curriculum documents. Other places like Japan, South Korea, Taiwan, and Singapore have also implemented curriculum reforms with an emphasis on creativity development in a top-down mode. With governmental support, keen efforts were put in these Asian regions in promoting creativity education.

However, in addition to point out teachers and traditional practice as impediments to enhancing creativity in the classroom, there is little discussion in the initiatives on guidelines of pedagogical strategies to adopt for fostering creativity. On the other hand, there is little response from school teachers to the urge of enhancing creativity through education. As mentioned earlier, varied terms and disparities were created due to different approaches and foci of creativity research. Therefore a comprehensive framework is proposed to offer a more consistent rhetoric. While in the East, a framework is suggested to render a clearer guideline of pedagogy in facilitating learner creativity, as well as to challenge the perceptions and ways of teaching/ learning taken for granted in many Asian regions where creativity is often discouraged.

Theoretical Assumptions of the Framework

There are varied explanations and theories of creativity; for instance, some psychologists believe creativity to arise from unconscious drives, while some psychological researchers defined creativity as a syndrome or a complex. Some other researchers deem creativity as thinking skills, a product of creative thinking, or personal qualities. The varied views and definitions of creativity imply different research approach to creativity. Then what is the view of creativity within education? Although mainly drawing from theories of scholarly field of creativity studies, such as behaviourist, cognitive, social-psychological, or humanistic approach, the approach to creativity in education, as Craft suggests, has its unique concerns, including the relationship between creativity and knowledge, curriculum, and appropriate pedagogical strategies to foster creativity in the classroom. The perceptions of creativity this approach adopts are hence more relevant to educational values and settings. Generally there are two premises underpinning the approach of creativity in education: first is the view that creativity can be developed, and second is that all individuals have the potential to be creative.

Creativity Can Be Developed

The argument over whether creativity is amenable to education can be dated back to the nineteen century when the studies of human genius and creative achievement were the main concern. In the early twentieth century, the perception of the source for creativity has gradually shifted from inherited genius possessed by the highly talented individuals, to diverse human abilities. Owing to the attempt of psychometric researchers in measuring and fostering individuals' thinking abilities since the 50's, and to the later multidimensional theories of intelligence, more interest was given to developing creativity in education.

Educational researchers, for instance, Fryer maintains that creative skills could be taught through certain strategies: "Training in creative problem solving can enable people to be skilled in finding the best solution quickly...". Esquivel also emphasizes the role of educators in enhancing the creative potential of every student. In contemporary research, creativity is embraced as a multi-dimensional and developmental construct; it is believed that creativity is a developmental shift and a life long process.

Everyone Has the Potential to Be Creative

As mentioned, more attention was given after the 50's to enhancing creative development, and since then several waves of creativity in education occurred. In the earlier wave of promoting creativity, child-centred and innovative pedagogy were called for in the attempt to reform traditional school practice. Educators hold the view that children are naturally creative, open to experience, and tend to be attracted by novel things, and this natural quality will diminish unless it is nurtured by favorable environments created by adults. Humanistic scholars also see creativity as the natural urge of individuals to develop, extend, express and activate their capacities.

The latest wave in enhancing creativity began in the 90's due to the intense social, economic, and technological changes nowadays; creativity is reckoned as a basic capacity for survival as well as for future success. Csikszentmihalyi put it this way to show the altered status of creativity: "In the Renaissance creativity might have been a luxury for the few, but by now it is a necessity for all". At this point, the relationship between creativity and education is more than the previous goal, to encourage personal development and self-actualization, but to equip youngsters with the basic capacity for future life. Yet regardless in the earlier or recent urge for fostering creativity, the belief behind the efforts that every individual has the potential to be creative is unchanged.

Promoted Aspects of Creativity within Education

Psychologists have made a significant distinction between product-oriented and process-oriented creativity, focusing on different facets and values of novel invention Product creativity makes the assumption that creativity should be defined as the production of both novel and appropriate work. "Novel refers to original work; ... appropriate simply concerns the usefulness of the product towards a certain need". In contrast to the utility and productivity, process-oriented creativity focuses on the "mental process" involving creative potential to generate new ideas, solution of problems, and the self-actualization of individuals.

Other researchers draw a distinction between "big C" and "little c" creativity with the former having wider influence in society and the latter being relevant to everyday creativity. Instead of highlighting remarkable achievements, little c creativity (LCC) focuses on the agency of ordinary people and recognizes everyone's potential to be creative in terms of everyday problem-solving. To illustrate its features, Craft proposed the notion of "possibility thinking" as the core of LCC, involving nine qualities that manifest the aspiration of asking the question "*what if*" when facing blockage. Whether creativity is domain-specific or transferrable is another debatable issue. Although creativity is often related to arts or poetry for instance, and some researchers believe creative expression and outcome requires specific knowledge and skills, the qualities and capacities of everyday creativity, as Lucas maintains, "can be demonstrated in any subject at school or in any aspect of life".

In a recent study, a four c model of creativity is proposed based on the original distinction, for the reason of more precise judgment and measurement of creativity. Two other constructs are introduced: *professional* and *mini-c* creativity. Similar to the educational concern of LCC, mini-c intends to describe the creative insights experienced by the students and to "encompass the creativity inherent in the learning process". Because of its premise and concern, the concept of process creativity, LCC, and mini-c creativity are found useful in advocating educational efforts in creativity. It is the developmental process that is underlined, and therefore what really matters is the intention and evaluation of the agent, and as a result, the self-actualization. In recent years, LCC is also regarded as a life capacity for future success. Thus nurturing creativity through education is to support the individual's development in creative qualities to face everyday problem, to support their need for self-actualization, as well as enhance their capacities for future success.

Framework of Creative Pedagogy

Informed by the assumptions and the aspects of creativity nurtured within education, a framework of creative pedagogy is proposed to illustrates the relationship between creativity and pedagogical practices. *Creative pedagogy* is put forward to describe practice that enhances creative development through three interrelated elements—*creative teaching*, *teaching for creativity*, and *creative learning*. Rather than a situation in which teaching and learning are two parallel processes that rarely meet, the three interconnected elements complement and result in each other, rendering it a resonant process. A supportive climate for developing creative abilities and qualities is created through the interaction between inventive and effective teaching (by the creative facilitator), and creative learning (by the active learner).

Creative Teaching and Teaching for Creativity

A distinction is made in the NACCCE report between *teaching creatively* and *teaching for creativity,* defining the former as "using imaginative approaches to make learning more interesting and effective'" while relating the latter to the objective of identifying young people's creative abilities, as well as encouraging and providing opportunities for the development of those capacities. Albeit having different foci—creative teaching focuses on teacher practice, whereas teaching for creativity highlights learner agency —the two practices are seen interconnected and indispensible in this framework.

For the features of *creative teaching*, such as imaginative, dynamic, and innovative approaches, often inspire children's imagination and new ideas and lead directly to teaching for creativity. On the other hand, the pedagogical strategies of *teaching for creativity that* facilitate children's agency and engagement, such as strategies of learning to learn, or to exploring more new possibilities, often seek to be inventive in order to arouse curiosity and learning motivation.

In addition, a supportive ethos for nurturing creativity can be found in both practices. Through teaching creatively, teachers encourage learners' creativity by passing on their enthusiasm, imagination, and other talents; whilst creating a learning context for problem solving and appreciating learners' creative contributions are essential principles of teaching for creativity.

The pedagogical principles of foster children's possibility thinking identified by Cremin, Burnard, and Craft, are useful to describe how teachers create a supportive environment through effective strategies that prioritize children's autonomy. They maintain that the three principles, involving *standing back*, *profiling learner agency*, and *creating time and space*, help to encourage the children's questioning and active engagement in learning by passing the decision making and the responsibility for learning back to the child. In short, the two practices are interrelated and are salient elements of building a context for children's creative development and engagement.

Creative Learning

When considering pedagogy, most research and implications seem to focus on the teacher, classroom context, or teaching content, and few include the importance of learning until the complex model of pedagogy proposed in recent years. The neglect of a spontaneous and creative learning and its characteristics, such as autonomy, could result in difficulties in fostering children's creativity. Therefore *creative learning* is considered a salient feature in the framework of creative pedagogy.

Torrance contrasted *learning creatively* with *learning by authority* when arguing about giving children a chance to learn and think creatively. Children learn by authority when they are told what they should learn and accept the ideas from the authority (e.g. teachers, books); whereas in the other process, children learn by means such as questioning, inquiring, searching, manipulating, experimenting, and even aimless play. Children explore out of their curiosity, which is natural to human beings. Torrance also connected learning and teaching by suggesting that during the learning process, children's creative skills and methods are required; while at the same time the learning context, which is filled with curious problems to explore, stimulates spontaneous learning and flexes the capacities for learning and thinking creatively.

In more recent studies, several features of creative learning are revealed including playfulness, collaboration, development for imagination and possibility thinking, and supportive/resourceful context. These features of creative learning not only echo the previous argument, but imply the interplay between creative endeavours of teachers and learners.

Interplay between the Framework Elements

In an article of stressing creative and improvisational teaching, Sawyer criticizes that contemporary reform efforts has associated creative teaching with "scripted instruction", which emphasizes important skills for teachers yet often denies teacher creativity. This scripted approach is considered problematic for it suggests teachers as "solo performers reading from a script, with the students as the passive, observing audience". Thus Sawyer conceives of creative teaching as improvisational performance, highlighting the in-teractional, collaborative and emergent nature of classroom practice.

Adding to the view of seeing creative teaching as improvisa-tional process that allows "collaborative emergence", it is argued that the creative endeavors of both teachers and learners in an effective teaching/learning process are indispensable. In other words, the three elements of creative pedagogy interplay and contribute to each other, forming a dialogic and improvisa-tional process with creative inspiration, supportive teacher ethos, effective inquiry-based strategies, and learners' creative and autonomous engagement.

In short, instead of merely addressing one of the aspects of teaching practice that fosters creativity, the proposed framework of creative pedagogy embraces three features—creative teaching, teaching for creativity, and creative learning. It intends to describe the interplay between innovative teaching and effective strategies which facilitate and are responded by children's creative and active engagement, as well as to encourage a more comprehensive practice in developing learners' creativity.

Prospective Research in Creative Pedagogy

As argued, a framework of creative pedagogy is proposed to connect different foci of the implications for fostering creativity, and to promote the overlooked learning aspect as well. In addition, it is introduced to offer a clearer pedagogical guideline to encourage the educators/practitioners to re-examine educational views and methods of fostering creativity, especially in an Asian context. In fact, a study was conducted and in which a series of drama lessons based on the framework of creative pedagogy was designed and taught to understand the Taiwanese teachers and pupils' responses to a creative pedagogy in drama.

The finding shows that the pupils considered the lessons useful in developing certain creative qualities, such as imagination, independent thinking, and risk-taking. The participants also identified characteristics and strategies used in the lessons that made the development possible, such as innovation, playfulness, task-oriented, collaborative learning, and the teacher's guidance. Although most of the pupils conveyed their enjoyment of the lessons, tensions arose during the teaching/learning process, for instance, there were different views of the space and freedom offered, of the playfulness of the learning, and the strategies and ethos which may result in the teacher losing authority, to name a few. Based on these findings, more specific issues in fostering creativity through creative pedagogy are raised;

concerns of re-evaluation of teacher's role, ways of learning, and contextualization of creative pedagogy are therefore urged.

There are other concerns over creative pedagogy that could be addressed further in addition to the above study. The sus-tainability of the impact of a creative pedagogy used, for instance, could be investigated, especially when the pedagogy is adopted in a context that is less supportive to creative development. The perceptions of applying creative pedagogy are worthwhile to learn from participants with different positions in the educational system, such as academic researchers, policy makers, school principals, or parents, in addition to the pupils and their classroom teachers. It would also be useful to focus on studying teachers' responses through using creative pedagogy in teacher education to nurture their own creativity. In terms of cultural issue, it would be interesting to learn and compare the indigenous perceptions and practices of creative teaching in Asian countries with the *creative pedagogy theorized and applied in Western classrooms*, and the possible benefit and means of balancing between the two sets of values and practices.

References

Amabile, T. M. (1996). *Creativity in context.* Boulder: Westview Press.

Armstrong, T. (2000). *Multiple intelligences in the classroom.* Alexan-dria, VA: Association for Supervision and Curriculum Development.

Chen, L. (1997). *Teaching for creative thinking.* Taipei: Shtabook.

Choe, I. S. (2006). Creativity—A sudden rising star in Korea. In J. C. Kaufman, & R. J. Sternberg (Eds.), *The international handbook of creativity.* New York, NY: Cambridge University Press.

Collins, M. A., & Amabile, T. M. (1999). Motivation and creativity. In R. J. Sternberg (Ed.), *Handbook of creativity.* Cambridge: Cambridge University Press.

Craft, A. (2000). *Creativity across the primary curriculum: Framing and developing practice.* London: Routledge.

12

Learning and Teaching Skills for the Future

This literature review synthesizes published works on 21st century learning skills. There has been a signifcant shift over the last century from manufacturing to emphasizing information and knowledge services. Knowledge itself is growing ever more specialized and expanding exponentially. Information and communication technology is transforming how we learn and the nature of how work is conducted and the meaning of social relationships. Shared decision-making, information sharing, collaboration, innovation, and speed are essential in today's enterprises. No longer can students look forward to middle class success in the conduct of manual labor or use of routine skills – work that can be accomplished by machines or easily out-sourced to less expensive labor markets. Today, much success lies in being able to communicate, share, and use information to solve complex problems, in being able to adapt and innovate in response to new demands and changing circumstances, in being able to command and expand the power of technology to create new knowledge.

Hence, new standards for what students should be able to do are replacing the basic skill competencies and knowledge expectations of the past. To meet this challenge schools must be transformed in ways that will enable students to acquire the creative thinking, fexible problem solving, collaboration and innovative skills they will need to be successful in work and life. Some authors and organizations argue that 21st Century Learning Skills, the subject of this literature review, are critical for accomplishing the necessary transformation.

The Partnership for 21st Century Skills has developed a framework for 21st century learning, which describes the skills that students need to thrive in today's global economy. The North Central Regional Education Laboratory (NCREL) and the Metiri Group have also identifed a framework for 21st century skills, which is organized into four categories: digital age literacies, inventive thinking, efective communication, and high productivity. This literature review is organized in line with the framework developed by the Partnership r 21st Century Learning Skills. The literature review begins by defning 21st century learning skills, and then moves to address "Core Temes and Subjects," "Learning and Innovation Skills," "Life and Career Skills," and "Information, Media, and Technology Skills." The review concludes with discussions of 21st century support systems.

21ST CENTURY LEARNING SKILLS

The Educational Testing Service (ETS) in its publication, *Digital Transformation: A Literacy Framework for ICT Literacy,* defnes 21st century learning skills as the ability to a) collect and/or retrieve information, b) organize and manage information, c) evaluate the quality, relevance, and usefulness of information, and d) generate accurate information through the use of existing resources. NCREL identifes broader 21st century skills as achieving 21st century learning through digital age literacy, inventive thinking, efective communication, and high productivity. The Partnership for 21st century skills identifes six key elements for fostering 21st century learning: 1) emphasize core subjects, 2) emphasize learning skills, 3) use 21st century tools to develop learning skills, 4) teach and learn in a 21st century context, 5) teach and learn 21st century content, and 6) use 21st century assessments that measure 21st century skills.

What are 21st Century Learning Skills?

21st Century Core Subjects and Temes

Traditional education models have often focused on learning identifed content for subject areas (i.e. math, science, language arts, and social studies), and then assessing this content knowledge with quizzes, and tests at the end of a chapter or learning module. Desired outcomes within 21st century learning frameworks include learning traditional school subject and contemporary content themes in combination with the interdisciplinary 21st century themes. The core subjects and themes that frame 21st century learning include traditional core subjects while emphasizing civic literacy, global awareness, fnancial literacy, health literacy, and environmental literacy.

Civic literacy

Civic literacy speaks to the need for students to be able to understand and infuence civic decision-making. This theme focuses on the importance of staying informed and understanding governmental processes, being able to participate in civic life, and recognizing the local and global implications of civic decisions.

Donald Lazare's recent text, *Reading and Writing for Civic Literacy: The Critical Citizen's Guide to Argumentative Rhetoric* addresses a documented need for students to develop critical reading, writing, and thinking skills for participation in civic society. Lazare provides a number of lesson plans and classroom exercises for teachers to help students understand the ideological positions and the rhetorical patterns that underlie opposing viewpoints in current political debates.

Global awareness

The global awareness theme speaks to the need for students to be able to learn from and work collaboratively with individuals from diverse cultures, religions, ideologies, and lifestyles in an environment of openness and mutual respect. This theme also references the ways in which students utilize 21st century skills to understand and engage with global issues and diverse learning communities.

A nationwide poll of registered voters conducted in 2007 by the Partnership for 21st Century Skills, found that Americans are deeply concerned that the United States is not preparing young people with the skills they need to compete in the global economy. Gragert concurred, arguing that international collaborative problem solving is benefcial for students. In his study, Gragert noted that students who participated in international collaborative e-learning projects showed heightened motivation in class, improved reading and writing skills, and enhanced engagement. Adams & Carfagna argues that cross-cultural deliberation through Web 2.0 technologies helps to break down stereotypical notions regarding cultures other than one's own.

Financial Literacy

Financial literacy speaks to the set of skills individuals need to make informed economic decisions. Research indicates that there is considerable defciency in fnancial literacy among students and adults in the United States. Findings from the Jump$tart Coalition's biennial fnancial literacy tests of high school seniors in the contiguous United States show that students correctly answered 50 percent of the questions in 2002 (Jump$tart Coalition, 2002). Similarly, the Institute of Certifed Financial Planners, in a survey of Certifed Financial Planners (CFP) found that fnancial literacy is a major problem when it comes to making individual fnancial decisions. Other studies fnd that low-income consumers, those with less education, and African Americans and Hispanics also tend to have below-average fnancial literacy scores.

In recent years, supporters of fnancial education, defned as knowledge that helps people make sound, informed fnancial decisions, has been reinforced by the fndings of studies that show that fnancial literacy training has had a positive impact on fnancial knowledge. Braunstein & Welch argue, however, that an increase in fnancial knowledge does not necessarily translate into improved fnancial behavior. Instead, they contend that causality may be reversed since people may gain knowledge as they save and accumulate wealth, or there may be a third infuence, namely, family experiences and economic socialization, that afects both knowledge and behavior. Further examination of the relationship between the nature of economic socialization and fnancial literacy is much needed.

An emergent body of research suggests that poor job attendance and performance may be linked more closely to fnancial distress than to demographics. Financial education has been shown not only to enhance students' knowledge levels, but also to have a lasting positive impact on their fnancial behaviors. As schools work to prepare graduates to be efective workers, fnancial competency (i.e., managing money, understanding banking, using credit wisely, understanding taxes and insurance, understanding investing and homeownership, and understanding the implications of consumer fraud and identity theft) is an important curricular objective to consider.

Health Literacy

The emphasis on health literacy addresses the need for individuals to be able to access and use high quality information to make health-related decisions. This includes a working knowledge of ways to access health information and services and a working knowledge of preventative health measures.

Safeer & Keenan argue that inadequate health literacy can result in "difculty accessing health care, following instructions from a physician, and taking medication properly. Berkman et. al. published a report on literacy and health outcomes that was requested by the American Medical Association and funded by the AHRQ. This report addresses two key questions: Are literacy skills related to: (a) Use of health care services? (b) Health outcomes? (c) Costs of health care? (d) Disparities in health outcomes or health care service use according to race, ethnicity, culture, or age? For individuals with low literacy skills, what are efective interventions to: (a) Improve use of health care services? (b) Improve health outcomes? (c) Afect the costs of health care? (d) Improve health outcomes and/or health care service use among diferent racial, ethnic, cultural, or age groups? In 2003, the National Center for Education Statistics published *The Health Literacy of America's Adults: Results from the 2003 National Assessment of Adult Literacy*. This represented the frst release of the National Assessment of Adult Literacy (NAAL) health literacy results. The results are based on assessment tasks designed specifcally to measure the health literacy of adults living in the United States. For the purposes of this study, health literacy was reported using four performance levels: Below Basic, Basic, Intermediate, and Profcient. The majority of adults (53 percent) had Intermediate health literacy. About 22 percent had Basic and 14 percent had Below Basic health literacy. Relationships between health literacy and background variables.

The U.S. Department of Health and Human Services Ofce of Disease Prevention and Health Promotion's *Quick Guide to Health Literacy* provides a basic overview of key health literacy concepts and techniques for improving health literacy through communication, navigation, knowledge-building, and advocacy. It also provides the information for teachers and administrators to become efective advocates for improved health literacy.

Environmental Literacy

In January 2003, the National Science Foundation released a report of its Advisory Committee for Environmental Research and Education. The Committee found that "in the coming decades, the public will more frequently be called upon to understand complex environmental issues, assess risk, evaluate proposed environmental plans and understand how individual decisions afect the environment at local and global scales." The authors argued that environmentally literate individuals at the start of the

21st century will need to be able to understand and discuss both man-made and natural environmental issues and propose or debate alternative solutions to these problems. Tw o years later, the National Environmental Education & Training Foundation, concluded in a national survey, *Environmental Literacy in America 2005,* that "while the simplest forms of environmental knowledge are widespread, public comprehension of more complex environmental subjects is very limited."

Environmental literacy, in 2010, for the frst time, has been included in the U.S. Department of Education budget. In response to this Obama administration initiative, Senator Jack Reed responded, "This budget takes an important step toward boosting environmental education in the classroom and giving more kids the opportunity to get out and learn about the natural world around them. Environmental education can help raise student achievement in other core subjects like math and science. This is a smart investment in our children's future and the future of our planet."

David Orr, describes the need for and debate over environmental literacy in his book *Ecological Literacy*:

"The crisis of sustainability and the problems of education are in large measure a crisis of knowledge. But is the problem as is commonly believed, that we do not know enough? Or that we know too much? or that we do not enough about some things and too much about other things? Or is it that our scientifc methods are in some ways fawed? Is it that we have forgotten things we need to remember? Or is it that we have forgotten other ways of knowing that lie in the realm of vision, intuition, revelation, empathy, or even common sense? Such questions are not asked often enough.

Orr cites Garrett Hardin's defnition of ecological literacy as "the ability to ask 'What then?'" Hardin also cites the ability to read and calculate (literacy and numeracy), ecological literacy (the intimate knowledge of our landscapes, and an afnity for the living world). Orr, states that teachers need to both present the environmental issues in terms of systems and in an interdisciplinary fashion. This approach does not allow for the simplifcation of problems to a level where their connections to the context (i.e., land, water, environment, sense of place) are lost. Orr faults analytical modes of teaching that abstract problems from the context in the perceived interest of clarity and simplicity. He believes that this clarity is deceptive, because, devoid of context—and hence apparent relevance—the ideas do not stay with the students – they are not made relevant and connected to their daily lived life.

Stephen Schneider argues that we should not expect students to gain a detailed knowledge about the content of all environmentally relevant disciplines. Instead, he proposes that students should be taught how to ask three questions to teachers/experts that include "what can happen," "what are the odds," and "how do you know." He argues that students do not need to know the technical aspects of opposing views, but they should have the skill to evaluate the credibility of processes and arguments. Schneider defnes environmental literacy as the capability for a contextual and detailed understanding of an environmental problem in order to enable analysis, synthesis, evaluation, and ultimately sound and informed decision-making at a citizen's level. This means that "environmentally literate" students will have the knowledge, tools, and sensitivity to properly address environmental problems, and to conscientiously include the environment as one of the considerations in their work and daily living.

Environmental literacy is about practices, activities, and feelings grounded in familiarity and sound knowledge. Just as reading becomes second nature to those who are literate, interpreting and acting for the environment becomes second nature to the environmentally literate citizen. Environmental literacy provides students with the ability to understand and utilize the language of the environment, and respond to its grammar, literature, and rhetoric. It involves understanding the underlying scientifc principles, value systems, and the cultural, aesthetic, ethical and emotional responses that the environment invokes.

In the edited work, *Teaching Environmental Literacy: Across Campus and Across the Curriculum contributing* scientists, policy-makers, artists, and historians, as well as experts in law, economics, and language argue that environmental issues are profoundly entwined with all aspects of society and should not be limited to a few science or science policy classrooms. They argue that environmental literacy needs to be taught across the curriculum.

In 2008, The National Science Teachers Association published *Resources for Environmental Literacy: Five Teaching Modules for Middle and High School Teachers*. This resource collection focuses on biodiversity, genetically modifed foods, earthquakes, volcanoes, tsunamis, and global climate change. The authors state that the resource materials are designed to build skills in critical thinking and analytical reasoning about complex issues. Likewise, Emma Wood Rous, in her 2000 text, *Literature and the*

Land: Reading and Writing for Environmental Literacy, 7-12, provides pedagogical techniques and sample interdisciplinary lesson plans that support environmental literacy.

Visual Literacy

The graphic user interface of the internet and the convergence of voice, video, and data into a common digital format have increased the use of visual imagery dramatically. Advances such as smart phones, digital cameras, graphics packages, streaming video, and common imagery standards, allow for the use of visual imagery to communicate ideas. There is conficting evidence regarding whether younger and non-traditional learners prefer image-based over textual content for learning. Many authors argue that students need good visualization skills to be able to decipher, interpret, detect patterns, and communicate using imagery. In *Visual Literacy: Learn to See, See to Learn,* author Lynell Burmark claims that teaching visual literacy can enhance student learning in K-12 classrooms and also improve students' options in the workplace. Burmark argues that with access to print materials and internet sites, an image-rich curriculum can reach more students and teach them more quickly and meaningfully than traditional written student reports and text-based, verbal instruction. Some authors have cited a demand for textual content, but after further investigation, the preference for textual content refected low levels of access to web-based content.

Critical Learning and Innovation Skills

Communication and Collaboration

Learning is a fundamentally social activity—whether in schools, workplaces, or other environments. The communication and collaboration skill sets refer to the ability of individuals to communicate clearly, using oral, written, and non-verbal languages, and collaborate efectively and responsibly with diverse populations. In the area of communication skills, Eisenkraft argues that the growing diversity of the U.S. student population poses new communication challenges. Eisenkraft provides the example of the ways in which earth science and physics textbooks often refer to ice on glaciers or waves on a beach, yet many students across the country have never actually been to a mountain or to the beach. Similarly, chemistry books, when discussing the concept of balancing a chemical equation, often suggest that it is similar to baking bread, in which one combines certain amounts of various ingredients.

Most students today purchase bread and are unfamiliar with baking, Eisenkraft said. The world of people adding and mixing measured ingredients to make bread, he said, "is not the America we live in," yet textbook authors assume it is when they try to communicate with students. Although communication and problem-solving skills have always been important, Eisenkraft argues, that society now demands that everyone to have these skills, not just an educated elite.

While education has focused on the fundamentals of good communication – speech, writing, and reading- the demands of social relations and global economy call for a much more diverse set of communication and collaboration skills. Trilling & Fadel argue that today's student should be able to:

Communicate Clearly

- Articulate thoughts and ideas efectively using oral, written and nonverbal communication skills in a variety of forms and contexts.
- Listen efectively to decipher meaning, including knowledge, values, attitudes and intentions
- Use communication for a variety of purposes [e.g., to inform, instruct, motivate and persuade]
- Utilize multiple media and technologies, and know how to judge their efectiveness a priori as well as assess their impact
- Communicate efectively in diverse environments [including multi-lingual]

Collaborate with Others

- Demonstrate the ability to work efectively and respectfully with diverse teams
- Exercise fexibility and willingness to be helpful in making necessary compromises to accomplish a common goal
- Assume shared responsibility for collaborative work, and value individual contributions made by each team member

Tese communication and collaboration skills can be learned through a variety of methods (e.g., project-based learning, problem-based learning, and design-based learning). Research on teaching communication and collaboration skills encourages direct and mediated communication, working with others on team projects, and performance-based learning and assessment.

Critical thinking and Problem Solving

Critical thinking and problem solving skills include the ability of individuals to a) reason efectively, b) ask pointed questions and solve problems, c) analyze and evaluate alternative points of view, and d) refect critically on decisions and processes. The P21 initiative specifcally focuses on the ability of learners to: a) reason efectively, b) use systems thinking, c) make judgments and decisions, and solve problems. Trilling & Fadel defne critical thinking as the ability to analyze, interpret, evaluate, summarize, and synthesize information. What gives these, perhaps traditional, critical thinking skills a twist in the 21st Century is the availability of advanced technologies for accessing, manipulating, creating, analyzing, managing, storing, and communicating information.

Creativity and Innovation

Just as business and industry must constantly adapt to the rapid shifts in this 21st Century, so must education. This calls for a culture of innovation informed by data, research, and critical and creative thinking. This skill set promotes creative thinking and the ability to work creatively with others.

Creativity is often described as an essential skill that can and should be fostered. In a review of the interconnection between technology, learning and creativity, Loveless shows how technology allows individuals to produce high quality work in a range of media that provide opportunities for creativity.

Lack of attention to developing creativity and innovation skills is often based on a common misperception that creativity is only for artistic-types and geniuses – that creativity is something one is born with or without. Creativity can, Triling & Fadel argue, be nurtured by teachers and learning environments that encourage questioning, openness to new ideas, and learning from mistakes and failures. Creativity and innovation skills can be developed, like other skills, with practice and over time. Tough it is difcult to assess creativity, there are multiple instruments and assessments that have been designed to measure creativity in specifc felds such as problem solving and design.

Life and Career Skills

The 21st century life and career skills focus on the ability of individuals to work efectively with diverse teams, be open-minded to varying ideas and values, set and meet goals, manage projects efectively, being accountable for results, demonstrate ethical practices, and be responsible to both one's self and the larger community.

Leadership and Responsibility

Leadership and responsibility skills include the ability of individuals to work with the interest of the larger community in mind, to inspire others by example, and to capitalize on the strengths of others to achieve a common goal.

Productivity and Accountability

Skills that fall into the "productivity and accountability" category include: setting and meeting goals, prioritizing needs, managing time, working ethically, and collaborating and cooperating with colleagues and clients. The Partnership for 21st Century Skills maintains that students should be able to manage projects; set and meet goals; prioritize, plan, and manage work; produce results; multitask; work positively and ethically; be accountable for results; and collaborate and cooperate efectively with teams.

Social and Cross-cultural Kkills

21st century social and cross-cultural skills reference the ability to work well with colleagues, present oneself professionally, and respect and embrace social and cultural diferences. This ability is an essential 21st century life skill. Understanding and embracing cultural and social diferences and using those diferences to develop new ideas and new solutions to problems are increasingly important in social spheres as well as in the workplace. Students should be able to interact efectively with others, conduct themselves in a respectful and professional manner, work efectively in diverse teams, respond open-mindedly to diferent ideas and values, and be able to work efectively with people from a range of social and cultural backgrounds.

Information, Media, and Technology Skills

Media Literacy

The literature on 21st century media skills argues that it is essential for individuals to be able access, understand, and analyze media and media messages. This skill set includes the ability to understand media bias and the ways in which media infuences beliefs and behaviors. A media literate individual will be able to understand ethical issues surrounding the production of and use of various media forms and critique the inclusion or exclusion of opinions or factual information in media reports. 21st century media skills also refer to the ability of individuals to efectively create and deliver media products. Learners need skills in critically evaluating and creatively producing representations in a variety of media.

Information Literacy

Information literacy forms the basis for lifelong learning. It is common to all disciplines, to all learning environments, and to all levels of education. It enables learners to master content and extend their investigations, become more self-directed, and assume greater control over their own learning.

In order to thrive in a digital economy, students will need digital age profciencies. It is important for the educational system to make parallel changes in order to fulfll its mission in society, namely the preparation of students for the world beyond the classroom.

Information literacy is "the ability to recognize when information is needed and have the ability to locate, evaluate, and use efectively the needed information". Information literacy skills include: accessing information efciently, evaluating information critically, and using information accurately and creatively. Tese literacies form the basis for lifelong learning. They are common to all disciplines and to all learning environments. Information literate individuals are able to:

- Determine the extent of information needed
- Access the needed information efectively and efciently
- Evaluate information and its sources critically
- Incorporate selected information into one's knowledge base
- Use information efectively to accomplish a specifc purpose
- Understand the economic, legal, and social issues surrounding the use of information, and access and use information ethically and legally

Due to the increasing volume of information available, teachers, students, and other stakeholders are faced with diverse, abundant information choices.

Additionally, evermore so, information comes to individuals in unfltered formats, raising questions about its authenticity, validity, and reliability. The uncertain quality and expanding quantity of information pose large challenges for the efectual application of relevant information. The mere abundance of information will not in itself create a more informed citizenry without a related set of abilities necessary to use information efectively.

Big6, an approach to teaching information and technology skills, defnes information literacy as the ability to 1) defne information problems and identify information needed, 2) understand information seeking strategies, 3) locate sources and fnd information within sources, 4) use information, 5) synthesize information, and 6) evaluate or judge information and/or processes.

The American Library Association (ALA) Presidential Committee on Information Literacy, Final Report states, "To be information literate, a person must be able to recognize when information is needed and have the ability to locate, evaluate, and use efectively the needed information." In 1992, the Colorado Study found signifcant links between student success and school library programs. In school library programs where a School Library Media Specialist (SLMS) teaches information literacy skills and information problem solving to both teachers and students, student achievement has been bolstered, resulting in a 10 to 20% boost in reading scores, improved performance on state and local assessments (compared with performance in library impoverished schools. The fndings of this study indicate that collaboration between school librarians and teachers are instrumental for student success because they foster student engagement, utilize active learning models, and employ strategies for information problem solving.

In 1998, AASL published *Information Power: Building Partnerships for Learning,* a guide for school library media specialists in helping students develop information literacy skills and thrive in a learning community not limited by time, place, age, occupation or disciplinary borders. The guidelines of *Information Power* also emphasized the importance of collaboration — joining teachers and school librarians to identify student information needs, develop curricular content, teach to state and national education standards, and compile a variety of print and non-print recourses for standards-based instruction and research.

The Best Practices Initiative Institute for Information Literacy, Association of College and Research Libraries published *Characteristics of programs of information literacy that illustrate best practices: A guideline.* This text ofers a presentation of characteristics that represent a metaset of elements of exemplary undergraduate information literacy programs and philosophies. Bordonaro, K. & Richardson, G. have developed and disseminated a multistep process to integrate library instruction and information literacy skills training into an undergraduate education. Teir research found that scafolding is important to support the research process and refection is important to shape the process.

To measure information literacy, DeMars, et. al. discusses the reliability and validity of a computer-based test – the Information Seeking Skills Test (ISST) to measure students' ability to fnd and evaluate information. The Educational Testing Service (ETS) has also introduced the ICT Literacy Assessment, designed to measure students' abilities to fnd, use, manage, evaluate, and convey information efciently and efectively.

Grassian argues that incorporating information literacy goals, standards, and benchmarks throughout the curriculum is the best approach to help students learn how to fnd, evaluate, make efcient use of, and cite electronic materials responsibly. Schools and school libraries with highly trained staf can act as a catalyst for the incorporation of information literacy standards and increased student achievement and lifelong learning. Efective school librarians, in collaboration with the classroom teacher, can positively impact the ability of all students the ability to identify information needs, seek out resources to meet those needs, and then analyze, synthesize, evaluate, and communicate the resulting knowledge.

Technological Literacy

The use of social media – from blogging to on-line social networking to creation of all kinds of digital material is central to many teenagers; lives.

21st century learning initiatives, informed by emergent research on how people best learn, leverage emerging technologies (e.g., computers, smart phones, and Web 2.0 tools) and embraces the collaborative, participatory learning made possible through Web 2.0.

Web 2.0 technology enables users to produce and share content in new ways and in real-time: user-generated content creation and 'remixing' become creative and engaging practices that challenge the traditional relationships between teachers and students in providing information and content for learning.

E-learning, defned by is the accessing of information, instruction, and/or interaction through the Internet or Intranet using instructional materials and tools such as web-based resources, e-mail, discussion boards, blogs, chat or video. In 2008, the State of Hawai'i's House of Representatives passed legislation mandating that the Hawai'i Department of Education increase e-learning opportunities for students by furthering the development of online programs.

Downes, Anderson and Walton et. al. argue that learners' familiarity with web 2.0 technologies opens up a new space for and style of learning. This new style of learning focuses on collaborative knowledge building, shared assets, problem solving, and the breakdown of distinctions between knowledge and communication (e.g., the production and utilization of podcasts, blogs, videos, and interactive tutorials).

Watson, Gemin, & Ryan argue that e-learning will transform all forms of education and learning in the 21st century. Ellis argues that a commitment to teaching 21st century skills will enable educational leaders to a) improve teaching an course quality, b) move to performance and competence based modes of learning, c) ensure that every student is college or work ready, and d) enable educators to be more fexible and creative in the ways they assist and engage students with learning disabilities and students that are needing a more challenging curriculum.

Collaborative, computer-based learning environments can work to stimulate student learning and the process of inquiry. McFarlane notes, "It seems that use of ICT can impact favorably on a range of attributes considered desirable in an efective learner: problem-solving capability; critical thinking skill; information-handling ability".

In supporting digital and learning literacies, support staf and faculty should work to: design fexible learning opportunities, situate those learning opportunities, where possible and appropriate, in authentic contexts, continually review how technologies are integrated into the curriculum, support students to use their own technologies and to develop efective strategies for learning with technology, use assessment and feedback to encourage innovation in learners' approaches to study, reward exploration as a process, empowering students to navigate increasingly complex learning landscapes, and support student self-assessment and review.

Game-Based Learning

Research shows that learning content through virtual environments enhances student learning. Simulation games in online "virtual" environments can be infuential learning tools. Such games give students a chance to take on new identities and sink, virtually, into situations in which they can apply knowledge in ways not possible in most students' real lives. The choices a player makes within a virtual simulation game transform the virtual environment, which give students something rare: a world in which their personal actions dramatically alter events.

Simulation environment and modern video games are often difcult to master. They require students/players to be skilled at pattern recognition, sense-making of unfamiliar environments, and multitasking. They also often require the user to be a risk-taker. In game play, players immerse themselves in complex, information rich, dynamic realms where they must sense, infer, decide and act quickly. When they fail, they must repeat the task, learning from that failure and working towards mastery.

McFarlane argues that the gaming generation is bottom-line oriented. He states that students often want metrics and want their performance measured – if the form of measurement is meaningful to them. Game designers at top gaming companies work to design good (engaging) learning environments; environments that are create new challenges for players that are neither too difcult nor too simple. As the players improve, the gamers expect the challenges to become more demanding—but at just the right pace. The skills needed for gaming refect many of the 21st century skill sets discussed in this review. Translating this into classroom pedagogy is critical for reaching students who learn well in this type of environment.

Support Systems

The vision, mission, and values of educational agencies are crucial for framing an agenda for 21st century learning work. Once these statements or goals have been developed, education leaders can then align them with their strategic plans, strategies, and accountability systems.

21ST CENTURY LEARNING ENVIRONMENTS

The Partnership for 21st Century Skills (P21) defnes 21st century learning environments as "the support systems that organize the condition in which humans learn best – systems that accommodate the unique learning needs of every learner and support the positive human relationships needed for efective learning" and learning communities that encourage and enable students and educators to attain the skill-sets that the 21st century requires. This includes a number of important elements such as the physical environment, a school's daily operations – including scheduling, courses and available activities, technology infrastructure, school culture, community involvements, and school leadership. P21 states that 21st century learning environments are *system of systems* that:

1. "Creates learning practices, human support and physical environments that will support the teaching and learning of 21st century skill outcomes
2. Supports professional learning communities that enable educators to collaborate, share best practices, and integrate 21st century skills into classroom practice
3. Enables students to learn in relevant, real world 21st century contexts (e.g., through project-based or other applied work)
4. Allows equitable access to quality learning tools, technologies, and resources
5. Provides 21st century architectural and interior designs for group, team, and individual learning.
6. Supports expanded community and international involvement in learning, both face-to-face and online."

Cornell argues that 21st century learning needs to take place in contexts that "promote interaction and a sense of community [that] enable formal and informal learning." Similarly, Sack-Man, the author of *Building the Perfect School* and Susan Black, author of *Achievement by Design* both argue that the qualities of *where* we learn afect the quality of *how* we learn. Sack-Min encouraged school districts and planners to "design for fexibility." At learning styles continue to change, learning spaces will need to be able to adapt. To achieve this fexibility, architects are designing classrooms with moveable furniture and walls that can easily be reconfgured.

Konings surveyed tenth-grade students and teachers about their desired learning environments. In his fndings, he noted that educator's perceptions of what learning environments should be like were vastly diferent from students' preferences. He concluded that when students had input into the design of their environments, they felt more successful and invested in their learning. Similarly, when a frst-year high school teacher asked students to list factors that would make them more successful in learning, the students did not ask for more time to complete assignments and similar supports. Students stated that their learning would be best furthered in an environment that they designed and in which they could pursue their personal interests in addition to their schoolwork.

Practices for Implementing Modern Skills

How do we best prepare our students for a future of work that does not yet exist, careers that have not yet been created, and an economy that prizes creativity and innovation? Emerging research encourages teachers and other educational stakeholders to a) focus on real-world problems and processes, b) support inquiry-based learning experiences, c) provide opportunities for collaborative project approaches to learning, d) and focus on teaching students how to learn (above "what" to learn). Linda Darling-Hammond, in her recent work, *Powerful Learning – What we Know about Teaching for Learning*, provides a meta-review of accumulated research on project-based learning, problem-based learning, and design-based learning.

Project-Based Learning

The research on project-based learning has illustrated signifcant benefts for students who work collaboratively on learning activities in contrast with students who work alone. An additional research fnding was that students who have difculties with traditional classroom/ textbook/lecture learning beneft signifcantly from a project-based learning experience which more closely aligns with their learning style and preference. Best practices for project-based learning include a) tying project outcomes to curriculum and goals, b) employing questions or posing questions to introduce students to central concepts and principles, c) student responsibility for designing and managing much of their learning, and d) basing projects on authentic, real-world problems and questions that students care about.

Problem-Based Learning

Problem-based learning, a form of project-based learning, allows teachers to develop, and students to focus, on complex, real-world problems using a case study approach. When students work in small groups to research and pose solutions to problems, both a collaborative and multifaceted environment is created. Within this environment, students can explore multiple solutions and best practices for tackling projects. Studies and meta-studies of research that has focuses on problem-based learning have found that for factual learning, problem-based learning has similar impacts to traditional learning methods, but that problem-based learning does exceed traditional learning methods when skills such as critical thinking, communications, collaboration, and applying knowledge to real world situations are measured.

Design-Based Learning

Design-based learning has been shown to have the most impact in the areas of math and science. Popular design-based learning activities include robotics competitions wherein student teams design, build and then pilot their robots in a series of competitive challenges. Research has found that students who participate in learning by design projects have a more systematic understanding of a system's parts and functions that control groups.

Obstacles to collaborative and inquiry-based learning include a) the ability of teachers to choose activities and/or topics that beneft from difering viewpoints and lived-experiences of students, b) the need to strategically select students who will work well together and set ground rules so that all students may have the opportunity to participate, and c) encouraging multiple strategies to encourage deeper discussion and better learning for all group/ team members.

How might we best prepare our teachers to support student acquisition of 21st century skills? Teachers of 21st century skills will need to be experts and have expertise in teaching the same 21st century skills that they are encouraging their students to excel in. Teachers will have to take conscious eforts to communicate and collaborate with each other and with students; become fexible with managing new classroom dynamics; be able to support and enable independent student learning, and be willing to adapt their teaching styles to accommodate new pedagogical approaches to learning. For the above to occur, teachers will need professional development opportunities and strong support systems.

The professional development of our nation's workforce must be a top priority and teachers will need to become 21st century learners themselves. Developing successful 21st century teacher education programs and initiatives requires fexible and coordinated leadership. All of those involved in education need to be able to refect and learn from each other's experiences as new methods and processes are piloted and implemented.

Assessment of Skills

Assessment of student skills and knowledge is essential to guide learning and provide feedback to students, teachers, and parents on how well students are achieving set standards. In moving to design assessments to measure 21st century skills, the NEA states that a comprehensive approach to assessment, involving measurements that assess 21st century skills, is necessary to ensure accountability of schools in the 21st century. The P21 initiative recommends:

- Assessment systems be based on multiple measures of students' abilities that include 21st century skills.
- Assessment of 21st century skills should be listed as an integral part of the academic assessments in math, reading and science.
- Reporting requirements should be expanded to include information on whether the student is achieving 21st century skills.
- Funds should be made available for pilot projects that examine the use of assessments that measure 21st century skill competencies in high school students.
- Funds should be allocated for an international benchmarking project that allows U.S. high school students to be compared to their international peers in terms of competencies in 21st century skills.

Learning.com's 21st Century Skills Assessment instrument measures and is aligned to the ISTE NETS-S 2007 standards. The assessment is aligned to all 24 standards in six strands: creativity and innovation, communication and collaboration, research and information literacy, critical thinking, problem solving and decision-making, and technology operations.

Elena Silva, an advocate for the meaningful assessment of 21st century learning states that school systems should be investing in curriculum and professional development, but not forgetting to invest in rethinking traditional forms of student assessment. Silvia argues that the potential exists today to produce assessments that measure thinking skills and are also reliable, valid and comparable between students and schools—elements integral to eforts to ensure the accountability and equity mandated both locally and federally. Silvia states that eforts to assess these 21st century skills are still in their early years and that school districts will have difculties in developing the ability to deliver these assessments at scale.

According to Silva, a central challenge is the cost of assessment design and development. Although higher-level skills like critical thinking and analysis can be assessed with well-designed multiple-choice tests, a 21st century assessment instrument would need to move past multiple-choice testing and include measures that support greater creativity, show how students arrived at answers, and even allow for collaboration. Such measures, however, cost more money than state and federal policymakers have traditionally been willing to commit to assessment design and delivery. Silva argues that to move from traditional forms of assessment, we would need a coordinated public and private strategy (including intensive research and development) for assessment systems to change.

Cramer in his article, "Digital Portfolios: Documenting Student Growth" discusses the digital portfolio process as a 21st century form of assessment. Prior to beginning the portfolio process, students are trained in basic web design to build and maintain digital portfolios. Cramer argues that this process is not only useful for classroom instruction, but that these skills equip students with tools they will most likely use in college and the professional world. Cramer sees the digital portfolio development as an opportunity to provide students the skills necessary to be independent and use their own knowledge to present themselves and their work to others. Cramer claims that the digital portfolio process provides the students with two sets of skills: self-presentation and technology know-how. "Trough creating and maintaining digital portfolios, students are engaged in a process of synthesizing and presenting their academic work and growth in an increasingly professional manner. Tese skills associated with web design competence are an important way we give the students the technological and professional resources that they will draw upon throughout their lives."

Cramer states that digital portfolios have had a positive impact on student achievement across the curriculum. He believes that the public aspect of high stakes of the digital portfolios is a powerful motivator. Teachers, parents, as well as members of the community are able to access students' work and students are able to share their work with possible employers or internship providers.

Professional Development

Students may not master 21st century skills without the support of teachers who are well trained and supported in this type of instruction. 21st century professional development opportunities prepare educators to integrate 21st century skills into learning standards and classroom instruction. The P21 initiative recommends that:

- Funds be allocated for professional development of 21st century skills and establishment of 21st Century Skills Teaching Academies.
- Higher education institutions be supported in identifying and disseminating the best practices for teaching and assessing 21st century skills.
- Higher education institutions be encouraged to ensure that all pre-service teachers graduate prepared to employ 21st century teaching and assessment strategies in their classrooms.

Trilling & Fadel argue that successful professional development programs tend to be:

- Experimental, engaging teachers in the concrete tasks of designing, implementing, managing, and assessing learning activities and projects, and observing other teachers methods and skills
- Grounded in teachers' own questions, problems, and issues as well as what evidence-based research has to ofer
- Collaborative, building upon the collective experiences and expertise of other teachers and the wider community of educators
- Connected to a teacher's own work with students and the teacher's curriculum
- Sustained and intensive, with ongoing support by modeling, coaching, mentoring, and collaborative problem solving with other teachers
- Integrated with other aspects of school reform and transformation.

Bybee & Starkweather argue that teacher and support staf professional development used to focus mainly on how to use technology, and that today, the focus now is on instructional strategies and needs. The authors state that technology education professional development needs to focus on how to use technology to improve student achievement and how to teach a standards-based lesson infused with technology. The P21 initiative states that, "all professional development eforts should exist as part of an aligned system of teaching and learning that includes 21st century skills standards, curriculum, instruction, and assessments". Bybee & Starkweather, in the same vein as Cradler et. al., encourage administrators and education stakeholders to recognize the technology-related professional development to be ongoing. The author's encourage school systems to move away from short-term learning experiences and towards on-going support systems.

Research has shown that professional development sessions must be followed up with regular classroom visits or professional development workshops to provide support and mentoring. The authors contend that classroom visits help teachers translate what they learn in professional development sessions into actual classroom practice. Guskey claims that this is the piece that is usually missing in most professional development programs. Another key element of sustained professional development is collaboration. In the Summer 2003 issue of the *Journal of Staf Development*, Stephanie Hirsh states, " To meet [the NSDC goal of having all teachers experience high-quality professional learning], every teacher must be a part of a learning team-a team of teachers who meet almost every day about practical ways to improve teaching and learning."

In working to build professional development learning communities, P21 recommends working with the most capable and energetic people frst. Build their capacities and provide opportunities for these teachers to model both their teaching and curriculum. P21 then recommends having the early group of teachers who have began the professional development be placed within already existing learning communities. Technology (including online learning and mentoring) can be an important tool to help with collegiality and sustained learning P21 cites the My eCoach model, developed by Barbara Bray. This resource is based on a "coach the mentors" approach, in which teachers collaborate online to develop inquiry-based units and curriculum tools supported by virtual coaches who are being mentored by the My eCoach team.

The above discussion directed attention to the need to reshape teacher practice through developing 21st century skills literacies. While recognizing the importance of 21st century professional development, some researchers remind us that this potential, or need, is often unrealized due to the reality that educators are often not prepared or able to harness 21st century technologies and the possibilities they enable. Guskey argues that to teach 21st century skills, teachers need to be provided with on-going professional development that is supportive and allows teachers to question, practice, and explore emerging technologies. Guskey states that before a teacher can efectively teach and encourage 21st century learning, they must have the interest, motivation, and support to do so.

Failure to implement 21st century pedagogy and efective technology integrations is often attributed to educators being unprepared for the changes demanded by and formed by "technology infusion. Barnett states that too often, teachers are eager to infuse Web 2.0 technologies, but lack the skills and technological and pedagogical knowledge to efectively introduce these technologies into the classroom. Rakes & Casey caution that if educators are pushed into adopting Web 2.0 and other multimedia technologies without support and clear understanding of purpose, then transformation of both teaching practice and student learning will be unlikely. The focus of these authors reiterates the above insistence of the importance of focusing on on-going educator support and development. Tus teachers can begin with supplemental use of 21st century skills and move to full integration.

The P21 research brief on 21st century professional development provides both "guiding recommendations" and "promising directions." The eleven guiding recommendations are 1) develop intensive teacher professional development programs that focus intentionally on 21st century skills instruction, 2) integrate 21st century skills into teacher preparation and certifcation, 3) build capacity, 4) develop district leadership teams to infuse 21st century skills throughout the school district, 5) invest in information communications technologies (ICT), 6) develop professional learning communities around specifc 21st century skills, 7) train administrators around how to lead 21st century skills initiatives, 8) ofer professional development to state departments of education staf, 9) engage colleges of education for 21st century skills leadership, 10) integrate 21st century skills into teaching standards, and 11) leverage the reach of the Web to distribute resources. For each of the guiding recommendations, the P21 group provides corresponding models and/or best practices.

This review of the literature about 21st century skills suggests that educational decision makers need to acknowledge that the academics of yesterday are not sufcient for today The current state of research on the impact of 21st century skill acquisition of student achievement is steadily expanding, with current research seeking to document the longitudinal efects of the acquisition of 21st century skills on student success and workforce development.

Demand for 21st Century Skills

A survey of manufacturers conducted by Deloitte Development found that 80 percent reported shortages of skilled employees across all occupations in their frms. In terms of the kinds of skills needed, the respondents most frequently cited basic employability skills, including attendance, timeliness, and work ethic; problem-solving skills; ability to collaborate; and reading, writing, and communication skills. Tese skills are quite similar to the central 21st century skills identifed above. A 2009 study by Andrew, DeRocco, & Taylor found that manufacturers view innovation as integral to company growth, competitiveness, and shareholder value. Deloitte Development survey respondents indicated that the education and skills of the workforce are the single most critical element of successful innovation, while also reporting a lack of skilled workers. Andrew, DeRocco & Taylor argue that companies whose workforces lack 21st century skills are at a disadvantage to compete globally and have difculty in dealing with such challenges as the convergence of technology and manufacturing and the need to quickly move new products and services to market. The authors conclude that it is imperative to better educate the workforce not only in science, but also in 21st century skills.

In 2006, Caser Lotto & Barrington conducted a survey of 400 business executives and managers, asking respondents to rank the relative importance of 20 skills and felds of knowledge to the job success of new workforce entrants at three education levels: high school, two-year college or technical school, and four-year college. The respondents ranked three skills among the top fve most important skills and felds of knowledge for all three groups of new entrants:

(1) professionalism/work ethic,

(2) teamwork/collaboration, and

(3) oral communication.

In comparison, science knowledge was ranked 17th in importance in the list of 20 skills and felds of knowledge for high school graduates and 16th in importance for two- and four-year college graduates. When asked which skills and knowledge felds would become even more important over the following fve years, critical thinking/problem solving, information technology application, teamwork/collaboration, and creativity/innovation were at the top of the list, and science knowledge was ranked 16th in growing importance.

Given the economic and political challenges of our times, students will need plenty of practice developing and fne-tuning their 21st century skills to become better problem solvers and more creative innovators. Current research on 21st century skills and skill acquisition is focusing on social and cross-cultural interaction, developing and piloting programs and curriculum for students to develop leadership and responsibility skills, and the development of a body of research that can support the preliminary research that illustrates the impact of 21st century learning skills on student achievement and workforce development.

References

Falk, John H., and Lynn Dierking. *Lessons Without Limit: How Free-Choice Learning is Transforming Education.* Walnut Creek, CA: AltaMira Press, 2002.

McFarlane, A. (2003). Assessment for the digital age. *Assessment in Education: Principles, Policy & Practice, 10,* 261-266.

NCREL & Metiri Group. (2003). *enGauge 21st century skills: literacy in the digital age.*

Paige, J. (2009). The 21st Century Skills Movement. *Educational Leadership, 9*(67).

Silva, E. (2009). Measuring Skills for 21st-Century Learning. *Phi Delta Kappan, 90*(9).

Trilling & Fadel (2009). *21st Century Learning Skills.* San Francisco, CA: John Wiley & Sons.

Bibliography

Adey, P.S., Shayer, M (1994) *Really Raising Standards: Cognitive intervention and academic achievement.* London: Routledge.

Amabile, T. M. (1996). *Creativity in context.* Boulder: Westview Press.

Anderson, L. W. & Krathwohl, D. R. (Eds.). (2001). A taxonomy for learning, teaching and assessing: A revision of Bloom's Taxonomy of educational objectives: Complete edition, New York: Longman.

Angelo, T. A. & Cross, P. K. (1993). *Classroom assessment techniques* (2nd ed.). San Francisco: Jossey-Bass.

Armstrong, T. (2000). *Multiple intelligences in the classroom.* Alexan-dria, VA: Association for Supervision and Curriculum Development.

Binet, A., and Simon, T. (1916) *The development of intelligence in children.* Baltimore: Williams and Wilkins.

Blagg, N., Ballinger, M. and Gardner, R. (1988) *Somerset Thinking Skills Course Handbook* Oxford: Basil Blackwell

Bloom, B. S. (Ed.) (1956) *Taxonomy of Educational Objectives, the classification of educational goals - Handbook I: Cognitive Domain.* New York: McKay

Bonwell, C. C. & Eison, J. A. (1991). Active Learning: Creating Excitement in the Classroom. *ASHE-ERIC Higher Education Report No. 1.* Washington, D.C.: George Washington University.

Chen, L. (1997). *Teaching for creative thinking.* Taipei: Shtabook.

Choe, I. S. (2006). Creativity—A sudden rising star in Korea. In J. C. Kaufman, & R. J. Sternberg (Eds.), *The international handbook of creativity.* New York, NY: Cambridge University Press.

Clasen, D. R. & Bonk, C. (1990). *Teachers tackle thinking.* Madison, WI: Madison Education Extension Program.

Collins, M. A., & Amabile, T. M. (1999). Motivation and creativity. In R. J. Sternberg (Ed.), *Handbook of creativity.* Cambridge: Cambridge University Press.

Costa, A (2001) *Developing Minds: A Resource Book for Teaching Thinking* (3rd edition) Alexandria, VA. Association for Supervision and Curriculum Development

Craft, A. (2000): *Creativity across the primary curriculum: Framing and developing practice.* London: Routledge.

Dawes, R. M. (1988).*Rational Choice in an Uncertain World.* Orlando, Fla.: Harcourt Brace.

De Bono, E (1976) *Teaching Thinking*. London: Maurice Temple Smith.

De Bono, E (1987) *CoRT thinking programme: workcards and teachers' notes* Chicago: Science Research Associates

Dewey, J. (1909) *How We Think* Boston, MA: D.C. Heath and Co.

Elder, L. & Paul, R. (Winter, 1997). "Critical thinking: Crucial distinctions for questioning," *Journal of Developmental Education 21*(2), p. 34.

Ennis, R. H. (1958) 'A Concept of Critical Thinking' *Harvard Educational Review* Vol. 32, No.1, pp.81-111.

Ennis, R. H. (1996) *Critical Thinking* New Jersey; Prentice Hall.

Falk, John H., and Lynn Dierking. *Lessons Without Limit: How Free-Choice Learning is Transforming Education.* Walnut Creek, CA: AltaMira Press, 2002.

Fink, L. D. (2003). A self-directed guide to designing courses for significant learning. Retrieved May 13.

Fisher, A (2001) *Critical Thinking: An Introduction* Cambridge: Cambridge University Press.

Frensch, P. A., & Funke, J. (Eds.). (1995). *Complex problem solving: The European Perspective*. Hillsdale, NJ: Lawrence Erlbaum Associates.

Gardner, H (1993) *Multiple Intelligences: the Theory in Practice.* New York: Basic Books.

Glaser, E (1941) *An Experiment in the Development of Critical Thinking* New York: Teachers College, Columbia University

Halpern, D. F. (1996).*Thought and Knowledge: An Introduction to Critical Thinking.* (3rd ed.) Mahwah, N.J.: Erlbaum.

Hamers, J.H.M and Overtoom, M.Th. (Eds.) (1997) *Teaching thinking in Europe. Inventory of European programmes.* Utrecht: SARDES

Hayes, J. (1980). *The complete problem solver*. Philadelphia: The Franklin Institute Press.

Jung, C. G., (1971). *Psychological Types,* Princeton University Press, Princeton, NJ.

Kalsbeek, D., (1987). "Campus retention: The MBTI in institutional self-studies," in Provost, J., and S. Anchors (Eds.), *Applications of the Myers-Briggs Type Indicator in Higher Education*, Consulting Psychologists Press, Palo Alto, CA,, pp. 31-63.

Kolb, D. A., (1985).*Learning Style Inventory*, McBer & Co., Boston.

Kolstoe, O. P., (1975).*College Professoring: Or, Through Academia with Gun and Camera*, Southern Illinois University Press, Carbondale, IL.

Kurfiss, J. G., (1988). *Critical Thinking: Theory, Research, Practice, and Possibilities*, ASHE-ERIC Higher Education Report No. 2, Association for the Study of Higher Education, Washington, DC.

Lawrence, G., (1982). *People Types and Tiger Stripes: A Practical Guide to Learning Styles*, 2nd ed., Center for Applications of Psychological Type, Gainesville, FL.

Lawrence, G., (1984)."A synthesis of learning style research involving MBTI," *J. Psychol. Type*, 8, 2

Lawson, A. E., Abraham, M. R., and Renner, J. W., (1989). *A Theory of Instruction: Using the Learning Cycle to Teach Science Concepts and Thinking Skills*, Monograph *1*, National Association for Research in Science Teaching, Cincinnati, OH, 1989.

Lipman, M (1991) *Thinking in Education* Cambridge: Cambridge University Press.

Lochhead, J., and Whimby, A. (1987). "Teaching Analytic Reasoning Through Think-Aloud Pair Problem Solving." In J. E. Stice (ed.), *Developing Critical Thinking and Problem-Solving Abilities.* New Directions for Teaching and Learning, no. 30. San Francisco: Jossey-Bass.

Lowman, J., (1985).*Mastering the Techniques of Teaching,* Jossey-Bass, San Francisco.

Lynch, A. Q., (1987)."Type development and student development," in Provost, J., and S. Anchors (Eds.), *Applications of the Myers-Briggs Type Indicator in Higher Education*, Consulting Psychologists Press, Palo Alto, CA, pp. 5–29.

Marzano, R.J., Pickering, D.J., and Pollock, J.E (2001) *Classroom instruction that works: Research-based strategies for increasing student achievement.* Alexandria, VA: Association for Supervision and Curriculum Development

Maslow, A., (1970). *Motivation and Personality*, 2nd ed., Harper and Row, New York.

Mayer, R. E. (1992). *Thinking, problem solving, cognition*. Second edition. New York: W. H. Freeman and Company.

Mayer, R. E. (1992).*Thinking, Problem Solving, Cognition.* New York: Freeman.

McCaulley, M., (April 1976). "Psychological types in engineering: Implications for teaching," *Eng. Educ.*, 66, 729

McFarlane, A. (2003). Assessment for the digital age. *Assessment in Education: Principles, Policy & Practice, 10,* 261-266.

McGuinness, C (1999) *From Thinking Skills to Thinking Classrooms; A Review and Evaluation of approaches for developing pupils' thinking* Research report No 115; Nottingham: DfEE Publications.

McPeck, J (1981) *Critical Thinking and Education* Oxford: Martin Robertson

NCREL & Metiri Group. (2003). *enGauge 21st century skills: literacy in the digital age.*

Newell, A., & Simon, H. A. (1972). *Human problem solving*. Englewood Cliffs, NJ: Prentice-Hall.

Paige, J. (2009). The 21st Century Skills Movement. *Educational Leadership, 9*(67).

Perry, W. G., Jr., (1970). *Forms of Intellectual and Ethical Development in the College Years: A Scheme,* Holt, Rinehart and Winston, New York.

Phillips, J. L., Jr., (1981). *Piaget's Theory: A Primer*, W.H. Freeman, San Francisco.

Piaget, J., (1950). *The Psychology of Intelligence*, Harcourt and Brace, New York.

Silva, E. (2009). Measuring Skills for 21st-Century Learning. *Phi Delta Kappan, 90*(9).

Sternberg, R. J., & Frensch, P. A. (Eds.). (1991). *Complex problem solving: Principles and mechanisms*. Hillsdale, NJ: Lawrence Erlbaum Associates.

Swartz, R, Fischer, S., and Parks, S (1998) *Infusing the Teaching of Critical and Creative Thinking Into Secondary Science* Pacific Grove, CA: Critical Thinking Books and Software.

Trilling & Fadel (2009). *21st Century Learning Skills.* San Francisco, CA: John Wiley & Sons.

Wagner, R. K. (1991). Managerial problem solving. In R. J. Sternberg & P. A. Frensch (Eds.), *Complex problem solving: Principles and mechanisms* (pp. 159-183). Hillsdale, NJ: Lawrence Erlbaum Associates.

Watson, G and Glaser, E.M. (1980) *Watson Glaser Critical Thinking Appraisal,* Cleveland, Ohio: The Psychological Corporation

Index